SELLING APARTHEID

"Ron Nixon has pieced together the compelling tale of the apartheid government's extensive and underhand attempts to win international support and fight off sanctions, showing both the scope and the limitations of a global propaganda campaign that lasted over 40 years. With great detail from previously unexamined archival documentation, he shows how the Pretoria government poured millions into everything from above-board lobbying to covert ownership of newspapers and news agencies, often using African Americans to provide cover – sometimes unwittingly – for its attempt to undermine the anti-apartheid movement.

"This is a tale of intrigue, rich characters and large chequebooks, played out in all the Western capitals. At the end, they succeeded only in delaying the inevitable collapse of apartheid, though they sowed much confusion along the way and left behind some scarred reputations. This book is for those who want to understand the full intricacies of the Washington–London–Bonn–Pretoria relationship during the years of white minority rule, and the tough strategic and moral questions it raised."
– Anton Harber, Caxton Professor of Journalism, Wits University

"This is an important story that needs to be told about the apartheid government's global lobbying effort ... It's an important lesson on how organizing, protests and the arrests of regular people set off a cascade of events that trumped lobbying and money."
– Eleanor Holmes Norton, US House of Representatives

"Ron Nixon has made a major contribution to the scholarship on the apartheid era and the struggle for liberation in South Africa. By examining the efforts of the apartheid regime to mask its own inhumanity and racist oppression, Nixon helps us understand the sorts of elite international alliances constructed to suppress the liberation movement and move it in a non-threatening direction ... One cannot understand the South African freedom movement without understanding the issues that Ron Nixon so effectively presents to the reader."
– Bill Fletcher Jr, former president of TransAfrica

T0150515

SELLING APARTHEID

South Africa's
Global Propaganda War

Ron Nixon

PlutoPress
www.plutobooks.com

Published in the United Kingdom in 2016 by Pluto Press
345 Archway Road, London N6 5AA
www.plutobooks.com

First published in South Africa by Jacana Media (Pty) Ltd in 2015
www.jacana.co.za

British Library Cataloguing in Publication Data
A catalogue record for this book is available from the British Library

ISBN 978 0 7453 9914 0 Paperback
ISBN 978 1 7868 0001 5 PDF eBook
ISBN 978 1 7868 0003 9 Kindle eBook
ISBN 978 1 7868 0002 2 EPUB eBook

This book is printed on paper suitable for recycling and made from fully
managed and sustained forest sources. Logging, pulping and manufacturing
processes are expected to conform to the environmental standards of the
country of origin.

Typeset by Jacana Media, Johannesburg, South Africa

Simultaneously printed in the European Union and United States of America

Contents

Introduction

'We are here in the interest of millions of suffering South African children who are already the poorest and most helpless and the most vulnerable in South Africa, [who will] be further harassed and suffer all the more with a further round of U.S. sanctions.'

— *The Reverend Kenneth Frazier,*
founder of the Wake Up America Coalition

On the morning of 8 June 1988, dozens of children from Washington DC schools spread out across the well-manicured lawns of the United States Capitol. Holding hands, the students walked one by one into the domed building. This was no ordinary field trip. The children weren't there just for a civic lesson—they were also there to deliver a message. Each child carried a small black doll to hand to the law-makers. Each doll represented a child who would be harmed by the sanctions that Congress had imposed on South Africa two years earlier in protest against the country's apartheid government. The message behind the dolls—part of a lobbying campaign called Operation Heartbreak—was simple: sanctions against South Africa would do more harm than good.

The organiser of the event was the Reverend Kenneth Frazier, a former Methodist minister and failed congressional candidate, as well as the leader of the group behind Operation Heartbreak, which called itself the Wake Up America Coalition. Despite his opposition to a policy meant to weaken South Africa's white-dominated government, Frazier was also black.

Operation Heartbreak and the Wake Up America Coalition would vanish as quickly as they had sprung up. Within weeks, the House of Representatives would pass a tougher sanctions act, and apartheid would finally be dismantled in 1994.

Years later the event would be revealed as part of an elaborate campaign aimed at turning an unlikely coalition of black Americans against further US sanctions against South Africa. In part, that meant isolating African Americans from prominent African opponents of apartheid, like Nelson Mandela and the African National Congress (ANC).

With plans hatched by officials in Pretoria and aided by an army of lobbyists in Washington, the apartheid government waged a relentless campaign for the hearts and minds of the black American community by appealing to the economic suffering of fellow blacks in South Africa—the very victims of apartheid. As Donald Johnson, a California political organiser hired by the South African government, put it, 'black Americans can work it better than anyone'.

The US campaign targeting black Americans was part of a larger and longer propaganda push by the apartheid regime to improve its image. The South African government and its allies made similar moves in Britain, France, Germany and Australia. Official estimates from the former South African Department of Information put annual spending on the campaign at about $100 million a year (in 1980s dollars). An investigation into secret funding projects by the South African Truth and Reconciliation Commission (TRC) in the 1990s estimated that the amount spent on these projects was R2.75 billion (about $270 million) between 1978 and 1994. But even the TRC admitted that this figure probably underestimated the total sum spent by various departments.

The true amount may never be known because dozens of records of secret projects were destroyed by officials in the 1970s and before the handover to the ANC-led government in 1994. Even official records about the sums of money expended by US lobbyists hired by the South African government, which are housed at the US Justice Department, vastly underestimate the amount spent because they were self-reported. Foreign lobbyists rarely had their records examined unless there was a complaint. Moreover, at one point US officials stopped collecting records on the amount spent by the agencies of the apartheid government because they were given diplomatic status and not required to report their spending.

The South African propaganda campaign devised to sell racial separation was a vast machine. As with Nazi propaganda, art, politics and sport were all used to promote the regime's message and ideology. But the South African campaign, which began shortly after the National Party took power in 1948, was much broader in scope and took advantage of technologies not available to the Nazis, raising the propaganda effort to unprecedented levels.

This campaign would not reach its zenith until Eschel Rhoodie, an ambitious former journalist and government press officer, became secretary for information in the early 1970s. Before then, Rhoodie had published a book, *The Paper Curtain*, in which he outlined the need for a special programme that would use hundreds of millions of dollars and unconventional methods in a global information war to counter the regime's critics and what Pretoria considered the 'hate South Africa campaign'. From its origins as an ideological manifesto appearing in a small book, the campaign would grow into a worldwide media and lobbying operation run with military precision. A large focus of the campaign was on the US because, as Rhoodie wrote, 'America dominates western thought as far as Africa is concerned.' James Sanders has described Rhoodie as the Joseph Goebbels of the apartheid government and *The Paper Curtain* as the *Mein Kampf* of the propaganda campaign.

Not even the exposure of the secret programme by South African journalists in the late 1970s, and the ensuing scandal that brought down a prime minister and a high-ranking cabinet member and sent Rhoodie on the run before his eventual arrest and trial, would stop the campaign. In fact, it would expand and morph into a much larger and subtler operation, hidden behind front groups and individuals with seemingly little connection to Pretoria. It would end in the early 1990s, only after domestic problems caused the government to focus its energies on issues at home.

Along with its own institutions, the South African government would coordinate its public relations campaign with a worldwide network of supporters. These included global corporations with business operations in South Africa, conservative religious organisations and an unlikely coalition of liberal US black clergy and anti-communist black conservatives aligned with right-wing Cold War politicians in the US and the UK who opposed sanctions against South Africa.

Some of the people in the global propaganda war were willing participants—public relations firms, lobbyists, filmmakers and journalists—who were paid handsomely for their services. Others, like the black children who delivered dolls to members of Congress in a failed lobbying effort, played an unwitting part. In the US, in a stunning example of the Washington influence game at its most cynical, the campaign even involved many prominent civil rights leaders, some of whom had once fought alongside Martin Luther King Jr. The apartheid agents would also make their presence felt in London, Paris, Berlin, Amsterdam and Sydney.

To be sure, foes of apartheid also made their presence felt in the same capital cities. The ANC, for example, maintained lobbyists in Washington, and anti-apartheid groups such as the American Committee on Africa in the US and the Anti-Apartheid Movement in Britain also lobbied law-makers. Over the years, critics of the South African government poured hundreds of thousands of dollars into outreach, organised mass demonstrations, staged boycotts and hired their own lobbyists.

Still, the efforts of these groups paled in comparison with the massive resources brought to bear by Pretoria in defence of apartheid. Most of the anti-apartheid groups operated on shoestring budgets. The ANC spent a few thousand dollars each year on one or two representatives in the US. The South African government, on the other hand, was able to finance its massive propaganda operations with its abundant supply of minerals, spending three to seven million dollars a year on lobbying in the US alone.

What follows is the stories of the individuals and institutions— who maintained complicated, and sometimes hidden, connections to Pretoria—and their failed efforts to turn American and world opinion about apartheid on its head.

1

Apartheid Is Good for Blacks

'We shall steadfastly refuse to allow any county, power or organization to determine our destinies—that being a right we reserve to ourselves as a free and independent nation.'
– D.F. Malan, 4 June 1948

When the National Party came to power in May 1948, it paid only modest attention to promoting its image to the outside world. The party, under the leadership of Daniel François Malan, a former newspaper editor and Dutch Reformed Church cleric, had won the election by playing to white dissatisfaction with domestic and economic problems in South Africa after World War II.

A strong turn-out from the rural Afrikaner population had led Malan and his supporters to a victory that few South Africans—and not even some in the party—had predicted. After years in opposition, the National Party was ready to set about transforming the country into a bastion of white dominance, under the banner of Afrikaner nationalism, on the basis of the policy of apartheid. Prior to 1948, South Africa had long pursued a system of racial segregation, but under apartheid this was to be tightened, formalised and extended in unimaginable ways.

The Malan government didn't completely ignore the need to have an overseas propaganda effort. It reorganised its Information Office—not to be confused with the Department of Information, which was created in 1962—to concentrate on expanding its messaging abroad. The Office produced booklets and other promotion materials about South Africa and its new government.

One of the first changes made at the Information Office was transferring its overseas information officers, who were formerly under the Department of External Affairs, to the State Information Office, which was under the direction of the Department of the Interior. The director of the Information Office was then given access to the heads of all government departments and was instructed to come up with an overall media plan to coordinate the government's public relations efforts abroad. The budget for this office and its international propaganda activities was about $146,000 (about $1.4 million or R14.8 million today). A large part of this modest sum was used for efforts aimed at the US and the UK.

Malan considered the US a critical ally and sought to win its backing by working to convince the American government that black rule in Africa would amount to a takeover of the continent by communism, and that white rule was the only way to ensure that that didn't happen. In order to protect South Africa against growing calls for sanctions by an increasingly hostile United Nations, Malan sought America's friendship by participating in the Korean War in 1950. South Africa provided a squadron of pilots to help in the war effort.

Keeping the UK on its side was also a key focus of the Malan government. He courted British protection on the United Nations Security Council by keeping South Africa in the British Commonwealth, even though there was considerable opposition in his party to remaining part of this successor to the British Empire.

In the late 1940s there was actually little need for a sophisticated propaganda apparatus aimed at the great powers. Much of Africa and Asia was still colonised by European powers, whose colonial governments were often not very different from South Africa in terms of racial policies. Even the US, which had emerged as a superpower after World War II, was still a long way from being racially integrated. President Harry S. Truman had appointed the first federal black judge, William H. Hastie Jr, and a few months after the National Party's victory he had signed an executive order which abolished segregation in the US military. Still, most blacks in the US, particularly in its southern region, lived in conditions similar to their counterparts in South Africa. Blacks were barred from certain neighbourhoods; and 'Colored' and 'White' signs announced segregated drinking fountains and bathrooms.

Yet even the Truman administration was somewhat concerned about the harshness of the apartheid laws and the racial policies of the new South African government, for the US was trying to convince the world of its own progress in moving toward an integrated society. But most of Truman's worries about South Africa centred on a possible loss of access to strategic minerals, such as uranium, which were critical to powering the growing nuclear arsenal of the US military and which South Africa could provide. The Truman administration also worried that the Malan government might be distracted by its preoccupation with its racial policies and pay less attention to the larger issue of stopping communist expansion in Africa.

Despite these concerns, many in the Truman administration expressed sympathy for the new South African government and its decision to rigidly separate the country's population by race. Robert McGregor, an American diplomat in Durban, wrote to his seniors in Washington that it was 'quite possible, even likely that we would act in the same manner if we endeavoured to govern as a white race among a black population five times as numerous'.

Dean Acheson, the American secretary of state, who was sensitive to the racial situation in the US and its impact on American foreign policy—even writing that racism in the US 'jeopardizes the effective maintenance of our moral leadership of the free and democratic nations of the world'—nevertheless saw the apartheid government as a critical ally against Soviet expansion. Acheson believed that communists dominated black liberation movements like the ANC, which received their orders from Moscow. Truman himself put aside his feeling about apartheid, saying that South Africa and other African countries could not be allowed to fall into the hands of the Soviet Union because 'We would lose the source of our most vital materials including uranium which is the basis of our atomic power'.

Much to their surprise and delight, it was a black American whose support for apartheid provided a major public relations coup for the South African government in the early 1950s. Max Yergan hardly seemed like the man who would serve as a spokesman for the apartheid government or defend its policy of racial segregation. Himself barely a generation removed from slavery, he graduated from college—a rare feat for a black American in the 1910s—and joined the Young Men's Christian Association, being posted to India as a missionary. Following work in Britain's East African colonies, Yergan applied for a post in South Africa. After protracted talks among officials at the YMCA and numerous conversations between the organisation and the South African government, Yergan was approved. He arrived in Cape Town in January 1922 and then settled in Alice in the Eastern Cape, home of Fort Hare Native College, now Fort Hare University, set up to provide higher education to black South Africans. A good number of black South African leaders attended the university, including Nelson Mandela. The Yergans' house and Max's office were on the campus of Fort Hare.

For the next 14 years, Yergan would travel, by foot, horse and car, throughout the Eastern Cape and other parts of southern Africa, teaching and observing the conditions of blacks in the country. It was during this time that he also met and befriended a number of individuals who would play a crucial role in the history of South Africa, including Davidson Don Tengo Jabavu, a professor at Fort Hare and later president of the All African Convention; John Langalibalele Dube, founding president of the ANC; Dr Alfred Bitini Xuma, who would later become president-general of the ANC during the 1940s; and Z.K. Matthews, a professor at Fort Hare and another future ANC leader.

No one was more taken by the black American than the young Govan Mbeki, who would become a leader of the ANC and of South Africa's Communist Party as well as father of Thabo Mbeki, South Africa's second black president. The 24-year-old Govan, who was a student at Fort Hare, was a regular visitor to the Yergan household and often accompanied Max on his trips through the Eastern Cape. Mbeki recalled that Yergan fed him with literature, including Lenin's *The State and Revolution*. Another Fort Hare student equally impressed with Yergan was Wycliffe Tsotsi, who remembered Yergan as being a staunch foe of segregation, but someone who was secretive about his feelings, mindful of the watchful eye of the South African authorities. Yergan's meetings with some of the future leaders of the ANC and the All African Convention did not go unnoticed. From the time he set foot in South Africa, the government, or black informants who worked for them, monitored nearly all of his activities.

The experience in South Africa radicalised Yergan. He had arrived in the country as a young Christian idealist who believed that his missionary work could make a difference in the lives of Africans there. But as time passed, he began to see that despite his best efforts, the conditions of black people in the country remained largely unchanged. They continued to live in segregated areas; they were at the bottom of the pile economically; and they had few political rights.

Yergan began to believe that the religious works and teachings of the YMCA would not be enough to alleviate the problems facing blacks. This loss of faith in his missionary work also happened to coincide with Yergan's embrace of Marxism. He allegedly became a Marxist after making a trip to the Soviet Union in 1934. 'He was a changed man,' Mbeki said in an interview with Yergan's biographer. 'He was no longer the Max Yergan that we knew.'

In a series of letters and personal pleas made when he travelled back to the US for vacation, he urged the YMCA to do more to challenge the country's segregation policy and the deplorable living conditions of blacks. But the organisation refused to budge, not wanting to upset the South African government. In 1936, Yergan, after considerable thought and reflection, issued his resignation. In his resignation letter he wrote:

> The government in South Africa is not only not interested in the development of Africans but is quite definitely committed to a policy which is destructive of any real growth among Africans of that country ...
>
> In terms of the effective arrangements operating both the material resources as well as the great mass of the population are exploited by and in the interest of the overseas imperialist power, Great Britain, and the local governing class. To make this possible, Africans have been robbed of their land, deprived daily of their labor with exceedingly inadequate compensation and are being reduced to a level worse than serfs. And the business of any government, representative of the theory and practice of imperialism and the deeply rooted convictions of the dominant class in South Africa, is to maintain the status quo.

In an interview that was published in *Imvo Zabantsundu*, a Xhosa-language newspaper, on 17 April 1937, after returning home, Yergan elaborated further on his decision to leave both South Africa and the YMCA. 'I cannot go on as I am in the face of the so-called liberalism which is condoning the increasing political and economic repression of the Africans,' he said. 'The time has come when the African natives must be assisted in their right to organize themselves whereby they can act united in resisting the powers that exploit them.'

Returning to the US in 1936, he began to lay the groundwork for an organisation to do just that. Together with the famed actor, singer and political activist Paul Robeson, Yergan set up an anti-colonialist and pan-African body called the Council on African Affairs (CAA) in the same year. The two black Americans couldn't have complemented each other better. Robeson, because of his international reputation, brought instant recognition to the new organisation. He would be the face and chief spokesman for the new group. In contrast, Yergan was the consummate organiser and, because of his time in both East and South Africa, was considered one of the foremost authorities on issues related to the African continent. But more than knowledge, he had connections with various figures involved in African opposition movements, particularly the ANC, and with the Communist Party.

The new body created by the two men was initially called the International Committee on African Affairs but the name would later be changed to the Council on African Affairs in 1941. With its headquarters in the Harlem neighbourhood of New York City, then the cultural and political centre of black America, the CAA became what the historian Hollis Lynch called the most 'important American organization concerned with Africa'. It would serve as the precursor to the worldwide anti-apartheid movements that emerged during the 1960s and would provide them with a blueprint for attacking the apartheid system, with its focus on organising mass protests, sit-ins and demonstrations, and enlisting celebrities, to bring attention to racial discrimination and government repression in South Africa.

For the new organisation, Yergan recruited a veritable who's who of black America to serve on its board, including Ralph J. Bunche, who had toured South Africa in the 1930s and who would become the first black American to win the Nobel Prize. W.E.B. Du Bois, co-founder of the National Association for the Advancement of Colored People and renowned educationist and writer, served as vice-chair of the CAA African Aid Committee. As South African representatives there were Xuma and Jabavu as well as Rosebery Bokwe, one-time treasurer of the ANC in the Eastern Cape.

South Africa was a major focus of the CAA, and its two lobbyists at the United Nations worked closely with diplomats from the newly independent India, which was beginning to make its voice heard at the international body. The CAA also fought against South Africa's attempts to legally annex South West Africa (now Namibia), which it then administered under a mandate from the League of Nations.

The CAA sponsored a number of educational conferences that would bring to the US some of Yergan's old colleagues from South Africa, including Alfred Xuma and D.D.T. Jabavu, for speaking tours. The CAA's action on the South West African vote at the United Nations received worldwide press coverage, including in South Africa. It also drew praise from the ANC. During its 1947 annual conference the ANC passed a resolution that read, 'Congress desires to make special mention of the Council on African Affairs for its noble efforts to defend fundamental human rights.'

By now, the CAA was also catching the attention of the South African and US governments, both of which placed the group and its members under surveillance. The South African Department of External Affairs sent one of its officials, Robert Webster, who was the consul-general in New York, to attend the CAA's Madison Square Garden rallies to gather intelligence. Webster reported that the movement against South Africa had 'reached dangerous proportions' and concluded that the aim of the participants seemed to be 'Africa for communist-organised labour-controlled black Africans'.

US intelligence was more aggressive than its South African counterparts. The Federal Bureau of Investigation (FBI) had begun to monitor the movements of both Robeson and Yergan as early as 1942 because of their activities in the CAA. The FBI's director, the notorious J. Edgar Hoover, ordered a full-scale investigation of the CAA, believing it to be an 'active front' for communism. The telephones of both men were tapped, and the bureau bugged their homes, went through their trash and opened their mail, 'looking for the identities of espionage agents'.

The surveillance of Yergan, Robeson and the CAA escalated after a speech on 12 March 1947 by President Truman to Congress, which many consider to mark the beginning of the Cold War. Truman made it clear that his administration would consider as subversive any groups that criticised its foreign policy while it was engaged in a battle with the Soviets for the hearts and minds of countries in Africa and Asia. In November the attorney general listed the CAA as one of the many 'front' organisations that he called 'totalitarian, fascist, communist and subversive'.

While Paul Robeson was unfazed by the listing and continued to speak out, the escalating pressure unnerved Yergan. Yergan tried to get members of the CAA to 'disavow any communist or fascist ties', but the majority, including Robeson, refused to be 'redbaited' into stopping their criticism of the US government's foreign policies. A fight soon ensued between the pro-Yergan faction and Robeson supporters, with each hurling accusations at the other side. The biggest complaint was over the issue of money; more specifically, Yergan's spending of CAA funds for his personal use. Finally in May 1948, Paul Robeson demanded that Yergan 'relinquish all financial and other records' and vacate the CAA offices, effectively firing his former partner.

Yergan didn't go quietly. Almost overnight he would undergo a startling transformation. Once a committed foe of the colonial powers in Africa and of US government policies that supported them, Yergan now fashioned himself as an American patriot and staunch opponent of communism.

As his fight with Robeson and others at the CAA escalated, he came up with a plan he thought would protect him from both the accusation of financial mismanagement and a potential government investigation and criminal charges. He walked into the federal building in Manhattan and began informing on former colleagues to the FBI. He told the FBI that Robeson and others in the CAA had 'met repeatedly with the Communist Party leadership and members of the Soviet Consulate in

New York to determine how best to funnel money to the anti-apartheid movement in South Africa', particularly the ANC. Yergan's successor as executive director was later called before a congressional committee to produce all correspondence between the CAA and the ANC.

It seems the FBI had also learned that Yergan was trying to extort money from a former lover, the wife of Frederick Vanderbilt Field, wealthy scion of the Vanderbilt family, who was the main financial backer of the CAA. In exchange for his testimony at congressional hearings and information he provided on individuals and organisations of which he was once a member, the FBI made the charges of blackmail go away and helped him get a visa to visit South Africa. He was clearly in their debt and would remain so until he died in 1975.

Shortly after approaching the FBI, Yergan wrote to the South African embassy in Washington on 30 March 1949, seeking a visa to visit the country so he could enlighten Africans about the dangers of communism. A sceptical D.D. Forsyth, South Africa's secretary for external affairs, fired off a letter to the US ambassador in Cape Town, asking if Yergan's change of heart was indeed genuine. The ambassador, after checking with his superior, Dean Acheson, the American secretary of state in Washington, informed a delighted Pretoria that the transformation was indeed true. Yergan was no longer the man they knew from his days in South Africa or the activist who had drawn world attention to the problems facing black South Africans. He was now a committed Cold Warrior dedicated to the destruction of communism. The South African government quickly approved Yergan's visa.

It was a startling turnaround for a man who had been one of the government's most prominent global critics. Getting Yergan on its side was a major public relations coup for Pretoria. For one thing, it removed a prominent international critic, and it aligned the US and South African governments more closely in their fight against communism by having Yergan address black Americans and Africans about the Red threat. Secondly, it put an approving black face on the country's racial policies.

The worldwide propaganda campaign had begun.

After his 1949 visit, Yergan returned to South Africa in 1952. During this time he addressed a meeting at the Bantu Men's Social Centre in downtown Johannesburg, which was attended by many of the young lions in the ANC, including Nelson Mandela. It was a busy period for the president of the ANC Youth League and he really didn't have time to come and hear a lecture. South Africa was in the midst of the Defiance Campaign, a call for mass protest by the ANC and the Indian Congress to defy unjust and discriminatory laws. Chief among these were the pass laws, which controlled the movement of Africans by requiring black South Africans over the age of 16 to carry at all times, and produce on demand by any policeman or white person, what was in effect a domestic passport while they were in designated 'white' areas. The law stipulated where, when and for how long black people could remain in such areas. The Defiance Campaign also targeted segregated railway stations, post offices and other public facilities where segregation applied.

Despite his work as the national volunteer-in-chief for the campaign, Mandela had come to the Bantu Men's Social Centre, along with Walter Sisulu and Barney Ngakane, a neighbour of Mandela from the Orlando section of Soweto, because Max Yergan was familiar to the young men, many of whom had grown up in the Eastern Cape or studied at Fort Hare.

After giving a few obligatory thanks, and greetings to people he recognised in the audience, Yergan launched into his speech. Given his background as a teacher and organiser in the Eastern Cape, Mandela, Sisulu and many others in the audience expected Yergan to offer his support for the Defiance Campaign and criticise the restrictive laws applied to Africans. But after speaking about his past work in South Africa for a few minutes—in what Mandela and the others thought was a brilliant speech—Yergan instead delivered a blistering attack on communists. He lectured those in attendance about the evils of communism and warned that it was detrimental to the aspirations of blacks. He spoke about how Soviet agents working in Africa were using black liberation movements, not to bring about racial equality, he said, but to sow discord among blacks and whites.

Mandela and Sisulu were stunned. It was not what they had expected to hear from a man who had for years criticised the racial policies of South African governments, and had been closely aligned with the Communist Party. He didn't sound like a man who had for years worked tirelessly in advocating the rights of black South Africans.

After Yergan's speech, Mandela later recalled, many of the black politicians and businessmen present stood up and politely applauded. But Barney Ngakane, Mandela's neighbour, was having none of it. Before Yergan could leave the stage, Ngakane launched into an attack, asking why Yergan hadn't addressed the Defiance Campaign, the pass laws, the poverty, the lack of political rights. How could he not talk about the fact that American business was helping to prop up the apartheid regime?

Walter Sisulu would later recall that Yergan even attempted to talk the organisers of the Defiance Campaign out of continuing with the mass protests. 'His warning to us in our activities sounded far more like the warnings of a US Government spokesman than from a Negro participating in any movement for Negro rights,' recalled Mandela. Mandela was half right.

Less than a year later, Yergan would again draw the ire of Mandela, Sisulu and former American colleagues for the comments he made in an interview of 7 May 1953 with an American magazine, *U.S. News and World Report*. In it Yergan declared that the South African government deserved the world's understanding, rather than scorn, for its policy of apartheid. He also repeated his claims that the ANC and the Indian Congress were communist-dominated front groups, more interested in fomenting dissent than promoting racial equality. In view of the communist influence in these organisations, Yergan said the South African government was 'completely justified in its policy of suppressing communist influence'.

The article brought an immediate rebuke from anti-apartheid

activists in South Africa and the US, among them Walter Sisulu and Z.K. Matthews. 'In so far as South Africa is concerned, Dr Yergan, apart from oppressive policies of the Nationalist government toward the non-European, has either deliberately distorted the true position to suit his special mission or he has accepted *in toto* a statement from government officials,' said Sisulu. Yergan's friend Z.K. Matthews also added: 'I resent the suggestion that the African people need communists to teach them to defend their rights.'

The criticisms seem to have had little effect on Yergan. He also provided information to the Central Intelligence Agency (CIA) that proved what he called the communist takeover of the ANC. He named as communists the ANC leaders John Marks, David Bopape and Moses Kotane, who were banned under the Suppression of Communism Act. Yergan's information, shared with the CIA, about communist influence in the ANC would play a major role in the US government's later classification of the organisation as a 'terrorist group'. The ANC would remain listed as such until President George W. Bush removed the designation in 2008 before he left office.

* * *

Yergan's new outlook may have disappointed his former friends and colleagues, but the South African government was elated. Yergan's turn had come at a most opportune time. In the early 1950s the country began to find itself under increasing attack internationally from newly independent countries like India just as attitudes about race in the US and Europe had started to change. In 1952, at the urging of India and 12 other countries, the UN established a commission to study the 'racial situation in South Africa' and report its conclusions at the next meeting of the body's General Assembly. South Africa voted against the measure, while the US and 20 other countries abstained.

Behind closed doors, the US was worried about its association with

South Africa and what sort of impression this would create for the newly emerging countries. A few officials had even given consideration to voting for an earlier United Nations measure to put the apartheid issue on the agenda. According to a State Department cable of 29 September 1952, some diplomats at the US embassy in New Delhi suggested that voting for the measure would 'go a long way toward convincing Arabs and Asians US continues to maintain principles and would put the US in an advantageous position 'to dispel belief skilfully and ruthlessly fostered by Commies [that] the US [has] an interest in furthering cause of White race in ... growing struggle against colored people'. But the US ambassador in South Africa rejected the idea. 'I am convinced that any action condemnatory of South Africa at this juncture will lead South African Govt very seriously to consider withdrawal from UN,' wrote Waldemar J. Gallman. Behind the scenes, the US worked to derail any attempts to take punitive actions against Pretoria.

Despite the US backdoor diplomacy at the United Nations, international pressure was mounting on the South African government over apartheid. Having Yergan travel the world voicing support for the South African government helped, but Pretoria knew it needed to do more.

A succession of South African prime ministers had served as their own foreign minister, but J.G. Strijdom, newly elected in 1954 after the resignation of D.F. Malan, decided that he needed a separate person for the position, someone who could not only represent his government on diplomatic missions, but intensify its campaign to deflect growing international criticism. The man Strijdom chose was Eric Louw.

Louw was a well-known figure in South Africa and abroad. He had been a member of the South African parliament, an accomplished foreign diplomat and a rising star in the National Party when he was chosen for the position. He had served in the US and Canada as the South African trade representative, and had opened the country's first diplomatic ties with the US in 1929, appearing in a ceremony with President Herbert Hoover. Louw travelled widely in America, and newspaper articles from the time show that he and his wife were popular hosts at their residence in Washington.

Despite his background as a diplomat, he could come across as combative and short-tempered to friend and foe alike. For all his faults, he was a proud Afrikaner and strong defender of apartheid and, when given control of the ministry, was told to 'breathe fire and enthusiasm' into the department. According to James Barber and John Barratt, 'For the first time there was a minister, and a forceful one, responsible for foreign affairs, who was backed by an expanding department staffed by able men.'

Louw was credited with making the ministry more proactive in defending the apartheid government from foreign attacks. One of the first changes he made was to revamp the government's information services, securing additional staff and money to try to transform the country's image aboard. In spite of the government's stance on race, Louw made attempts to reach out to newly independent African countries such as Ghana, sending a message to congratulate Kwame Nkrumah on his appointment as first president of the new country.

The US became a particular focus for Louw, as American businesses had begun to increase their investments in South Africa and the two countries were also strengthening their military ties. This focus was given added significance by the presence of the United Nations in New York, with its multitude of diplomats. Louw recognised that the kind of propaganda campaign he sought to launch needed more than just government information officers—he required expert help, and found it among the various advertising and public relations firms in New York City's Madison Avenue. The South African government had previously rejected overtures from American public affairs companies that pitched their services. It felt that the firms would not have 'enough sympathy and understanding for South Africa's problems'. Louw quickly began to change that.

Records from the US Department of Justice show that in the US the

South African government began to increase its spending on lobbying by hiring American firms and increasing the budget for the country's own information office. In 1950 the Information Office within the Department of External Affairs, which represented the government's own lobbying efforts in the US, spent about $30,000 and had ten employees. The South African Tourism Corporation, which would play a major role in worldwide propaganda efforts, registered to lobby for the first time. It spent about $71,000 annually and employed ten people.

By the end of the decade, the apartheid government would employ about six US public relations firms and spend three times the amount on lobbying that it had in 1950, although the sum may have been much larger because not all the lobbyists filed reports with the Department of Justice as required. The Information Office's American staff was increased to 26.

Louw also hired Films of the Nation Inc., a distributor of short feature films, to produce movies that showed South Africa in a more positive light to American audiences. The lobbying firms of Dow, Lohnes & Albertson, and Krock-Erwin Associates, were also retained to shore up the country's image and to court friendly American politicians and businessmen. The new effort was part of what Louw called a counter to the 'completely distorted and false' picture that had been spread abroad about the racial policies of the National Party.

Louw also launched another, less public effort to both win American support and deflect criticism. South African diplomatic officials in the US were tasked with collecting information that would show America's 'discriminatory practices in regard to race, colour, class, caste, religion, politics or sex'. The instructions also called for compiling information on 'restrictions or limitations on the freedom of movement, of speech, of religion, of political expression'. This included gathering evidence on race riots in the US, monitoring restrictions on black Americans' and other minorities' voting rights, and reporting the US government's crackdown on so-called subversive organisations. 'It is time that events within their own country should be a lesson to the Americans in the grace of humility when expecting other countries to achieve what they themselves have difficulty in doing,' one embassy employee wrote.

* * *

Lobbying wasn't left entirely up to the South African government. After sitting on the sidelines for decades, the South African business community also began to play a major role in countering negative publicity about the country. In December 1959 a new organisation was launched that would later play a prominent role in helping to block international economic sanctions. A group of businessmen, led by the Anglo American Corporation's Harry Oppenheimer, started the South Africa Foundation. According to an investigation by the British anti-apartheid group the Africa Bureau, Piet Meiring, director of the Department of Information, and Eric Gallo, a businessman who made a fortune from the black South African music market, also played a part in founding the group.

Major-General Sir Francis de Guingand, former chief of staff for Field-Marshal Montgomery, and a personal friend of Franklin D. Roosevelt, was picked to lead the foundation. Guingand's friendship with the American president would give him unequalled access to the corridors of power in Washington, even years later.

The founders of the group, which consisted of both English and Afrikaans speakers, represented South Africans from across a broad range of political persuasions. The businessmen argued that the government needed to make some concessions to blacks and smooth over some of the rougher edges of apartheid. The foundation would even on occasion publicly criticise the government, but it never criticised the system of apartheid itself during this period.

Leaders of the foundation added that its function was 'imbued with the ideal of presenting South Africa's case at home and overseas' by countering outside 'pressures' and 'misunderstandings'. Its goal was to build relationships with friendly businessmen in the US and Europe, particularly the UK, and to stave off international criticism or actions that affected the South African economy. Criticising apartheid was one thing, but international activists whose campaigns affected the balance sheets of South African companies or its economy were something else.

The apartheid government and its business allies were now armed and ready to wage propaganda warfare.

2

In Defence of Apartheid

'Never, except in a state of war, had there been such concentrated opposition against a state.'
– Eric Louw

For years, the pressure among South Africa's oppressed majority had been building. Tired of having their movements restricted and of enduring unequal treatment in a segregated society, black South Africans began staging a number of acts of civil disobedience to protest against the notorious pass laws. The largest of these demonstrations had been the 1952 Defiance Campaign, as a result of which 8,000 people, including Nelson Mandela and Walter Sisulu, were arrested and jailed.

On 21 March 1960, the Pan Africanist Congress (PAC), a group that had split from the ANC a year earlier, called for a day of demonstration against the pass laws and urged its followers to present themselves at police stations across the country without their passes and invite arrest. At the township of Sharpeville in what is now Gauteng province, a group of protesters gathered outside the police station and, as the crowd began to grow, police reinforcements were called in. Eventually police opened fire and, when the shooting stopped, nearly 70 people were dead, including eight women and ten children. Another 180 people were injured.

The response among South Africa's black population was immediate, and the following week there were more demonstrations, protest marches, strikes and riots throughout the country. On 30 March 1960, the government declared a state of emergency, detaining more than 18,000 people. A week after the state of emergency came into force, the government banned both the PAC and the ANC. Some of the leaders of these organisations were arrested, while others went into exile abroad.

A storm of international protest followed the Sharpeville shootings, including sympathetic demonstrations in many countries and sharp condemnation by the United Nations. Medical reports leaked to the media showed that nearly 70 per cent of those killed or injured had been shot in the back as they tried to run away. A spokesman for the US State Department issued a statement condemning the shootings:

> The United States deplores violence in all its forms and hopes that the African people of South Africa will be able to obtain redress from legitimate grievance by peaceful means. While the United States, as a matter of practice, does not ordinarily comment on the internal affairs of governments with which it enjoys normal relations, it cannot help but regret the tragic loss of life resulting from the measures taken against the demonstrators in South Africa.

But the State Department's spokesperson had jumped the gun. The statement had been issued without the approval of President Eisenhower or the secretary of state, Christian A. Herter. Both later apologised to the South African government for the 'breach of courtesy between nations'. Still, the damage was done internationally.

On 1 April 1960, the United Nations Security Council passed Resolution 134, which called on South Africa to abandon apartheid. Even the US—one of the apartheid government's staunchest allies at the UN—voted for the resolution, though both France and Britain abstained. British Prime Minister Harold Macmillan wrote in his diary that 'feeling against South Africa is swelling to really dangerous proportions'.

The Sharpeville shootings marked a turning point in South Africa's history. The massacre finally caused the PAC and ANC to abandon non-violence as a means of achieving their goals, and both turned to armed resistance the following year. Internationally, South Africa found itself increasingly under siege and isolated in the global community. The Sharpeville massacre, as it came to be known, was a public relations nightmare for the apartheid government, further proof to the world of the violence inherent in the country's repressive racial policies. Along with critics like India, South Africa also had to contend with the reactions of several newly independent African countries, which pushed for action against Pretoria.

In the US, media coverage after the Sharpeville shootings was widespread, with nearly all magazines and newspapers running articles on apartheid, giving unwanted exposure to South Africa's racial policies. A broad range of well-known Americans, ranging from civil rights leaders like Martin Luther King Jr to the conservative evangelist Billy Graham, condemned the South African government and called for an end to apartheid.

In response, the government went on the defensive with its usual mixture of bombastic public statements and a public relations campaign to repair and improve its damaged international image. The first thing it did was to launch an international speaking campaign featuring high-ranking government officials to defend the nation's racial policies. Officials were dispatched to colleges and universities and political and social clubs in both the US and Europe. In the US, most of the speaking tours were centred on Washington and New York.

The foreign minister, Eric Louw, himself travelled to the US to inform Americans of what he called the truth about South Africa. As he said at the time, 'Never, except in a state of war, had there been such concentrated opposition against a state.' In a speech to the National Press Club in Washington, he told those in attendance that Americans would take a similar approach to race if they were faced with a hostile black majority. As his officials had done in the past when confronted about the country's racial policies and security measures, Louw raised the spectre of communism. He said that South Africa's strategic position was of the greatest importance to Western countries as a bastion of freedom and democracy against the Soviet Union, which was bent on spreading its influence in the region. He concluded by saying, 'I suggest that the Union of South Africa is an ally worth having—and worth keeping.'

In April 1960, a month after Sharpeville, the NBC broadcast a television series called the 'Winds of Change' about South Africa, which referred in critical terms to the 'terror and bloodshed' of Sharpeville. Louw was incensed. He dispatched the South African ambassador in Washington, Wentzel du Plessis, to meet with Caltex, a division of the American oil giant Texaco with significant investments in South Africa and a major advertiser for NBC, to see if the company might exert some pressure on the television network.

But the government knew that it needed to do more than try to strong-arm its American counterpart. It needed a more subtle approach to repair its image. Consequently, it turned to one of America's premier image-makers at the time for help. It hired the Hamilton Wright Organization, a New York public relations agency with experience in representing unpopular foreign countries, to launch a major campaign that would create a more favourable image for the South African government both within the US and globally. The Hamilton Wright Organization has been called the first international public relations firm. It represented a host of foreign governments, including Communist China.

To burnish South Africa's image, the firm produced articles and took photos featuring smiling black Africans that were widely distributed through several newspaper syndicates, including the United Press

International News Service; these were sent to 1,300 newspapers in the US and another 1,000 abroad. It also distributed articles penned by writers on its payroll or friendly reporters through the Associated Press, which served 1,400 US papers and another 1,500 internationally. It produced photo essays in magazines such as *National Geographic*, *Life* and *Look*, which drew attention to the scenic beauty of South Africa. It commissioned friendly articles about South Africa from journalists who were taken on trips to the country paid for by the firm with funds from the South African government, mostly from the Department of Information, which was set up in 1962 as a separate agency from the Department of Foreign Affairs.

More importantly, the firm produced newsreels and short films that were shown in American movie theatres as well as on television. These high-quality movies, which were narrated by André Baruch, a famous radio talkshow host and narrator who worked for two major television networks, NBC and ABC, were shot in both black-and-white and colour. They were released through all the major Hollywood production companies, including 20th Century Fox, Universal, MGM, Paramount and Warner Brothers, and seen by more than 200 million people worldwide. The films were also distributed through production companies in Spain, Germany, France, Belgium and the Netherlands.

Hamilton Wright Sr, the firm's president, told the South African government that, despite the costs, an extensive international propaganda campaign was needed. 'When you are in the front lines you must use heavy artillery and lots of it,' he wrote to officials at the Department of Information.

Almost no one realised at the time that seemingly harmless films on South African gold or diamond mining or wildlife were propaganda paid for by the apartheid government. Hamilton Wright wanted to keep it that way. The firm took pains to list itself as the producers of all the films, articles or photos that it distributed to media organisations, not the South African government, even though US law required that political propaganda be labelled as such. In a letter of 2 May 1962 to a US television station, Wright admitted that he had 'deliberately left off' the fact that a film called *South Africa Today* was paid for by the South African Information Service.

Writing in November 1961 to Piet Meiring, director of the Information Service, Hamilton Wright Sr boasted about the firm's ability to achieve the government's political goals without being overtly political:

> What most of this work proves—beyond doubt—is the value of positive nonpolitical propaganda to create an effect essentially political. Political propaganda as such would have been largely ineffective. But institutional publicity—touching on South Africa's general life, economic, social and cultural accomplishments, tourist attractions, sports, festivals, etc.—can tend to soften hard political attitudes, make for good feeling, and tend to correct misinformation about the country.

But South Africa's lobbying efforts were dealt a serious blow in 1963 when Senator James Fulbright opened a series of congressional hearings into the activities of American lobbying and public relations firms that represented foreign governments, and called the Hamilton Wright Organization to appear before it. Fulbright was particularly concerned about contracts the firm had with the South African government to promote propaganda campaigns that were largely hidden from the American public.

The firm denied wrongdoing. But under questioning from Fulbright, Hamilton Wright Sr admitted that he often failed to disclose the fact that hundreds of films and articles distributed through Hollywood studios and American newspapers and wire services neglected to declare that the South African government funded them. Asked about the omission, Hamilton Wright Sr replied: 'If we put this on there, it would kill us, it would put us out of business.' Wright further explained that moviegoers would not pay money to see a 'piece of propaganda'.

'That is actually what's happening, isn't it?' Fulbright asked.

Replied Wright Sr, 'Well ...'

'The only difference is that you don't tell them [that it is propaganda],' Fulbright offered.

The hearings also revealed that the Hamilton Wright Organization had hired the children of some movie studio executives to curry favour, paid writers for articles in newspapers and magazines that did not disclose they had been produced and paid for by a foreign government, and sponsored a number of junkets for journalists to travel to South Africa. The journalists were then expected to come back to the US and write positive stories about that country.

Letters between Hamilton Wright Sr and South African officials also revealed that the firm invited leading editors at various newspaper syndicates and their wives to travel to South Africa as the firm's guests. 'The returns are fabulous,' Wright Sr wrote to Willie le Roux, an official with the South African Information Service in New York. According to Wright, the information about the editors' trips was to be kept confidential. 'It would be inadvisable to have news of this arrangement now being discussed in New York "leak out"—especially to competitive USA newspapermen,' he wrote to the secretary of the Information Department in Pretoria, in a letter of 10 May 1962.

In a touch of irony, the hearings revealed that the Chinese government, which Hamilton Wright also represented, was reportedly 'hurt' that the company was acting on behalf of South Africa as well, complaining that the firm was making films about how well South Africa 'treats its Negroes'.

Under repeated questioning from Fulbright, Hamilton Wright Sr and his son Hamilton Wright Jr, who also testified, insisted that they had not acted illegally and had not produced political propaganda for South Africa. Ultimately, the committee did not find that the firm had broken US laws requiring the disclosure of propaganda—though it did determine that the firm had engaged in questionable practices by concealing the source of funding for its news articles and films.

Despite the Fulbright Committee's finding, the damage was done. For the first time the American public was given a behind-the-scenes look at the South African government's attempt to influence US foreign policy. A grassroots campaign by anti-apartheid groups in the US that had formed in the wake of the Defiance Campaign and the Sharpeville shootings called for a boycott of theatres showing movies produced by the Hamilton Wright Organization. At the same time, the Public Relations Society of America, a trade group of PR professionals, suspended the firm from membership for violation of its code of ethics. Despite the public criticism and the suspension, Hamilton Wright Sr was unrepentant. The firm would disband a few years later, with Wright insisting that the hearings had unfairly damaged his firm's reputation.

Although the work of the Hamilton Wright Organization on behalf of the Pretoria government proved to be fatal to the company, it did little to change the relationship between the US and South Africa, nor did it stop South African efforts to counter what it considered to be negative international criticism of its internal racial policies.

* * *

In the 1960s South Africa was the biggest Cold War trading partner of the US in Africa, and America depended on it for reliable uranium supplies, ports of call for the US Navy ships, and its four missile-tracking stations.

The election of a new president, the liberal Democrat John F. Kennedy, in January 1961 didn't change the US approach to dealing with South Africa. Despite the Kennedy administration's reaching out to what the young president called in a speech of 1962 'an extraordinary group' of African leaders building new countries 'fresh from winning their independence', the US government remained largely silent on the fate of millions of black South Africans living under the yoke of apartheid.

The ANC and its leaders like Mandela were widely believed to be agents of the Soviet Union, and as such were not included in the president's embrace. 'Mandela, a probable communist ... is believed to have been responsible for much of the ANC's success in seizing the initiative from anti-communist groups,' the CIA said in its *Current Intelligence Weekly Summary* of 21 May 1961. The report called Mandela 'an able organizer' and cast doubt on his commitment to non-violence. It said he might only be interested in a veneer of peaceful intent, which hid a more violent streak. 'Mandela allegedly hopes violence can be avoided, since peaceful demonstrations would increase the ANC's aura of respectability.'

On 5 August 1962, when South African authorities arrested Mandela, who was then on the run, it was reportedly with the help of a CIA informant working in the ANC or as an associate of Mandela. Though the connection has never been properly documented, some former American intelligence officials privately say that they understand it to be true.

The CIA was not alone in its belief that Mandela and the ANC were under the influence of communism. A report by the US Joint Chiefs of Staff came to a similar conclusion. Notwithstanding its belief that the liberation movements in South Africa were largely inspired by communism, the Kennedy administration did impose a limited arms embargo against South Africa—it was voluntary and did not include military contracts between the two countries that had been previously negotiated, nor did it include spare parts or maintenance contracts.

Despite pressure from African leaders and many African Americans who called on Kennedy to use US economic pressure to eliminate apartheid, the president resisted, saying sanctions would be 'bad policy and bad law'. And despite the arms embargo he had imposed on Pretoria, the two countries continued to have solid military ties and significant intelligence sharing. Formal diplomatic relations between the two countries were also strengthened by major private American investment in South Africa, which made the US its second-largest trading partner after Britain. When Kennedy was killed by an assassin in 1963, his successor, Lyndon B. Johnson, kept to the anti-communism track.

* * *

Even after the exposure of the Hamilton Wright Organization, Pretoria continued to employ a number of American public relations firms to promote its agenda. It also began to rely on home-grown non-governmental bodies concerned to promote South Africa abroad. One of these institutions was the South Africa Foundation. Since its founding in the 1950s, this business-funded group had worked tirelessly to sell South Africa and obstruct or stall international efforts that might harm trade with and investment in the country. By 1963, the foundation had its lobbying operations up and running in capital cities like Washington. In meetings with US policy-makers and other corporate leaders, officials of the foundation agreed that the South African government should moderate its racial policies, but stopped short of calling for the end of apartheid or full rights for blacks.

One of the foundation's key officers was the American mining magnate Charles W. Engelhard, who had extensive business holdings in South Africa. Engelhard had first travelled to South Africa in 1947, just before the National Party took power. He had gone to establish a foothold for his father's company in exploiting the country's large deposits of minerals including gold, diamonds, platinum and uranium. In 1949 Engelhard set up a company in South Africa called Precious Metals Corporation to make gold statues for resale. The company was supported by Robert Fleming & Co., a London merchant bank, founded by the grandfather of Ian Fleming, author of the James Bond novels. Engelhard and the younger Fleming would strike up a friendship, and the author would use the American businessman as the inspiration for his Goldfinger villain in the James Bond novel of the same name.

After the Sharpeville shootings, Engelhard led a group of private investors who lent the South African government $150 million to help stabilise the economy after many international investors had pulled out. Engelhard also persuaded the Kennedy administration to back South Africa in its application for an $18.8 million loan from the International Monetary Fund. A 1961 article in *Time* magazine called Engelhard one of the most powerful businessmen in South Africa. In 1966 he had investments worth $130 million tied up in South African mining companies.

But Engelhard wasn't just a businessman with investments in South Africa; he was also a key officer in the South Africa Foundation, which sought to influence world opinion in favour of the country. Engelhard had met Harry Oppenheimer, who set up the South Africa Foundation, in 1955 during one of his many trips to South Africa. The two men had hit it off well and soon became business partners. Engelhard would gain a seat on the board of Anglo American, Oppenheimer's giant mining company, and he also became chairman of the South Africa Foundation's American committee.

In that role, he became an active supporter of South African causes by using his contacts in the highest levels of American government. State Department records show that Engelhard consistently sought to influence US policy towards South Africa, encouraged greater investment and promoted a positive image of the country. He told the *New York Times* that he had joined the foundation because news coverage of South Africa and its racial policies was biased. The situation in South Africa was no different from what was occurring in the US, he said.

Engelhard was a major contributor to Kennedy's Democratic Party and had organised the Business and Professional Men and Women Committee for the presidential and vice-presidential campaigns of both Kennedy and Lyndon Johnson. After Kennedy's death, Engelhard turned his attention to the newly elected President Johnson and continued to push for American economic investment in South Africa. Engelhard was a constant presence in the Johnson administration, especially when it came to its dealings with South Africa. Anti-apartheid activists in meetings with the State Department complained about the 'influence Mr Engelhard had on the USG [US government]' and said the businessman 'consistently turned up in respect to American relations with Africa', in particular South Africa. Although he didn't always get his way, Engelhard would, during the 1960s, help to thwart the efforts of anti-apartheid activists to influence the US government in its policy towards South Africa. His work in the South Africa Foundation was crucial in this regard.

To help create a favourable image of South Africa, the foundation had since its beginnings sponsored a number of trips for American and European businessmen as well as politicians to see the country for themselves. The visitors stayed in the best hotels. They met with top officials in government and with prominent local businessmen. Meetings were also arranged with black leaders who were friendly towards the regime. After completing the trips, which were carefully constructed to show the softer side of South Africa, many of the businessmen and legislators returned home and spoke in favour of the country, its prosperity and economic prospects.

One such visitor was Max Yergan, a long-time spokesman for the apartheid government, who arrived in South Africa at the end of November 1964 as a guest of the South Africa Foundation for a month-long tour. Yergan had visited the country numerous times before. In 1957 he had even brought his white wife with him. Apparently unaware that Yergan was a partner in a 'mixed' marriage, which was then illegal in South Africa, the embarrassed South African government came up with an interesting solution. A visit to Uganda was hastily arranged for Mrs Yergan, while her husband continued on his trip to speak about the dangers of communism to black Africans.

The November 1964 trip would prove beneficial for both the South

African government and Yergan, who was embarking on a new career as an anti-communist conservative spokesman. At a news conference over tea and biscuits at the Parktown residence of the head of the South Africa Foundation, Yergan, flanked by the foundation's staff, heaped praise on the apartheid policy, saying it gave Africans 'more dignity and self-respect'. 'South Africa has the right to demand and receive more informed and objective understanding of her situation,' he said. One black South African interviewed by the *New York Times* said Yergan's statements stunned him. 'How can a Negro talk like that?' the man asked. 'I thought they were on our side.'

Yergan's speech wasn't the only controversy that arose during his 1964 trip. A week before the press conference, Yergan had made a visit to the so-called autonomous homeland of Transkei, where he stayed in a hotel that was reserved for whites only and from which even the black head of Transkei was barred.

Yergan's speech and his trip were widely publicised abroad 'Apartheid Gives Negroes Dignity, Sociologist Says,' announced a *New York Times* article, which was picked up by news organisations around the world. Yergan repeated his support for apartheid and its homeland policy in a stop in London after his South African tour. 'Separate development is a recognition and respect of the black man's ambition to develop to the fullest extent,' he said in an interview at the St James' Court Hotel.

A year after his South African and London speeches in defence of apartheid, Yergan joined with William Rusher, a prominent American conservative and publisher of the right-wing *National Review* magazine, to form the American African Affairs Association. The purpose of this body, according to its leaders, was twofold. The first was to speak calmly and rationally to Americans about developments in Africa; the second, to help Africa 'work constructively towards the betterment of its people'. But as the black columnist Carl Rowan would point out in an article of March 1966, the association served as little more than a vehicle that was 'primarily interested in defending South African apartheid' and other settler regimes in southern Africa.

The group defended South Africa before the United Nations, undertook tours of the country sponsored by the South African Information Department to highlight its positive aspects, and produced a stream of glossy publications, including a booklet entitled *Some American Comments on Southern Africa*, which quoted a variety of former American diplomats and newspaper columnists who opposed sanctions against South Africa.

The American African Affairs Association was also used to organise tours and meetings for South African government officials and academics visiting the US. In 1971 it sent a three-man fact-finding team to southern Africa headed by Dr Alvin J. Cottrell, director of research at the Center for Strategic and International Studies at Georgetown University. Cottrell would later file a report that allegedly found 'communist activity' in the Indian Ocean area and touted the value of South Africa as an ally in the region.

The association's work on behalf of South Africa was not free. According to investigative reporters Russell Howe and Sarah Trott in their book on foreign lobbying in Washington, *The Power Peddlers*, the American African Affairs Association received about $40,000 of its $160,000 annual budget from the South African government. Louis Gerber, an official with the South Africa Foundation, told the authors that he depended on the association for lobbying. Its actions tied the organisation directly to the apartheid government.

Yergan would continue to play a major role as a spokesman for South Africa. Though he would be vilified by former colleagues, he was much admired by the South African diplomatic corps. Among his personal papers at the Moorland-Spingarn Research Center at Howard University are several invitations to attend receptions at the home of the South African consul-general in New York and for cocktails with visiting South African dignitaries.

Though he never said anything publicly, there are signs that Yergan may have regretted at least some of his actions. In 1975, shortly before his death, Yergan wrote a letter to an ailing Paul Robeson. In it, he seemed to want to make amends with his former friend. 'I am at times deeply pained that a long and cherished friendship with you was interfered with,' he wrote. 'And to make it clear that it is my deep desire to withdraw, wipe out and apologize for anything that I ever said or did which could interfere with our friendship.' Both men would die not long afterwards.

* * *

While the South African government's public relations campaigns and diplomatic efforts may have been effective for some time in forestalling American and European political and economic demands for change, grassroots opposition to apartheid continued to grow. Opposition was particularly strong in the American black community as it began to push for an end to segregation and racial policies in the US and to link their own struggles for civil rights to the broader liberation struggle in Africa.

Martin Luther King Jr had had early exposure to South Africa and the ANC. His father, Martin Luther King Sr, had corresponded with Walter Sisulu in the 1940s, and in 1948 the senior King invited Albert Luthuli, later president of the ANC, to his church in Atlanta, Georgia.

King Jr became an active supporter of anti-apartheid campaigns in the US and abroad. He lent his name to a number of rallies and fundraising efforts to give support, both financial and political, to blacks in South Africa. One of the most significant was an international campaign called the 'Declaration of Conscience on South Africa', organised after the South African government launched a pre-dawn raid in 1956 and arrested 156 leaders of the ANC, the Indian Congress and other anti-apartheid groups, and charged them with treason. Among those arrested were Nelson Mandela, Z.K. Matthews, Oliver Tambo and Walter Sisulu.

With former first lady Eleanor Roosevelt, King served as co-chair of the campaign, which called on world leaders to join a 'worldwide protest against the organized inhumanity of the government of the Union of South Africa'. One hundred and twenty world leaders would sign the declaration. The campaign received numerous statements of solidarity from churches, labour unions, local governments, student groups and artists. It earned a sharp rebuke from Eric Louw, the South African foreign minister, who claimed that the campaign was led by communist sympathisers, who were 'propagating their doctrine of universal equality in the guise of protest against racial discrimination'.

The declaration of conscience campaign wouldn't be the last time that King became involved in anti-apartheid activities or tried to link the struggle of blacks in America with those in South Africa. King and Luthuli, both Nobel Prize winners, exchanged letters on numerous occasions. Luthuli had also travelled to America in 1961 and, with King, issued an appeal for action against apartheid. Each would praise the other: according to Luthuli, King's book *Stride Toward Freedom* had influenced him; while King declared that had he been in South Africa, he would have joined Luthuli in fighting against apartheid.

The two issued a joint letter in 1962, calling for sanctions against South Africa, a boycott of South African products and an end to trade and investment 'until an effective international quarantine of apartheid is established'. The two men added: 'The apartheid republic is a reality today only because the peoples and governments of the world have been unwilling to place her in quarantine.'

During a meeting in 1962 with President Kennedy in the Oval Office, King actively pushed the president to invoke sanctions or, at the very least, issue a resolution against the South African government for its treatment of black people. Kennedy declined. 'We do not believe [sanctions] would bring us closer to our objective—the abandonment of apartheid in South Africa,' Kennedy said. 'We see little value in a resolution which would be primarily a means for a discharge of our emotions, which would unlikely to be fully implemented and which calls for measures which could easily be evaded by the country to which they are addressed—with the result of calling into question the whole efficacy of the sanctions process.'

In spite of Kennedy's reluctance to take a harder stance against apartheid, Martin Luther King Jr remained undeterred. He continued to speak out against South Africa's rulers, whom he called 'spectacular savages and brutes' and a 'monstrous government'.

In December 1964, en route to Sweden to receive the Nobel Peace Prize, King made a speech praising South African leaders such as Nelson Mandela and Robert Sobukwe, 'rotting away in Robben Island prison'. He compared the situation in South Africa to the problems blacks faced in the American South. 'Clearly there is much in Mississippi and Alabama to remind South Africans of their own country, yet even in Mississippi we can organise to register Negro voters, we can speak to the press, we can, in short, organise people in non-violent action,' he said. 'But in South Africa even the mildest form of non-violent resistance meets with years of imprisonment, and leaders over many years have been restricted and silenced and imprisoned.'

In a speech on 10 December 1965 King called apartheid an attempt to reach into the past and 'revive the nightmarish ideology and practices of Nazism'. 'In South Africa today all opposition to white supremacy is condemned as communism and, in its name, due process is destroyed, a medieval segregation is organised with 20th century efficiency and drive, a sophisticated form of slavery is imposed by a minority on a majority, who are kept in grinding poverty,' King said.

These speeches may have been one reason King was later denied entry into South Africa. After he was invited to speak to students at the University of Cape Town, King applied for a visa to visit the country. In his letter of 9 February 1966 to the consulate in New Orleans, King said he would only stay in the country for a few days and would only be there as a lecturer. But he did add that he wanted to exchange cultural and human rights concerns, and would be interested in spending some hours talking to religious leaders during the visit. But a month later, an official at the consulate advised King that his visa request had been denied, without offering an explanation. King, who was assassinated in 1968, never had another chance to go to South Africa.

Many other black American leaders spoke out during this period against the apartheid government. Malcolm X, national spokesman for the Nation of Islam, urged African Americans to pressure their government on behalf of black South Africans. 'Twenty-two million Afro-Americans in America can become for Africa a great positive force—while in turn the African nations could and should exert a positive force at diplomatic levels against racial discrimination,' Malcolm X said during a speech at the University of Ghana in May 1964. 'All of Africa unites in opposition to South Africa's apartheid and to the oppression in the Portuguese territories. But you waste your time if you don't realize that Verwoerd and Salazar [the Portuguese dictator], and Britain and France, never would last a day if it were not for the United States support. So until you expose the man in Washington DC you haven't accomplished anything.'

In addition to the civil rights movement, a number of multi-racial non-government organisations sprang up in protest against the apartheid government. One of the most prominent was the American Committee on Africa. This organisation had grown out of a loosely affiliated group called Americans for South African Resistance, formed in support of the 1952 Defiance Campaign. It would later expand its focus to support liberation movements across the African continent, but South Africa remained a key focus.

The committee was one of the first to call for economic sanctions and divestment by American companies in South Africa. While this initially had very little effect on corporate investments, it would later result in churches, universities such as Michigan State and Columbia (in 1978), cities such as San Francisco (also in 1978), and several American state governments, including Michigan (in 1982), selling their stock in companies that did business in South Africa.

As the 1960s gave way to the 1970s, American blacks began to insert their voices into the construction of US foreign policy by a means that had not been previously available: through legislative politics. The struggle by King and others had led to the passage of numerous laws outlawing segregation in America and giving blacks full voting rights. This, in turn, would lead to the election of black legislators at the local, state and federal levels. With an increase in their numbers, newly elected black congressmen began to exert their influence on US foreign policy and called for increased political and economic action against the government of South Africa.

At the same time, black liberation struggles in the US and Africa created a backlash. White American fears of growing black militancy led to allegations of communist influence on the civil rights movement. In almost a mirror image of South African practices, any organisation or individual that advocated equal rights for blacks was labelled communist.

Almost immediately after Martin Luther King Jr and a group of Southern black ministers formed the Southern Christian Leadership Council (SCLC) in 1957, FBI memos show that its agents began to warn that the group was 'a likely target for communist infiltration'. King himself would later be accused of collaborating with communists. By November 1963, all his phones, both at home and at the SCLC's offices, would be wiretapped.

The National Association for the Advancement of Colored People (NAACP), another civil rights organisation, which had supported black South Africans and the ANC as far back as the 1930s, was also accused of being a communist front organisation. Eugene Cook, attorney general of the state of Georgia, one of the most frequent critics of the NAACP, launched investigations into its activities in the 1950s and 1960s. During a speech to law enforcement officers Cook told them that the 'racial aims of the Communist Party of the United States and the NAACP are virtually identical'. 'Through its activities, the NAACP is causing strife and discord between the white and negro races in the South and is disrupting relations between these races which have been, and at present are, harmonious and friendly in every respect,' Cook added.

The racial situation in the American South as well as the rest of the US played into the hands of the South African government, which found ready allies in American conservatives and segregationist politicians. American conservatives wrote glowingly in support of South Africa throughout the 1960s. Many of them travelled to the country either as guests of the South Africa Foundation or of the apartheid government itself.

Following a trip to South Africa in 1963, William F. Buckley Jr, a conservative commentator and founder of *National Review*, wrote in support of Pretoria's homelands policy and credited the government for trying to help blacks. 'We should try at least to understand what it is they are trying to do, and deny ourselves that unearned smugness that the bigot shows,' he wrote in *National Review*.

Another influential conservative, Russell Kirk, wrote that giving blacks the vote in South Africa would bring about 'anarchy and the collapse of civilization'. The ultra-conservative John Birch Society also lent its support to the South African government's cause. The society, founded in 1958 to fight what it called a rising tide of communism in the US, and considered too right wing for even some conservatives, saw communist influence everywhere. Its official magazine frequently featured articles by George S. Schuyler, who, like Max Yergan, was a black American, and former liberal and socialist who later in life became vehemently anti-communist. A powerful writer, who contributed to the *Pittsburgh Courier*, one of the most influential black-owned papers of its time, Schuyler had once been an advocate of equal rights for blacks and used his columns to document racist attacks on blacks in the US and the treatment of blacks in Africa under European colonisation. Schuyler also worked for the National Association for the Advancement of Colored People, which had long been critical of South Africa's racial policies. But in the late 1940s, Schuyler began to shift his political views, perhaps because of an awareness that he had come under suspicion by American intelligence agencies like the FBI.

Whatever the reason for the change, Schuyler began to write articles that denounced black civil rights leaders, calling them race agitators who were stirring up blacks on behalf of communists. Martin Luther King Jr was a frequent target of his ire. In one editorial, Schuyler stated that King was undeserving of the Nobel Peace Prize. He also began voicing his support for apartheid. 'In South Africa you have a system of Apartheid,' he said in a radio interview. 'That's their business. I don't think it's the business of other people to change their society.'

Conservatives like Schuyler would become influential supporters of South Africa during the 1960s. But they weren't the only ones. Nowhere was support for South Africa stronger than in local governments and among politicians and groups fighting against racial integration, particularly in the American South. Many white Southerners could see much of themselves in South Africans. Like the white-led government in Pretoria, many white Southerners viewed the black liberation struggle as the work of outside agitators, mostly communist, who had come to stir up good blacks. They also saw black calls for equal rights as an affront to the Southern way of life.

The government of the state of Mississippi was one of the most vocal supporters of Pretoria, and while most Southern states resisted federal efforts to grant blacks political rights, none was more resistant than Mississippi. After the Sharpeville shootings, the Mississippi state legislature passed a resolution commending the National Party 'for its steadfast policy of segregation and the staunch adherence to traditions in the face of overwhelming external agitation'.

The state's conservative Senator James O. Eastland, a firm believer that segregation was the law of Nature and of God, visited South Africa in 1969 and offered his support. Most likely the trip was sponsored by either the South Africa Foundation or the government's Information

Department. Eastland saw many parallels between the state of Mississippi and South Africa: both, he felt, were under siege by outside forces intent on making those in power change the way in which they ruled and lived.

Further support in Mississippi came from a group of white businessmen and local politicians who made up the White Citizens Council. This anti-integration group, which had sprung up in Mississippi after the landmark 1954 Supreme Court decision in *Brown* vs *Board of Education* against segregated public schooling, soon spread across the US to gain more than 60,000 members.

According to research by Zoë L. Hyman, the council's support of apartheid went back to its founding. Its first newsletter dedicated two separate columns to South Africa. One of the articles linked together the efforts of segregationists in the American South and South Africa. The other featured a letter of support from a right-wing South African, S.E.D. Brown, who published the *South African Observer*, a Pretoria-based right-wing and anti-Semitic newspaper. In his letter, Brown congratulated the founders of the new organisation, saying: 'Many Whites in Africa will be heartened by the news that you are organizing as you are doing; because our local English newspapers—and the U.S. Information Service—give the impression that integration is becoming an accomplished fact in the U.S.A. The news of your fight will not only give a great measure of moral support here, but will help us to burst through the Press iron curtain.'

Another South African, John R. Parker, provided the White Citizens Council with a steady stream of materials. These played on the widespread fear of segregationists and white South Africans that they were unfairly judged and misrepresented, that independent African states were unstable, dangerous and anti-white, that the white race was superior and that whites in the US and South Africa shared a common bond. Parker also established a Society of the Two Souths, which functioned as a pen-pal matching service linking white South Africans and white American Southerners, a kind of low-tech FaceBook.

It is uncertain how much of an influence the group had on American public opinion outside the South. And since the individuals and groups who exchanged letters had similar beliefs, it is unclear how much the correspondence did to change policy or encourage actions in the American South or within the US federal government. By 1966 the group appears to have disbanded.

* * *

While the support of conservatives and Southern segregationists proved useful to South Africa during the 1960s, better was yet to come with the election of Richard Nixon to the White House in 1968, ushering in a new era in South African–American diplomatic relations. Pretoria was about to gain an important ally in the highest office of the American government.

Nixon had been a congressman on the infamous House of Representatives Committee on Un-American Activities, which had hounded liberal activists and groups with charges of communism. He had then served as vice-president under Eisenhower. During his run for president, Nixon had campaigned on a platform of 'law and order', in a direct reference to the racial riots and conflicts that were gripping America. Nixon had also employed what was later called a 'Southern Strategy', appealing to white fears of blacks, which resulted in many whites leaving the Democratic Party to join the Republicans. Nixon himself had little regard for blacks in his own country or anywhere else, saying they were 'just down out of the trees'.

By aligning himself with the South African government, Nixon felt that he had little to lose since he had very few ties to blacks in the US or in the African liberation movements. Nixon believed that his core constituents—conservatives and white Southern segregationists—would go along with increasing US support for Pretoria. David Newsom, the

Nixon administration's assistant secretary of state for African affairs, put it this way: 'there are a few of our citizens who view the white domination of Southern Africa with a certain nostalgia.'

Still, apartheid leaders were initially sceptical of Nixon, fearing that he would be 'tempted to appease liberal and Negro sentiment by taking a strong line' against South Africa's racial practices. Pretoria didn't need to worry. Seeking to distance himself from the foreign policy of the Kennedy and Johnson administrations, Nixon developed an approach that would draw the two countries closer together. Rather than isolate the South African and other settler governments in the region, Nixon sought to 'maintain public opposition to racial repression but relax political isolation and economic restrictions on the white states', according to a *Washington Post* editorial at the time. In a 1969 National Security Council memorandum, the new administration succinctly summed up what its new policy towards South Africa would be: 'The whites are here to stay and the only way that constructive change can come about is through them. There is no hope for the blacks to gain the political rights they seek through violence, which will only lead to chaos and increased opportunities for the communists.'

Before the policy was formally adopted, a dissatisfied official in the State Department said it would 'mire the United States deeper on the side of the oppressors'. But the internal criticism didn't seem to upset the Nixon administration. Instead, it sought increased communication and cooperation with the apartheid government. In a speech to Congress in 1971, Nixon said, 'the maintenance of contact and communications was essential if the United States is to exert a constructive influence on South Africa'.

One of the priorities of both the Nixon administration and the South African government was the fight against the spread of communism, which both felt had infiltrated black liberation movements in Africa. One of the main objectives of the Nixon doctrine towards southern Africa was to 'minimize the opportunities for USSR and Communist

China to exploit the racial issues in the region for propaganda advantage and to gain political influence with black governments and liberation movements'.

Trade between the two countries also increased. During Nixon's first administration, US investments in South Africa rose from $864 million in 1970 to $1.4 billion by the end of 1973. And while the US under Nixon did not break the arms embargo that the Kennedy administration had imposed, it did sell equipment, including planes, that could be used for military purposes. The administration also removed restrictions on loans through the Export-Import Bank.

Pretoria was elated to finally have someone in the White House it deemed sympathetic to the problems of South Africa. But Nixon's policies and the closer ties with South Africa would bring a chorus of criticism both domestically and internationally. Many black leaders who had been impressed by Nixon when he attended the independence celebrations of Ghana in 1957 expressed their dismay at the new president's South African policy. A *Washington Post* editorial said the administration essentially appeared 'to be opting for a strong status quo policy in black Africa and, where useful, small but increasing accommodations with white minority governments'.

Many leaders of the newly independent African countries also expressed their disappointment with the closer embrace of South Africa. But there was little that could be done. The nascent worldwide anti-apartheid movement had not yet reached the point where it could put political pressure on the US or European governments.

In the seats of power, particularly London and Washington, any talk of action against South Africa's repressive racial policies continued to take a back seat to the perceived threat of communism.

3

Taking the Offensive

'In countries abroad we must have every means at our disposal in order that we may present the image of South Africa as it is, namely that of a beautiful, prosperous country, in which law and order prevails ... where in an atmosphere of peace and calm, numerous people with different languages, cultures, religions and traditions are living together in an orderly manner ... an example to the whole world.'

– Dr Connie Mulder,
South African minister of information

Dr Petrus Cornelius ('Connie') Mulder didn't like what he was seeing. In 1971, three years after becoming the minister of information, Mulder took an overseas tour to gauge international opinion about South Africa. In country after country, he found an unfriendly press, political debates that centred on South Africa's racial policies, and a growing grassroots movement calling for economic and military sanctions against his country.

Mulder, then a rising star in the National Party, who had his heart set on one day becoming prime minister, didn't feel that the South African government diplomatic corps and information services were providing an adequate defence of the country abroad. One department in particular, his own Department of Information, was criticised for being largely ineffective in that regard, a view even shared by staffers within the department.

Mulder wanted to change that. In a report to the prime minister, John Vorster, he recommended an aggressive campaign that would 'buy, bribe, or bluff its way into the hearts and minds of the world' to counter the 'propaganda offensive against South Africa'. He called for a global public relations programme that would engage 'in the propaganda war and employ the same methods as our opponents'. Millions of rands would be needed to fight the information battle, Mulder told the prime minister. No holds would be barred, and much of the work would have to be done in secret. Vorster agreed and the plan was given preliminary approval. Mulder then set about putting his ideas into place.

Much of Mulder's ire was aimed at the growing anti-apartheid movements springing up in Europe and the US. In Britain, the Anti-Apartheid Movement was growing in strength and had launched a number of campaigns to disrupt South African links, especially trading links, with England. The organisation was founded in 1959 after the ANC president, Albert Luthuli, called for British people to boycott South African goods in shops. At the time Britain was the largest foreign investor in South Africa and South Africa was a major export market for British goods. The AAM launched a series of protests against South Africa, calling for economic sanctions and a boycott of South African products.

The AAM intensified its efforts after the Sharpeville shootings in an attempt to isolate the South African government and force it to grant full political rights to its non-white population. The movement played a major role in getting South Africa suspended from the 1964 Olympic Games. In one of its most successful campaigns, the group put a stop in May 1970 to the tour of an all-white South African cricket team to England.

In the US, after years of grassroots campaigning to pressure corporations and universities to withdraw their investments from South Africa, several anti-apartheid groups organised a Washington office, which gave them a presence in the nation's seat of power. Another body, the Interfaith Committee on Corporate Responsibility, a church-based shareholder advocacy group, founded in 1972, also played an important role in the anti-apartheid movement by targeting the shareholders of American companies with investments in South Africa.

But the biggest problem Pretoria had to contend with in America was the rise of black representatives as a force in US politics. Although it would be years before they could introduce legislation in Congress that would have an impact on South Africa, the black law-makers would be a consistent source of irritation for the apartheid government.

One of them, Charlie Rangel, a black Democrat from New York, repeatedly launched attacks on the National Aeronautics and Space Administration for supporting a segregated space-tracking station in South Africa that cost American taxpayers about $3 million per annum. Every year, beginning with his first year in Congress in 1971, Rangel sponsored bills that would cut off funding to the station, saying it was an egregious symbol of American support for apartheid.

Ronald V. Dellums, a black congressman from California, who was elected a year before Rangel, began introducing anti-apartheid legislation, calling for trade restrictions against South Africa and immediate divestment by American corporations. Although it would be many years before the legislation would pass, by introducing it every year Dellums kept the spotlight on the apartheid policies of the South African government and its US supporters in government and the business community.

As the number of black legislators increased during the early 1970s—there were nine black members of Congress in 1970—they joined together to form the Congressional Black Caucus, an active participant in the US anti-apartheid movement. In Congress, black caucus members introduced 15 bills targeting South Africa over a 14-year period, beginning in 1970. These newly elected black law-makers were instrumental in the creation of TransAfrica, the black lobbying group that led the fight for sanctions in the 1980s.

The most prominent of these black legislators and the most persistent critic of the apartheid government during this period was the congressman Charles Diggs, the first black American to serve on the House of Representatives Foreign Affairs Committee, whose subcommittee on Africa he chaired. South Africa was a particular focus of Diggs, who made numerous trips to the country. In 1971, Diggs oversaw a bipartisan delegation of law-makers to South Africa to observe at first hand the business practices of American companies operating there. The resulting 471-page report was released during a congressional hearing and proved embarrassing for both the US and the South African governments. Diggs called the situation for blacks in South Africa appalling. There was a 'blatant, ever-present and all-pervasive discrimination based on race, colour and creed', he said after the trip. American business interests, Diggs added, provided the means for the South African government to continue its oppression of blacks in the country.

Although Diggs and other black law-makers would be unable to get Congress to impose sanctions against South Africa in the 1970s, he held numerous highly publicised hearings through his subcommittee, keeping South Africa's racial policies and American business investment there in the spotlight. The hearings were crucial because for the first time US government officials and business leaders had to come before Congress and answer questions about their involvement with the apartheid regime.

Diggs pressured presidents from Richard Nixon to Jimmy Carter to deal decisively with the apartheid government, although they refused to do so. Diggs also became such a nuisance to Pretoria that he was subsequently banned from the country. Diggs went public with the banning, thereby causing a public relations embarrassment for the South African government. 'I was the biggest anti-South African around,' he said in an interview in 1978.

It was against this backdrop of growing protest in Europe and America that Dr Connie Mulder began assembling the necessary resources and personnel needed to carry out his plan for a global public relations offensive.

One of his first decisions was to hire the 38-year-old Eschel Mostert Rhoodie as head of the Department of Information. The appointment generated considerable controversy among the department's staff since Rhoodie was promoted over more senior members who were also considered for the position. His promotion would leave a trail of bruised egos and resentment that would later come back to haunt both Rhoodie and Mulder.

Before his appointment Rhoodie had been a journalist and low-level press officer within the Department of Information, with postings in Europe and the US, hardly the type of man expected to lead the propaganda war that Mulder envisioned. But what Rhoodie had that others lacked was a plan for how to wage this war. In 1969, he had written a book called *The Paper Curtain*, a manifesto that would in the main provide the blueprint for South Africa's information offensive for years to come. In the book, Rhoodie wrote that a paper curtain had been drawn over South Africa by international news outlets, which told lies about the country and spread communist propaganda. The solution, he wrote, was for the South African government to own its own media in order to tell its story or else buy people with power and influence in the media, those who could influence the editorial content of their publications.

Mulder had come across *The Paper Curtain* and was impressed by its proposal to counterattack the apartheid regime's opponents rather than simply respond to their criticism. In Rhoodie, Mulder found a kindred spirit, who also believed that the manner in which the Department of

Information carried out its duties was ineffective and outdated. Unlike South Africa's diplomats, Rhoodie believed that the department needed to play by a different set of rules:

> I specifically said to [John Vorster]: I want you to approve, not an information asset, but a propaganda war in which no rules or regulations count. If it is necessary for me to bribe someone then I would bribe him or her. If it is necessary for me, for example, to purchase a sable mink coat for an editor's wife then I should be in a position to do so. If it is necessary for me to send someone on a holiday to the Hawaiian Islands with his mistress for a month, then I should be able to do so.

Vorster and Mulder gave the go-ahead for Rhoodie's plan. Vorster also gave approval for millions of rands to be transferred from the defence budget to a secret fund at the Department of Information called the 'G' fund, to pay for a series of propaganda projects. Since the defence budget was covered by the Official Secrets Act, very few people besides Vorster, Mulder and Rhoodie knew all the details about the new propaganda campaign.

With his superiors' blessing and flush with millions of rands in a secret fund, Rhoodie began implementing his plan. The first order of business was to assess the view of South Africa worldwide in order to draw up a plan of attack. Rhoodie hired a New York public relations firm headed by the advertising expert Richard Manville at a cost of R280,000 (about R13.7 million today) to carry out a survey. The South African government's funding was hidden, and participants were told that the survey was being done on behalf of several countries.

The 20-volume report produced by Manville, which covered 16 countries, proved both illuminating and shocking. Apartheid government officials knew that South Africa was not well liked in the world, but had no idea just how disliked they were. The thousands of pages told them just how much of a pariah the country had become. One Department of Information official would later describe the survey as the equivalent of an X-ray that revealed not only broken bones, but alarming spots on the patient's lungs as well.

During a presentation for the heads of several government departments in a meeting in Cape Town, the American survey guru laid out his findings to a group of shaken bureaucrats. South Africa, Manville's survey found, was ranked as the most unpopular country in the world, except for Uganda, then ruled by the brutal dictator Idi Amin. The country was also less favourably regarded than the communist countries of the Soviet Union and China. But more than anything, the report showed that apartheid was 'the one word that popped into people's minds most frequently when questioned about South Africa'.

The report was crucial, Rhoodie said, in helping him carry out his plans for the new propaganda programme. The firm also helped the government put together a list of 40,000 organisations and individuals who were key decision-makers in the West.

With his battle plan in hand, for the next five years the suave, well-tailored and swashbuckling Rhoodie travelled the world as South Africa's secretary for information and most visible spokesman, with one purpose in mind: to sell the apartheid government and its policies of racial segregation.

To help carry out his grand plans, Rhoodie hired his brother, Deneys, and a close friend, Les de Villiers, as deputies. De Villiers was in charge of the secret 'G' fund. Of the three men, De Villiers had the most experience. He had served as the head of government information service in New York, and toured the country meeting with politicians, media people and a host of American businessmen who would later become involved in several of the apartheid government's secret propaganda projects. It was De Villiers who first met John McGoff, the right-wing American publisher who would play a central role in trying to buy newspapers in the US on behalf of the South African government.

With funding and trusted deputies in place, Rhoodie then began to set in motion more than 160 secret projects that would win over friends, buy favour and influence, and, ultimately, end the careers of Vorster, Mulder and Rhoodie himself. The main point of the projects was to let others, particularly well-respected individuals and institutions with seemingly no connection to the apartheid government, tell the South African story rather than having the government do the talking. Rhoodie and the Department of Information set up front companies so that funds could be routed through them, making it difficult to trace the money back to the South African government.

In *The Paper Curtain*, Rhoodie had demonstrated the increasingly negative coverage of South Africa in the local and world press: the first order of business therefore was to change this. At first he tried covertly to buy South African Associated Newspapers, which was then the leading English-language newspaper publisher, owner of the *Rand Daily Mail*, *Sunday Express*, *Sunday Times* and other major titles. When that failed, the plan was to establish a newspaper from scratch. This was an English-language tabloid called *The Citizen*, to counter attacks on the apartheid government by the English-language press, particularly the *Rand Daily Mail*.

The mostly Afrikaner government believed that it was papers like the *Rand Daily Mail*, the *Engelse pers* (English press), that kept reasonable Africans, Coloureds and Indians from seeing the benefits of separate development. *The Citizen* would do just the opposite. The man chosen to be the face of the new paper was Dr Louis Luyt, the fertiliser millionaire and one-time rugby player.

In an agreement signed on 2 April 1976, Luyt was established as the sole owner of the paper and chair of its board. The board also included the American publishers John McGoff, who owned a chain of small newspapers in the Midwestern US, and Beurt SerVaas, a former CIA agent and editor of an influential magazine, the *Saturday Evening Post*, which published articles supportive of the South African government.

Both men had business dealings in South Africa.

A second project of Rhoodie's was the Committee for Fairness in Sports. Supposedly headed by a private group of wealthy South Africans—Luyt was also a leading figure—the committee's mission was to counter the overseas campaign to boycott the country's sports teams and prevent them from competing in international sporting events. A significant member was the golf pro Gary Player. As part of government efforts to beat back calls for sanctions and to prevent American and European companies from withdrawing from the country, Player was asked to invite American CEOs to South Africa for a game of golf. With money from Rhoodie's secret funds, all-expenses-paid trips were provided for executives of companies such as Union Carbide, Bank of America and McDonnell Douglas, among others, to spend a week playing golf with Player.

The golf outings proved to be a major selling point with business executives. Several of them wrote glowing letters to US government officials about South Africa, asking for more lenient policies towards the apartheid regime. 'A personal invitation from Gary Player was worth ten invitations from the foreign minister,' a gleeful Rhoodie later boasted.

Other front groups established by Rhoodie in South Africa were the Foreign Affairs Association and the Southern African Freedom Foundation; two seemingly independent research groups which were also set up using secrets funds. The Foreign Affairs Association, which included Luyt among its members, was meant to serve as an 'independent clearing house for information on South Africa's contacts with the rest of the world'. It sponsored conferences worldwide and produced papers and books on the communist threat and the strategic importance of South African minerals to the US and other Western countries. The Freedom Foundation served a similar purpose, but was confined to the African continent. It promoted visits to South Africa by experts from other African countries.

Besides Gary Player, another well-known South African who would play a role in the information war was Dr Christiaan Barnard, the Cape Town surgeon who performed the first human heart transplant. Although Barnard was a vocal opponent of apartheid laws and treated both blacks and whites in his medical practice, the doctor agreed to help the government for patriotic reasons. Through Barnard's contacts, Rhoodie and other officials were able to meet heads of states that had often shunned contact with the South African government. Barnard would also play a key role in stopping a worldwide boycott of sea and air shipments to and from South Africa. Using his connections to the powerful American Federation of Labor leader George Meany, Barnard convinced the US labour unions that a boycott would actually hurt blacks more than it did whites. The boycott was called off. A gleeful Rhoodie would later say that 'Barnard thereby saved millions of South Africans' by helping to stop the boycott.

One of Rhoodie's first and perhaps most significant secretly funded projects in Europe was the UK-based Club of Ten. The organisation was supposed to be a group of British, South African and American businessmen concerned about the biased treatment of the apartheid government in the media. But despite its name, the Club was really the work of just one man, Gerald Sparrow, a former judge on the International Court in Bangkok. Sparrow was also a prolific writer who authored over 40 books, mostly about travel. Sparrow had first travelled to South Africa to write a book on tourism to the country on a six-week trip sponsored by the South African Tourism Corporation and the government-owned South African Airways. During his visit, Sparrow was approached by Connie Mulder, who set up a meeting between Sparrow and Eschel Rhoodie.

At the meeting Rhoodie outlined his project of a global advertising campaign that would trounce the enemies of South Africa, rout the Reds and 'quell those who dared to suggest that the government of South Africa was a tyranny in a democratic shell'. Rhoodie told Sparrow that writing letters to the editors of newspapers was hopeless because editors wouldn't print them, while articles written about South Africa were also ignored. The only way to counter the negative publicity was to buy full-page political advertisements in papers around the world. (Sparrow later noted that the papers would quickly accept the advertisements and compete with each other to offer the best space and terms.)

Sparrow suggested 'Friends of South Africa' as the name for the new front organisation. But Rhoodie came up with the 'Club of Ten' because he said it was very British-sounding and would promote interest and publicity. The publicly stated purpose of the Club of Ten would be tackling the global media for their bias, and the United Nations and the British and American governments for double-dealing and hypocrisy in their treatment of South Africa.

With funding in hand, and copy that was written by Rhoodie and Les de Villiers, Sparrow went on the attack. When *The Guardian* published a series of articles about the low wages earned by blacks in South Africa, the group took out advertisements in the *Daily Telegraph*, *The Times* and *The Guardian* itself, asking why the paper hadn't done the same for workers paid by British companies in India, Hong Kong, Ceylon or other countries in Africa. Other advertisements by the Club warned about communist activity in Africa and the strategic importance of South Africa.

The Club also took out full-page advertisements in papers elsewhere, including the *New York Times* and the *Washington Post* in the US, the *Montreal Star* in Canada, and major papers in West Germany, Holland, Australia and New Zealand. The advertisements ran to as much as $16,000 in some papers. In one year alone, the Club would spend about $100,000 in this way. The advertisements placed in these papers repeatedly attacked critics of the apartheid government and were seen by readers and opinion-makers in all the world capitals which the South African government wanted to influence.

Among those attacked by the Club of Ten was the World Council of Churches, particularly the WCC's Programme to Combat Racism, which provided direct humanitarian support to liberation movements like the ANC, and which had promoted several international campaigns for economic sanctions against the apartheid government.

From the beginning, anti-apartheid groups and, according to documents from the Wikileaks website, the US government itself thought the Club was little more than a front for Pretoria. But Sparrow and the South African government denied a connection. Press attention did, however, force the British Foreign Office to request a list of the group's members. Sparrow provided them with ten names, including those of Luyt, the South African fertiliser millionaire, and Lampas Nichas, a Greek immigrant to South Africa who had made a fortune selling potatoes. Nichas even travelled to Britain on 22 August 1974 to present a R50,000 cheque to Sparrow at the Royal Horse Guards Hotel as proof that wealthy South Africans were behind the venture and not the government, although the money he used was supplied by the Department of Information out of the secret 'G' fund. Three of the ten people on the list, including Luyt, were also members of the Foreign Affairs Association, another of the government's front groups. The British government took no further notice. Only much later would it be proved that the Club was the work of Pretoria.

In addition to the various front groups like the Club of Ten, Rhoodie also beefed up the government's direct lobbying and spying operations. In London two MPs in the ruling Labour Party were put on the South African government's payroll. Their job was to lobby for South Africa in the House of Commons and spy on anti-apartheid groups in the UK. Information from the two MPs was used to launch 'disinformation and disruptive' campaigns against anti-apartheid groups in Britain and Holland, including creating fake mail petitions, and cancelling meetings, all to cause confusion among the activists. The project, which was referred to in official documents as 'British parliamentary activities', cost about R46,000.

Leaders of the Liberal Party also felt they were being targeted by South African agents. Pete Hain, a leading participant in the campaign to stop tours of the UK by all-white South African sports teams, was believed to be one of the main targets of a South African smear campaign. For one thing, Hain was set up on a bank robbery charge for which he was later acquitted. In 1974, a photograph of Hain circulated in Britain that tried to tie him to a bombing in South Africa. The picture, which featured a dead baby, bore the caption 'A Victim of Liberal Terrorism'. A pamphlet entitled *The Hidden Face of the Liberal Party* was also widely circulated in an attempt to smear the party's leaders. Election documents later showed that a number of copies of the pamphlet had been entered on the expenses of Harold Gurden, a member of the Conservative Party and avid supporter of the South African government.

According to Rhoodie, in a second covert offensive in Britain, called 'Operation Bowler', money was funnelled through a conservative member of parliament for the purpose of bringing British MPs to South Africa. None of the MPs knew that the money was coming from the South African government.

Other secret projects in Britain involved the attempted take-over of the business publishing company Morgan Grampian. The company was the publisher of about 30 major journals and guidebooks. More importantly, it owned a major book publisher in the US that would have given the South African government a foothold there. Although the government failed to take over the company, it did manage to buy a 28 per cent stake.

The project actually made money for the government: it received nearly one million dollars, which was used to buy a South African publishing company, Hortors. The company set up a photo-news agency that had contracts to supply photos to numerous newspapers in the US including the *New York Times*, the *Washington Post* and the *Chicago Tribune*. None of the papers was aware that the South African government owned the photo service.

A secret effort in Germany involved taking journalists on annual trips to South Africa to win favourable coverage. Two Germans, Heinz Behrens, who had been with the German Press Agency, and a public relations consultant in Frankfurt coordinated the secret effort to bring about 15 German journalists and several politicians to South Africa on 'fact-finding' trips. In addition, Behrens wrote dozens of articles about South Africa and fed them to friendly reporters who published the work under their by-lines. Ironically, Gerald Barrie, who as auditor-general would play a role in exposing the so-called Information Scandal, had actually started the project while he was head of the Department of Information.

Anti-apartheid groups in The Hague were infiltrated and subjected to a dirty tricks campaign that included fake mailings and cancelled protests. In Japan a pro-South African group was formed that maintained contacts with Japanese unions, and an advertising expert was hired in Argentina who launched a year-long series of articles in nine papers in several South American countries.

In the US, Rhoodie and his department would launch a lobbying campaign that in its scope dwarfed their efforts in Europe and other parts of the world. Organisations such as Rotary and Lions International, which had branches around the world, were provided with speakers and sometimes money. Another part of the lobbying involved targeting Southern universities and small black businesses.

In one case, Ronald Farrar, then chairman of the department of journalism at the University of Mississippi, toured South Africa as a guest of the government and later wrote a number of favourable articles which suggested that the country had a free press, that whites had arrived in South Africa first, and that blacks were no longer required to carry passes. The articles were widely printed in several publications. When a local Mississippi activist distributed flyers debunking the claims in Farrar's articles, Farrar threatened to sue.

These public relations campaigns paled in comparison with the offensive which the South African government unleashed in Washington. The largest and most effective part of the lobbying campaign would involve prominent American businessmen, including Charles Engelhard; a former International Monetary Fund staffer, Albert S. Gerstein; film distributors; and dozens of lobbying firms with connections to both the Democratic and Republican parties.

One of the most prominent of these Washington lobbying firms hired by Rhoodie was Collier, Shannon, Rill & Edwards, which signed a contract to represent the South African government in 1974. The firm had close ties to the Republican Party. The man who would be the face of the South African public relations campaign in Washington was Donald E. de Kieffer of the same firm. Connie Mulder first approached De Kieffer, then a 28-year-old businessman with South African links and a former FBI agent, about becoming a lobbyist for South Africa in January 1974. The two men had met when Mulder was on a trip to Washington to meet with US officials. Mulder liked the young lobbyist, who had connections to many of the political power-brokers in the US capital. And almost as important, De Kieffer was married to a Japanese woman who had grown up in the state of Hawaii, which paradoxically made him the perfect political consultant for a South African government wishing to appear non-racist.

The records show that De Kieffer's firm was tasked to 'lobby for a reassessment of US policy towards South Africa, focusing on energy issues, mutual security and investment'. The firm said it would also contact public officials, media and education groups to project a positive image of South Africa in the US. The De Kieffer operation was directed by officials at the South African embassy or personally by Mulder in many cases.

From the start, the contract with the public relations firm was controversial. Officials at the South African embassy in Washington later said they had no knowledge of it and hadn't been consulted before it was signed, a fact that angered the diplomats, who claimed the

Department of Information was encroaching on their territory.

Still, the lobbying efforts by the newly hired PR firm proved to be highly successful and it would earn about R1 million over five years for its work. De Kieffer helped to arrange visits by Mulder to the US, where the information minister met with high-ranking American officials, including Vice-President Gerald Ford at the White House. Minutes from the meeting show that Mulder and the vice-president discussed the on-going arms embargo against South Africa, the US Navy boycott of South African ports and the country's strategic value to the US in its fight against communist expansion in southern Africa.

De Kieffer also arranged a meeting for Mulder with Thomas Morgan, chairman of the House of Representatives Foreign Affairs Committee. The meeting came just a few days after De Kieffer had given Morgan a monetary contribution for his election campaign. In 1974 he organised a meeting between Mulder and the Congressional Black Caucus. But Mulder failed to sell the merits of apartheid to the black law-makers.

De Kieffer also made inroads in Congress. He gave thousands of dollars in contributions to the campaigns of US senators and representatives. (He made sure to emphasise that the money for these campaigns was 'paid out of his pocket' and not from the South African government.) He also provided entertainment for members, including dinners, drinks and other social outings. His entertainment expenses on behalf of the South African government would jump from just over $2,000 in 1974 to nearly $18,000 in 1976, as records show. He helped as well to arrange for congressmen and their families to take fact-finding trips to South Africa. The trips would pay off when a political fight over recognising the black homeland of Transkei broke out in Congress. In 1976, when a resolution was brought up urging the US government not to recognise Transkei as an independent nation, De Kieffer managed to get the measure killed. The key to the resolution's defeat was the no vote of ten congressmen who had visited South Africa on government-subsidised trips.

De Kieffer also helped run another programme for the South African government that used intermediaries to fund many of the trips for members of Congress. One of the people involved in this effort was millionaire Werner Ackermann, husband of the South African opera singer Mimi Coertse. In early 1975, a number of high-profile American politicians and businessmen began receiving invitations from Ackermann to visit South Africa. Rhoodie would later reveal to the *Rand Daily Mail* that Ackermann had been reimbursed by the government for the trips. The list of invitees was provided by De Kieffer, who had done the same for other South African government front groups. Using businessmen like Ackermann to invite members of the US Congress may have been meant to get around the rules prohibiting representatives and senators from accepting gifts from foreign governments, such as travelling on junkets.

Not all members of Congress were willing to take the trips. When Ackermann reached out to Shirley Chisholm, a black Democrat from New York and frequent critic of South Africa, who was one of the people recommended by De Kieffer, the South African businessman was rebuffed.

In addition, De Kieffer hired Lester Kinsolving, a former Episcopalian minister, syndicated columnist and radio talkshow host, to take on a less visible lobbying role on behalf of the apartheid government. Kinsolving was given $25,000 in stock in several American companies including IBM, IT&T and the Southern Company, an electric utility—he called them 'lecture fees'—and expense money from De Kieffer in 1975 and 1976 to counter anti-apartheid groups, who were becoming more vocal. He also travelled to South Africa on a press junket paid for by the government. Kinsolving's job was to appear at the shareholders' meetings of 13 companies and defend the firms while church groups also present at the AGMs were pushing for resolutions to sever business ties with South Africa. He was meant to use his position as a former clergyman to provide a different viewpoint, one that opposed the boycott of companies doing business in South Africa.

Kinsolving, who today is a conservative radio talkshow host in Baltimore, has said that he never defended the racist system of apartheid, but wished to reveal the hypocrisy of the anti-apartheid movement, which never protested against African dictators like Idi Amin. The revelations of Kinsolving's lobbying by the *Washington Post* reporter Walter Pincus led to his press credentials being revoked in 1977 by the State Department Correspondents' Association, a group similar to the White House Press Association.

Kinsolving continues to deny that he was doing 'paid advocacy' for the South African government because, he said in a recent interview, the lobbyist who hired him never told him what to say.

* * *

South Africa's lobbying in the US wasn't left solely up to the government and its army of lobbyists. The South Africa Foundation, as usual, continued to play a critical role in the country's global information war. While it claimed to be independent of the apartheid government, the foundation did its part to support Pretoria's efforts to prevent any action that would cause harm to the country's image or its economy.

Leaders of the foundation in the 1970s believed that South Africa was being targeted by a well-funded international campaign, 'the like of which is possibly unequalled in history,' said Dr Jan Marais, president of the foundation, in a 1974 interview. Marais was also head of the Trust Bank, one of the biggest banks in South Africa at the time.

With more than 200 members representing some of the largest companies in South Africa, including members from companies in the US and Europe with South African interests, the foundation had access to large amounts of money to help promote the country. It spent R800,000 on lobbying and fact-finding trips for foreign dignitaries in 1975, and had R1.5 million in reserve.

In Britain, the foundation teamed with the United Kingdom-South Africa Trade Association to promote trade and investment in South Africa and opposition to sanctions. The foundation and the association jointly produced a magazine that promoted South African interests, and jointly arranged trade missions to the country. The two organisations also shared some of the same board members.

The foundation didn't just depend on the trade association to promote South Africa in the UK, but maintained its own offices in London. It regularly sponsored trips for British politicians, journalists and businessmen so that they could 'see the country for themselves'. By the mid-1970s the foundation had hosted about 100 politicians from countries around the world, as well as 75 editors, journalists and businessmen. Some of the most prominent guests of the foundation at that time were Sir Henry Plumb of the British National Farmers' Union, who was later a member of parliament for the Conservative Party and president of the European Parliament; Israel Wamala, a Ugandan-born journalist who headed the BBC's Africa Service, and would later aggressively question Prime Minister Vorster during a radio interview; and Sir Geoffrey Howe, later Britain's foreign secretary under Prime Minister Margaret Thatcher, who spoke out about apartheid but remained opposed to imposing sanctions. Dozens of other British politicians also made the all-expenses-paid trips. While some would be critical of the country, most of those who travelled would return home singing the praises of South Africa.

In the US, the foundation ran a similar operation. It sponsored trips to South Africa for members of Congress, particularly key conservatives and those sitting on key congressional committees. It also actively lobbied Congress and prepared talking points and fact sheets for friendly law-makers who would use the information to defend the South African government in congressional hearings. The foundation produced and distributed a number of publications for its American audiences including *South Africa International, Foundation News* and the *Information Digest*. Most of the organisation's budget in the US was spent on travel and entertainment.

The foundation's American director, John Chettle, was a constant presence at congressional hearings and on American television programmes, and a frequent speaker on US college and university campuses. Chettle, a native of Durban, said he had been recruited for the job after working for a number of years as an executive at the South African mining giant Anglo American. 'They asked me about working in the US to help explain the situation to businessmen and policymakers,' Chettle said. 'I told them that I would do it for a few years, which I did, but I eventually returned. I enjoyed the work.'

The foundation had gained a degree of credibility because it would often criticise the South African government. Prime Minister Verwoerd had once taken the foundation to task for trying to undermine the government. But while it may have occasionally had differences with the government, the foundation stopped short of supporting major changes such as full and equal political rights for black people.

Chettle and other officials did call for concessions to be made to black South Africans, such as easing or even abolishing entirely the pass laws. This stance helped the foundation reach into business and social circles unavailable to apartheid officials. Chettle and his colleagues were often invited to speak at business conferences, academic settings or other forums where they would try to convince attendees that the best way to help blacks in South Africa was to have American business invest more, not less.

In their investigation into foreign lobbying in the US, Russell Howe and Sarah Trott called the foundation a 'front group for the government'. 'It is well known in South Africa that the Foundation gets funding from the government,' the authors wrote in their book *The Power Peddlers*. But foundation officials denied the allegations. 'I have never seen any real proof that the South Africa Foundation was promoting government policy,' Chettle said in an interview in 2014. 'In fact we were often at odds with the government over several of its policies.'

Still, the work of the South Africa Foundation received favourable reviews from apartheid officials. And in its annual reports, the foundation often noted its cooperation with the Department of Information and South African embassies throughout the world, which assisted the group in the reception of foreign visitors.

Dr Connie Mulder, the information minister, praised the group for 'doing excellent work in the interest of South Africa', though he too denied there was a link with the government. Rhoodie said the foundation had the same goals as the government: it 'tries to do on a private basis what the Department of Information is doing on an official basis'. The foundation did draw unwanted public scrutiny to its lobbying activities in 1977 when the US Justice Department sued it for serving as a pass-through for money from South African business interests to pay for trips by members of the US Congress. The Justice Department investigation and subsequent lawsuit found that the South African Sugar Association (SASA) had paid for numerous trips to South Africa by members of the House of Representatives Agriculture Committee and their spouses. Included on the trips were William Poage, who served as chairman of the Agriculture Committee, and several other congressmen, who were offered a private executive jet to transport them on a round-trip between South Africa and Rhodesia. 'Knowing that the SASA hospitality so preferred would create a conflict-of-interest situation,' it was argued, the defendants 'arranged to make it appear outwardly that the foundation, rather than SASA, was host'.

The Justice Department investigation was limited and only charged the Sugar Association, the foundation and its director with incomplete reporting under the Foreign Agents Registration Act, a paperwork violation that did little to curtail lobbying by the group. None of the members of Congress involved were investigated for wrongdoing.

* * *

By the mid-1970s, things couldn't have been going better for the South African government. In its annual reports to the South African parliament, the Department of Information now boasted of a shift in international opinion about the country. This was especially true in the US, which South African officials considered crucial to winning the global propaganda war.

Spending by the government and the size of its operations in America reflected this belief. The Department of Information's budget had grown from just over $380,000 in 1969 to over $600,000 in 1976. The department maintained offices in Washington, New York and Los Angeles, and additional information officers were posted in consulates in Houston, Chicago and San Francisco.

For these outposts, the department ran several programmes whose purpose was to influence American opinion about South Africa. The offices distributed thousands of copies of government-produced publications, including those promoting the independence of Transkei, and a glossy magazine called *South African Panorama*. The department also produced a bi-monthly radio programme called 'South Africa Magazine' that was sent to hundreds of US radio stations, which often used them without listeners being told that the South African government had funded it. It further produced a series of short television programmes that were distributed through companies such as Association-Sterling Films, which was paid hundreds of thousands of dollars and which played a role similar to that of Hamilton Wright in the 1960s. 'Television is the most important publicity medium in the USA,' a Department of Information memo said. In 1974 alone, some 32 million Americans would view these films. In 1976 there were 1,160 screenings of documentaries produced by the South African Department of Information. These often depicted smiling whites, blacks in traditional dress or dancing, and plenty of wildlife. The 'soft' propaganda also featured films about the country's vast natural resources and its strategic importance to the US.

Rhoodie pushed information officers to get out of the office and meet with US government officials and ordinary citizens face to face. These 'contact tours' saw officers travelling to small towns and cities well beyond the major metropolitan areas of New York and Washington. In one year alone, South African officials—who were naturally a source of curiosity in the American heartland—visited 118 small US cities and towns. According to a 1975 Department of Information report, tours by the New York office alone 'indicate a rewarding result since the visits in most cases were followed by positive publicity for South Africa in the American press'.

By the mid-1970s total annual spending by the South African government had reached about $1.5 million per year (about $7.2 million today). But even that figure may underestimate the total amount of money spent. In boasting to the *Rand Daily Mail* in 1974, Rhoodie explained that '50 to 60 per cent of the Department's methods would be "hidden" not in the sense of secrecy or subversion, but on an indirect basis'.

With millions of dollars at his disposal and with the cooperation of groups such as the South Africa Foundation, Rhoodie felt everything was finally falling into place. The tide, for once, was turning in South Africa's favour. Rhoodie and the apartheid government were finally taking the fight to their enemies.

4

Operation Blackwash

'Before accepting the South African account I wanted to see the situation myself, and it was encouraging.'
– Andrew T. Hatcher,
African American lobbyist for South Africa

Outgunned by the millions of dollars the South African government was pouring into its propaganda campaign and equipped with few resources of its own, the anti-apartheid movement in America and Europe had limited success in keeping the South African situation at the political forefront of public attention. A few labour unions staged boycotts of South African products entering the US and UK, but this had a limited effect. The number of black American members of Congress continued to grow, but their efforts to persuade the various presidential administrations to impose sanctions had largely fallen on deaf ears and the grassroots movement pushing for sanctions and divestment had stalled.

The Soweto uprising in 1976 would change all that. On the morning of 16 June students from numerous schools in Soweto township outside Johannesburg began to protest in the streets against the introduction of Afrikaans as the language of instruction in education. The police fired into the crowds, killing nearly 200, including 13-year-old Hector Pieterson.

The photograph of Pieterson being carried by Mbuyisa Makhubo, a fellow student, as his sister, Antoinette Sithole, ran alongside became the iconic image of the uprisings. Pictures of the shootings were played repeatedly on television sets around the world and would galvanise opposition to the South African government and its race-based policies.

Anti-apartheid activists in the US pushed President Gerald Ford to mount some kind of punitive action against South Africa. But Henry Kissinger, the secretary of state and a holdover from the Nixon years, argued against it. One of the punishments suggested by members of Congress and activist groups was to expel South Africa from the International Atomic Energy Agency, in line with the international condemnation of the violence. But Kissinger also argued against that measure, reminding the Ford administration that South Africa was an important ally and Soweto was an internal matter. When Kissinger attended a meeting in Germany with Prime Minister John Vorster in late June 1976, he didn't even mention the Soweto killings, according to State Department documents.

The election of a new American president a few months after the revolt in Soweto offered some hope, and black leaders in particular began to push the new administration of Jimmy Carter for action. Blacks formed a sizeable part of the American electorate and were crucial to Carter's first election campaign and his prospects of a second term.

Carter took a different approach in dealing with the apartheid government from his predecessors. In one of his first speeches after becoming president he vowed that the US would no longer overlook the human rights abuses of allies like South Africa: 'For too many years, we've been willing to adopt the flawed and erroneous principles and tactics of our adversaries, sometimes abandoning our own values for theirs. We've fought fire with fire, never thinking that fire is sometimes best quenched with water,' Carter said.

The Carter administration's new emphasis on human rights led to a congressional requirement for the annual submission by the Department of State of 'a full and complete report' on human rights practices around the world, the first of its kind. Carter also ordered a ban on the sharing of intelligence between agencies like the CIA, the US military, the National Security Agency and the South African government. Yet despite the rhetoric and some cosmetic policy statements, Carter made few changes to the diplomatic relationship between the two countries.

Carter did vote for United Nations arms sanctions against South Africa and even discussed economic sanctions, but never implemented them. His ambassador to the UN, Andrew Young, a black American and confidant of Martin Luther King Jr, had cautioned the president against sanctions. Young, while calling the white South African government 'illegitimate', nevertheless did not believe that divestment or sanctions would help, telling Carter that the US did not want to 'back South Africa into a corner'. The Black Consciousness leader Steve Biko, who refused to meet with Young when the ambassador travelled to South Africa in 1976, said the American diplomat had 'no programme except the furtherance of the American system'.

In Pretoria, panic set in after the Soweto shootings. Even more than the Sharpeville massacre, Soweto quickly turned world opinion even further against the country. This time American and European governments were clearly no longer willing to look the other way.

As a result the apartheid government needed to counter, even more strongly than before, the view that South Africa was a racist society and blunt the calls for increased sanctions, which had escalated after the events of June. Shortly before the Soweto uprising the Department of Information had hired the New York firm Sydney Baron, one of the most prestigious and politically connected public relations businesses in the US. Baron was just one of many firms hired by the government, but it would be the most influential and play a key role in trying to change public opinion, especially among American blacks, in the 1970s. Baron was paid about $365,000 a year by South Africa. Despite some criticism for taking on this client, the firm's owner, after whom the company was named, said, 'Every client can't be Disneyworld ... clients have problems and problems are challenges ... South Africa is a very challenging one.'

Shortly after an arrangement was signed, the firm hired Andrew T. Hatcher, a 53-year-old black American, as its vice-president of international operations and the face of the campaign to discourage divestment and sanctions against South Africa. In his book *The Real Information Scandal*, Rhoodie later said that one of the main reasons Baron was hired was the presence of 'Hatcher, a Negro', who had 'invaluable political contacts'. Hatcher, a former editor at the *San Francisco Sun-Reporter*, had made history over a decade earlier when he was hired as the first black member of the White House press staff, serving as a deputy press aide to President Kennedy. Hatcher had joined the presidential campaign of the Massachusetts senator in 1960 as a speechwriter and member of the press staff. His presence on the team helped Kennedy in his efforts to appeal to black American voters in particular, whose support provided the margin of victory over Richard Nixon in a closely contested election.

One of the new president's first actions was to name Hatcher deputy press secretary, which broke the colour barrier for the press staff, previously all-white. The appointment made Hatcher a household name among blacks and one of the most high-profile African Americans in the world. A black journalist described Hatcher's appointment as 'comparable to Jackie Robinson when he broke into baseball's big leagues'. (In 1947 Robinson became the first black player in what had hitherto been an all-white major baseball league.) Hatcher would use his position to help black Americans gain access to the president. Famously, he would be the face of the Kennedy administration during some of the most critical moments of contemporary history, including the Cuban missile crisis.

Given his stature in the black community, the South African government hoped Hatcher's skin colour would help deflect criticism of apartheid and refute claims that the country was run by a racist government that denied black citizens their basic rights. The message from Hatcher was that the government was slowly making changes.

As lead man on the South African account, Hatcher helped organise a conference at which black businesses and corporations were encouraged to invest in South Africa. Unknown to the participants, the conference, which featured the former long-serving Treasury secretary William E. Simon, was paid for by the South African Department of Information. Another conference in Houston, Texas, featured former President Gerald Ford, who was paid $10,000 for his appearance. He was persuaded to speak by John McGoff, the conservative American publisher and South African government supporter, who was a close friend of the former president. Ford later said that he didn't know the South African government had paid his fee for speaking at the conference.

Hatcher's job also included setting up trips to South Africa for black American legislators and journalists so they could see conditions for themselves, although those who went averred that their movements were controlled and they were not allowed to visit places on their own. Only those journalists who could be counted on to write positively about South Africa were invited.

In the US, Hatcher was sent as spokesman to several black events, including a conference of 100 Black Men, a civic organisation he had co-founded in 1963 to help young African Americans. His appearance at the group's 1976 conference drew heckling from most of the audience and a small crowd carrying signs protested outside the event, with many questioning how a black man could lobby for South Africa. Hatcher described the audience of about 150 people as 'politely hostile'. 'We're talking about an emotional issue,' he said after the event. 'People seemed frustrated.'

Hatcher also made a number of press appearances on behalf of the South African government, including several bookings on national television morning news programmes. In one interview he told an audience that he had found considerable hope among blacks he had talked to in his visits to townships surrounding Johannesburg, Pretoria and Durban, saying that many local black leaders rejected the violence that had erupted after Soweto.

Hatcher's signature moment as a representative for the apartheid government came in June 1976 on NBC's 'Today' show when he debated with George Houser, a white anti-apartheid activist, who had founded the American Committee on Africa, an organisation that pushed for sanctions against South Africa. Houser said that violence in South Africa was escalating because of the government's continuing exclusion of blacks from power. Hatcher, who appeared on the show to defend the South African government, disagreed. He said that violence in South Africa was waning because the government was committed to changing apartheid laws and allowing blacks greater participation in politics and business. 'Before accepting the South African account I wanted to see the situation myself, and it was encouraging,' said Hatcher, who had recently made a trip to South Africa. He told the television audience that he wanted to save 'black South Africans from the George Housers of the world', implying that Houser was one of those white liberals who thought they knew what was best for blacks. A stunned Houser replied: 'to see a black man defending South Africa for money is not unlike seeing a Jew hired by the Nazis'.

In addition to his duties of defending the apartheid government, Hatcher was also tasked with vetting American journalists who wanted to go to the country after the Soweto killings. One journalist who wished to make the trip was Les Payne of *New York Newsday*. Payne, a black American, was a Pulitzer Prize-winning investigative reporter and had known of Hatcher because of his role in the Kennedy White House. When Payne applied for a visa at the South African embassy, the Department of Information assigned Hatcher to conduct a check and report back with a recommendation. When Hatcher discovered that Payne was a prize-winning journalist with a penchant for producing race-related stories, he recommended to the Information Department that Payne be denied entry. Despite Hatcher's opposition, Payne still managed to be issued with a visa on the recommendation of the South African minister of sport, Piet Koornhof, after the black American tennis pro Arthur Ashe, who knew Koornhof, had intervened on Payne's behalf.

Hatcher was then assigned to fly to South Africa with Payne, and chaperone him round the country. At Johannesburg airport, Hatcher introduced Payne to a man in a dark suit and sunglasses who called himself Mr Cloete from the Department of Information. (Payne believed the man was an agent of the Bureau of State Security.) Cloete and Hatcher again warned him sternly that Soweto was off limits. Instead, he was offered a month-long guided tour, drawn up by Hatcher, that included visits to gold mines, the black homelands, and the independence ceremony of Transkei, where Payne watched the lowering of the South African flag and the raising of the standard of the newly 'free' homeland. Throughout the tour Hatcher was with him constantly.

Payne recalled that during one of their trips he and Hatcher were in a taxi, and the driver, a black South African amazed at hearing a black American speak favourably of the apartheid government, asked Hatcher if 'he was with the people or the government'. 'I'm with the government,' Payne recalled Hatcher saying. The taxi driver shook his head in disgust.

Payne eventually managed to evade his guide and make a journey to several black townships, including Soweto. One of the stories he filed from his unauthorised journeys would cause the government some embarrassment. 'One of the troubling stories that nagged me making the rounds concerned the actual number of Africans police killed during the disturbance,' Payne said. 'The US media had settled on a figure ranging from 250 to 300, a figure they got directly from the Minister of Justice.' However, Soweto residents assured Payne that the numbers were much higher but they had no way of documenting this allegation. 'Rumours were flying around that bodies were taken out to sea and dumped from helicopters,' Payne said. To come up with concrete figures, Payne spent three weeks knocking on the doors of undertakers, morticians, inquest court clerks, eyewitnesses and relatives. His shoe-leather reporting was rewarded with the specific names, ages and circumstances of death at police hands of more than 800 Africans. 'I really pissed them [the government] off because I caught them in a flat-out lie,' Payne said. Payne would subsequently be banned from South Africa largely, he believed, at the instance of Hatcher.

Hatcher and his firm, Sydney Baron, would play other roles for the South African government, including trying to win international recognition for the Transkei bantustan, or ethnic homeland, set up by the government as a so-called self-governing independent African state. In reality, the Transkei, like the other bantustans, lacked meaningful economic or political power, and was little more than a puppet state controlled by South Africa.

At the South African government's expense Hatcher led a delegation of 14 Americans to the Transkei's independence ceremony in October 1976, over the objections of President Ford, who refused to recognise the 'homeland' as an independent country. Anti-apartheid activists travelling in southern Africa reported to the US embassy that Hatcher was handing out lapel pins with interlocking American and Transkei flags, which suggested US support, according to US diplomatic cables from the Wikileaks website. Hatcher also managed to get full-page advertisements about Transkei's independence in the *Wall Street Journal* and the black-owned *Ebony* magazine. But much of his outreach work was unsuccessful.

Most black journalists, like Ethel Payne, known as the 'first lady of the black press' and one of the first black women to work as a foreign correspondent, turned down the free trips Hatcher offered to South Africa because of the restrictions imposed. Payne ridiculed Hatcher in a column, calling his lobbying for South Africa shameful, and adding that he had taken the job because he had fallen on hard times.

Hatcher performed a number of other services for the South African government. He helped stop a proposed investigation by the House of Representatives into the lobbying activities of the South African government, monitored an anti-apartheid rally in New York City's Herald Square, and coordinated a television public relations campaign with Donald de Kieffer, another lobbyist hired by Rhoodie.

At about the same time as it hired Hatcher and Sydney Baron to represent it in the US, the South African government, with funds channelled through the Transkei, also hired several additional firms to help change the image of the homeland and sell it as an independent country. Bernard Katzen, a New York public relations man, who was paid $150,000 in 1979, was dispatched to the United Nations to 'encourage recognition of Transkei'. The most prominent Transkei lobbyist was Jay Parker, a black American, who was hired to promote the homeland as a 'non-racial state that had eliminated the South African system of apartheid'. According to documents at the Department of Justice, the government took on the lobbyist as an agent to represent the Transkei from 1977 through 1978. As part of his duties for the homeland, Parker distributed press releases, prepared speeches and issued brochures extolling the virtues of the new black republic.

Parker's job included monitoring the press, in particular the black press, and arranging meetings and receptions for Transkei officials, who sought recognition in the US. In particular his task was to persuade African Americans that the Transkei was entirely black-ruled and completely independent of the South African government. Parker ran the lobbying campaign through an organisation he had established, called Friends of Transkei. He also made television appearances on behalf of the South African government. He and Hatcher appeared on a CBS programme in October 1976 with Les de Villiers, South Africa's deputy secretary for information, to inform New Yorkers about the benefit of South Africa's homeland policies.

Parker, who was a protégé of Max Yergan and worked with the former apartheid apologist at the American African Affairs Association, was a long-time conservative. He was in fact an unlikely point of liaison with the wider US black community, where he had little support. In the early 1980s he would not endear himself to most black Americans by opposing a federal holiday for Martin Luther King Jr, arguing that the revered civil rights leader, who had criticised the Vietnam War, had given his 'full support to the North Vietnamese communists'.

While serving as a South African lobbyist, Parker created the conservative Lincoln Institute for Research and Education, which was founded to study public policy issues with an impact on the lives of black middle-class Americans. The institute published a quarterly journal, *Lincoln Review*, which consistently attacked the ANC, opposed sanctions against South Africa and denounced US civil rights leaders for their support of the anti-apartheid movement. In his 2009 biography, *Courage to Put My Country above Color*, Parker said he had sided with South African capitalists against Soviet-backed liberation movements such as the ANC. And while he thought apartheid denied black South Africans basic political rights, he did not want the country to fall into the hands of the Soviet Union.

But all this lobbying on behalf of the Transkei failed to move world opinion and the Transkei was never recognised abroad. In October 1976 the General Assembly of the United Nations, by a vote of 134 to 0, pronounced it a 'sham' and invalid and refused to recognise it. Even the US abstained from voting at the United Nations on the Transkei.

Failure to win international recognition for the Transkei wasn't the only problem for the South African government. The overall propaganda war wasn't working either and, although they didn't know it, things were about to get worse for Rhoodie and the South African government.

5

Muldergate

'I wish to state that, for years, the Department of Information has been asked by the government to take sensitive and even highly secret operations as counteraction to the propaganda war being waged against South Africa.'
— Eschel Rhoodie, secretary for information

Worldwide attention was again drawn to South Africa in 1977 when the Black Consciousness leader Steve Biko was killed while in police custody. Biko, who had been banned by the government, was arrested and fatally injured during interrogation by the security police. Although it was officially claimed that Biko died of a self-induced hunger strike, Helen Zille, a journalist at the *Rand Daily Mail*, obtained medical records from Biko's doctors that showed no sign of a hunger strike. Instead the death was the result of a brain haemorrhage from his being struck multiple times on the head. The South African minister of justice, Jimmy Kruger, told members of parliament: 'I am not glad and I am not sorry about Mr Biko. It leaves me cold.' This comment added to the international outrage and condemnation of the South African government. But an official inquest cleared the police of any wrongdoing.

Coming on the heels of Biko's death, the United Nations added to the apartheid government's woes by declaring 1978 the International Anti-Apartheid Year, which placed an even greater global focus on the government's racial policies. At about the same time, the secret projects hatched and carried out by the Department of Information, so crucial to the propaganda war, began to spiral out of control.

First, in Britain, a frustrated Gerald Sparrow resigned from the Club of Ten and wrote a book detailing the South African government's role in funding the group. Sparrow said he had been let go by the government after a disagreement with the Department of Information over the publication of a magazine which Rhoodie had disliked. But, more importantly, he said, he'd had a change of heart after he and his wife travelled to townships like Soweto.

The book, *The Ad Astra Connection*, gave a detailed account of the government's attempts to buy positive publicity by placing advertisements in newspapers around the world and attacking the government's opponents. The book, though, did not provide the necessary documentation to back up Sparrow's allegations. The Club of Ten would continue to exist and carry out its advertising campaigns after Sparrow left, but the disclosure was nevertheless damaging.

Even more damaging was what came next. During his time as secretary for information, Rhoodie had made his share of enemies within the government. Prompted by complaints and allegations by whistle-blowers, Gerald Barrie, the auditor-general, began looking into 'irregularities' and 'non-adherence to regulations and instructions' at the Department of Information. Barrie, who had been head of the department before Rhoodie, had himself participated in establishing several secret projects while director.

One of the projects had begun when Rhoodie, then working as a press officer at the South African embassy in The Hague, clandestinely negotiated an agreement with a Dutch publisher, Hubert Jussen, who agreed to help set up a new magazine called *To the Point*. This was a glossy news magazine that resembled *Time* or *The Economist*. Like other projects, *To the Point* was to be secretly financed by the South African government, with Jussen as the face of the publication. The magazine was established to counter some of the unfavourable press coverage that apartheid received overseas and provide the world with a 'balanced' view of the white minority regime. Rhoodie had sold the idea to the head of the Department of Information, Gerald Barrie. It also had the approval of Prime Minister Vorster, General Hendrik van den Bergh of the Bureau of State Security, and Dr Connie Mulder.

In February 1978, following nearly two years of investigation, Barrie delivered a damning report that detailed extensive misuse of government funds by Department of Information officials. A few months later, in April 1978, Kitt Katzen, an investigative reporter, published the first of several explosive reports in the Johannesburg *Sunday Express* that prompted parliament to begin its own official probe.

More details began to emerge about the secret projects and misuse of government funds as other reporters, particularly Mervyn Rees and Chris Day at the *Rand Daily Mail*, dug deeper into the scandal. The duo made inroads by tracking down employees at the Department of Information willing to talk. They also cultivated secret sources in other parts of the government, as well as in the National Party, who served the same role as Deep Throat in the Watergate scandal in the US.

Finally, they tracked down Rhoodie to Miami, where he was briefly in hiding, and then to the country of Ecuador, where he would eventually take refuge. Their interviews with Rhoodie would reveal the full scope of the scandal, which later came to be known as Muldergate, allowing the reporters to break numerous stories. These revealed that the government had shifted millions of dollars from the defence budget to fund about 160 secret projects for a worldwide propaganda campaign. Rees and Day likened the web of global projects to 'dozens of pieces that had been manipulated on a worldwide chessboard'.

Some of the projects were bizarre, like the attempt to finance a South Africa-supporting political party in Norway. Another eccentric and less than successful project was the funding of a cable television station in California to promote a positive view of South Africa. The station turned out to be a husband-and-wife team with a small viewership that reached a few hundred people. It eventually closed down.

But most of the money, as Rees and Day revealed from their interviews with Rhoodie, was used to purchase favourable coverage by bribing journalists in other countries or even, in some cases, trying to buy newspapers and other media outright. One of the largest of these projects, called Operation Star, involved a plan to buy a US newspaper. In 1974, the apartheid regime secretly gave the conservative Michigan publisher John McGoff, owner of the media company Panax, $11.3 million to buy the *Washington Star*, which was at one time a rival to the *Washington Post*. The son of a steelworker, McGoff had amassed a small publishing empire by the time he first went to South Africa at the invitation of Les de Villiers in the late 1960s. In South Africa, the publisher rubbed shoulders with top government officials, including Vorster and Mulder. McGoff, Mulder and Rhoodie would later buy a ranch together.

Despite his connections with those in power in South Africa, in the US McGoff was largely unknown, and in his hometown of Williamston, Michigan, he was considered a bit of a crackpot. He had once tried to have the town reject federal money for hot lunches for children because accepting it would amount to 'federal control'. All the same, the South Africans believed they had found the perfect man to carry out their plan to convert a respectable American newspaper into a propaganda tool.

McGoff had tried to get the papers he already owned to be receptive to a more benign view of the apartheid government. Former editors who worked for McGoff told the *Columbia Journalism Review* that after his various trips to South Africa, he would send them stories about the country. One recalled that after one visit McGoff wrote a 12-part series about the strategic importance of South Africa. Yet another editor, David Rood, said that he received several series from McGoff on the problems of southern Africa. When Rood objected, he was told to run the articles.

But even with McGoff's interventions, there was little chance that his small-circulation papers would have much value as propaganda tools. The reach of the papers did not extend beyond McGoff's home state. Then McGoff learned that the *Washington Star* was up for sale.

Purchasing the *Washington Star* made sense on several levels. For one, the paper's editorial policy had always been conservative, and so taking a favourable position towards South Africa would not have raised suspicion. Secondly, buying a paper in the American capital city would give the apartheid government access to and influence with its resident policy-makers and foreign diplomats. If the sale had been successful, the plan was to set up a South Africa desk at the paper to pump out positive news about the country.

McGoff, whose company was losing money at the time, made an offer of between $20 million and $25 million for the paper. But after lawyers for the family that owned the *Washington Star* looked over McGoff's financial records, they concluded that he didn't have the necessary capital. McGoff assured them that he had the wherewithal because the family that owned the American chemical giant Dow was backing him. (The family later denied that they had any involvement in trying to buy the *Washington Star*.)

The effort to buy the paper eventually failed, but McGoff had more luck with his second bid. He succeeded in buying the *Sacramento Union* in California with the money from Pretoria. Rhoodie later said the government had no idea McGoff was going to buy the *Union* and it lost money on the project. McGoff also used $1.5 million in secret funds from Pretoria to buy a 50 per cent interest in UPITN, a television news agency that operated from 1967 to 1985. United Press International, a competitor of Associated Press, and Independent Television News owned the other half of the news agency. At the time of the McGoff purchase, UPITN had clients in more than 100 countries and was the world's second-largest news film producer and distributor in the world. ABC News as a major American client.

After the South African funding was exposed, McGoff was investigated by the US Justice Department, which charged him with accepting millions of dollars from the South African government, alleging that he had taken the money without registering as a foreign agent. A federal court later dismissed the case against McGoff because the government had brought it after the statute of limitations had expired. But the Securities and Exchange Commission (SEC) also investigated McGoff on charges of failing to disclose that he had used money from the South African government to purchase newspapers and fund 'massive acquisitions' of stock in the company he owned, to enrich himself. 'The SEC further suspected that McGoff might have made an undisclosed agreement with South African officials to use Panax newspapers to promote South African interests,' the agency said in court records. After a lengthy fight with the SEC, McGoff eventually settled with the agency. McGoff did not admit or deny the charges but agreed to a court order barring any future violation of securities laws.

Despite the US and South African investigations, McGoff would continue to deny that the apartheid government had backed his media purchases. 'I have never taken a nickel from anybody outside this country,' he was quoted as saying in 1975. 'I am a patriot.'

After his brush with the US Justice Department, McGoff sold off parts of his media holdings to other chains and finally liquidated his newspaper group of daily and weekly papers. Nevertheless, he would continue to be an advocate for the apartheid government and continued to call for greater US investment in South Africa. He died of cancer in 1998.

In addition to the projects that involved McGoff, Rees and Day also found that the American financial magazine *Businessweek* featured prominently in the South African government's propaganda campaign. The Department of Information, over a three-year period, paid R300,000 to have an annual special supplement on South Africa included in the publication. Rhoodie told the reporters that the supplement had been an overwhelming success, generating thousands of letters in response to the first issue alone. But neither the magazine nor the writers producing the copy knew that the apartheid government was financing it.

According to Rhoodie, the covert campaign in the US had extended beyond attempts to buy newspapers and positive media coverage. Rhoodie also implicated Andrew Hatcher and his employer, the Sydney Baron public relations firm, in a scheme to influence US elections. In his book and in an interview in 1980 with the German magazine *Der Spiegel*, he alleged that $200,000 in South African covert funds was funnelled through Sydney Baron and used to help defeat Senator John Tunney. Tunney, a California Democrat, had angered the South African government in the 1970s by sponsoring legislation that temporarily cut off US aid to the Angolan rebel movement Unita, led by Jonas Savimbi, one of South Africa's clients.

Two years later the firm also targeted Iowa Senator Dick Clark, also a Democrat, who had sponsored legislation that cut off aid to Unita permanently. Clark had also called for an end to white rule in South Africa and, as chairman of the Senate Foreign Relations Committee's subcommittee on Africa, had held hearings to raise awareness about conditions in the country. According to Rhoodie, Clark's defeat in 1978 after a campaign in which he had been leading in the polls was due to the fact that the South African government had channelled $25,000 to his opponent.

During one of his trips to South Africa, Clark had come into contact with Steve Biko, who had just been released from jail two months before his final arrest and brutal police interrogation. Clark became a courier of sorts for Biko, taking back a memorandum to President Carter's incoming administration.

Clark's defeat was widely celebrated by government officials in South Africa, according to the *New York Times* correspondent Tom Wicker, who wrote that they could hardly contain their glee when informed of the results. Roger Jepsen, the Republican who defeated Clark, often mocking him as the 'Senator from Africa', would become an opponent of sanctions against South Africa. An investigation into the illegal South African funding was stopped after the US attorney in Iowa who was pursuing the allegations was removed from his job and replaced by a friend of Jepsen. The Federal Election Commission declined to investigate the accusations.

According to Rhoodie, the plan to funnel money to Clark's opponent was drawn up by Hatcher and Sydney Baron during a visit by the two men to South Africa in early 1978. The plan was discussed in a meeting with Vorster and Mulder. During the discussions, according to Rhoodie, Hatcher and his boss had reportedly boasted to Vorster that they had pulled off the defeat of Senator Tunney in the same manner in 1976. The two men allegedly told the South African prime minister that if he renewed the firm's nearly $500,000 annual contract, they would make sure Clark was taken care of.

Although Hatcher originally denied his role in the campaign to unseat Clark and Tunney, he later told the British journalist Anthony Sampson that on a visit to Pretoria he had promised Vorster that Clark would not survive the 1978 campaign. Jepsen, the man who unseated Clark, called the allegations totally false, adding that there 'was every reason to believe that there was absolutely no money put into my campaign from South Africa'.

Although Rhoodie failed to produce proof that the South African government tried to influence the 1978 Iowa Senate campaign, there is some evidence that South African interests or supporters attempted to change the outcome in Jepsen's favour. For one thing, during the campaign a flood of right-wing pamphlets criticising Clark for being soft on communism came into Iowa from the state of Ohio. No one seemed to know who sent them. A more direct South African connection can be traced to the visit to Iowa, a year before the election, by Jan van Rooyen, of the South African embassy in Washington, at the invitation of a conservative state senator, Stephen Bisenius. The state senator said he invited a number of government officials from different countries to talk about trade and investment because he was interested in selling local agricultural and other products abroad. 'It made sense to try to expand our business with countries like South Africa, and Clark didn't care,' Bisenius said in a 2014 interview.

While ostensibly present to talk about the possibilities of trade, Van Rooyen launched into an attack on Senator Clark for his support of black majority rule in South Africa. Van Rooyen asked his audience 'why Senator Clark finds South Africa such a fine problem, rather than dealing with the real problems this state might have'.

The State Department's under-secretary for political affairs, David D. Newsom, quickly fired off an angry complaint to the South African embassy and to Pretoria, objecting to Van Rooyen's speech. The US official charged that in making disparaging remarks about Clark, Van Rooyen had interjected himself into the American electoral process.

Bisenius would later be invited to a business conference that had been sponsored by the South African government and organised by Sydney Baron, the lobbying firm. One of the speakers was John McGoff, who used his time at the podium to attack Clark for interfering in South African politics. McGoff introduced Bisenius to several South African businessmen and representatives from Sydney Baron, including Andrew Hatcher. During the meeting Bisenius was repeatedly told that 'We don't get along with one of your Senators' and that Clark should be replaced in Congress by someone who was friendlier towards South Africa.

Rhoodie also claimed that South African interference in US politics wasn't limited to the two Senate campaigns. The firm also allegedly gave $20,000 to the campaign of Jimmy Carter in his 1976 presidential bid. South African officials had reached out to Carter through Sydney Baron earlier and an official from the Department of Information's New York office met with the future president in his Georgia office. 'But Carter's opinion, as was expressed to the Information ministry then and the position that he took as president, proved to be very different,' Rhoodie later recalled.

* * *

Muldergate would become one of the biggest political scandals in South African history. It reached into the highest offices in the apartheid government and brought down some of the most powerful men in the country at that time, including Rhoodie, Mulder and Vorster. More than anything, the scandal would destroy the widely held popular opinion that while apartheid-era leaders supported a harsh and repressive racial policy which denied blacks their rights, they personally weren't corrupt or out to enrich themselves. Muldergate proved just the opposite.

In Voster's place, P.W. Botha, a rival to Mulder, was elected prime minister after Vorster resigned. Botha promised a clean administration, but then shut down an investigation, headed by the well-respected Supreme Court judge Anton Mostert, that many believe would have implicated the new prime minister in the Muldergate scandal. Botha continued his political house-cleaning by disbanding the Department of Information and created a new department in its place. Incredibly, this new department, headed by Pik Botha, kept about 60 of the secret projects initiated by Rhoodie.

What is remarkable is that the scandal did little to hurt the international image of South Africa. Through the scandal, the world had been given a glimpse of the lengths to which the country would go to protect itself, and it gave further political ammunition to the still-growing anti-apartheid movement. All the same, the apartheid government managed to end the 1970s by holding off economic sanctions and other punitive actions against it. Muldergate was just a bump in the road. The apartheid propaganda machine continued to roll on.

6

Constructive Engagement

'We detest apartheid but believe we can do better with persuasion.'
— *President Ronald Reagan*

The election of President Ronald Reagan in 1980 brought a change in America's foreign policy towards South Africa. While Jimmy Carter had supported limited military sanctions and criticised the apartheid government for its racial policies, Reagan adamantly opposed any sanctions at all. Instead, the new president called for 'constructive engagement' with Pretoria, a policy that suggested dialogue with the South African government to encourage it to move gradually away from apartheid. Constructive engagement was the brainchild of Chester Crocker, a former professor at Georgetown University in Washington, who would serve as Reagan's assistant secretary of state for African affairs.

Crocker drafted a policy that included the relaxation of diplomatic and economic sanctions imposed under previous administrations, allowed more South African honorary consuls in the US, and relaxed controls on the export of non-lethal materials for the South African military and police and of equipment and technology with both military and civilian use. 'We detest apartheid but believe we can do better with persuasion,' Reagan wrote in his diary about the new policy.

The fervently anti-communist president was also intent on containing the Soviet Union and preventing what he called a 'domino effect' in Africa, whereby one country after another would fall prey to communism. Although he considered apartheid morally wrong and politically unacceptable, he saw South Africa as a key Cold War ally in the anti-Soviet fight and wanted to increase military and economic aid to the country.

In Britain, Margaret Thatcher, who had been appointed prime minister a year before Reagan's election, took a similar position. Not only did she see South Africa as a strategic Cold War ally, but she recognised that Britain was the biggest foreign investor in and principal trading partner of the country. There may have been a personal element as well. Thatcher's husband Denis had extensive South African investments himself. Margaret Thatcher opposed sanctions, saying they would cause more harm for blacks than whites and were unlikely to pressure the government in Pretoria to change its racial policy. 'So far as Britain is concerned, we believe that sanctions would only harden attitudes rather than promote progress,' Thatcher said.

In what the South African government considered a major diplomatic coup, in June 1984 Thatcher received a visit from P.W. Botha, the first South African leader to come to Britain since the country had left the Commonwealth in 1961. The two heads of government had a personal history. When Thatcher visited South Africa in 1974, Botha had been one of her hosts and, according to the journalist Gavin Evans, the South African leader had been impressed with the future British prime minister.

Although Thatcher told Botha that the policy of racial separation was 'unacceptable' and called for the release of Nelson Mandela, she nevertheless affirmed the UK's support for the South African government. Despite the request for Mandela's release, Thatcher and her government considered the ANC a 'terrorist organisation' and on numerous occasions sought to draw a link between the ANC and the Soviet Union. During one press conference Thatcher told reporters that there was considerable Soviet influence throughout Africa and 'a considerable number of the ANC leaders are communists'.

The South African government, for its part, in its communications with British and American authorities, played up the alleged communist ties of the ANC, the PAC and other anti-apartheid movements, arguing that the country served as a bulwark against an expanding Soviet push into Africa. South African officials also called for Washington to restore funding to its Angolan proxy, the rebel group Unita, which had been cut off in the 1970s, in its fight against the Soviet-backed MPLA, the ruling party in Angola.

Under Reagan the White House was more than happy to oblige Pretoria. The ANC, which Reagan called a group of 'Soviet-backed guerrillas', was put on the list of terrorist organisations during his term of office. Reagan also relaxed trade restrictions against the South African police and security forces, reversing a Carter administration policy that had been in place for four years. Covert aid to Unita was restored, and Reagan steadfastly resisted the call for sanctions, dismissing Bishop Desmond Tutu, a proponent of sanctions, as naive.

The Reagan administration, along with the British government, also began supplying Pretoria with intelligence about the ANC, and gave the government specific warnings about planned ANC attacks on targets in South Africa. A US intelligence official told the *New York Times* in an article of 23 July 1986 that the South Africans were given specific advance information about attempted bombings and other attacks. According to the *Times*, the National Security Agency intercepted communications from ANC officials in Zambia, Mozambique and Angola and passed the information on to the South African Directorate of Military Intelligence.

In addition, the CIA and other intelligence agencies monitored the international travels of Oliver Tambo and his staff and also shared this information with the South Africans. Many of the national security officials in Reagan's administration believed that the leadership of the ANC was dominated by communists. Giving the apartheid government information about the movement and communications of the ANC also served the US interest. 'We targeted the ANC. We considered them to be the bad guys, to be Soviet pawns, stalking-horses for the Soviets,' an intelligence officer told the *New York Times*.

But despite a friendly president in the White House and a new diplomatic relationship with the US government, Pretoria still took pains to bolster its already considerable lobbying presence in Washington. In the 1980s the lobbying campaign in the US would far exceed previous efforts, amounting in spend to nearly $7 million per year.

One of the first firms hired by Pretoria in the 1980s was the law office of John P. Sears. Sears was a well-known political operative in Washington. He had served as Reagan's campaign manager in the 1980 presidential election, which gave him unlimited access to the president and his staff. Sears was the highest-paid of the South African lobbyists, commanding an annual fee of $500,000. His job was to arrange meetings for South African diplomats with US Congressional representatives and senators to discuss legislation. Sears and his firm also wrote speeches for the South African ambassador and compiled lists of influential Americans to meet with South African officials.

Sears's contract was originally awarded to the firm he had co-founded with Philip Baskin, a major fundraiser for Democratic candidates, including the 1984 presidential hopeful, Walter Mondale. The firm of Baskin & Sears began lobbying for the South African government in 1981, two weeks before Reagan took office, but when another client of the firm, the city of Pittsburgh, found out about the South African connection, it threatened to withdraw its business. The controversy caused the two men to dissolve the firm. Baskin would later apologise, but Sears, after leaving the firm he had co-founded, started his own company, taking the South African contract with him. The business of lobbying for Pretoria was in fact so good that Philip J. Hare, who worked at the Sears firm, later left it and set up his own company, which also lobbied for the South African government.

Another lobbying firm linked to the Republican Party and hired by Pretoria during the Reagan years was United International Consultants, which was paid about $780,000 for a two-year contract. The firm consisted of Michael Hathaway and Joan Baldwin, long-time political consultants in Washington, whose jobs included lobbying against divestment legislation in the US Senate and at state and local government levels. Both were long-time supporters of South Africa. As a Senate aide and staff director for the Senate Energy and Natural Resources Committee, which had jurisdiction over strategic minerals policy, Hathaway had long argued that South Africa was important to the US because of its abundance of minerals, such as cobalt and uranium.

But Hathaway claimed his support of South Africa went beyond money. 'I want to stop this US trend of dumping on someone who is pro-US and anti-Soviet,' he said in an interview in 1985. 'Here you have an anti-Soviet government that's trying to end apartheid [alluding to P.W. Botha's current reforms], and every time they take a step they get kicked in the teeth.' The alternative to the white majority government was a 'bloody revolution and a Marxist dictatorship, à la Nicaragua and the Sandinistas'.

Hathaway's partner, Joan Baldwin, was a less visible media presence, but a familiar face to staffers and law-makers in the Capitol. She had served on the staff of the Senate Republican Policy Committee from 1956 to 1962 and again from 1973 to 1981, and also in the Nixon administration, which had taken a position on South Africa similar to Reagan's. Hathaway and Baldwin's long history as legislative staffers gave them free access to Republican senators, who controlled the Senate at that time.

While United International Consultants focused their lobbying on the US Senate, the firm of Pearson & Pipkin was hired to represent the interests of South Africa in the House of Representatives. The firm was paid about $300,000 a year plus $15,000 in expenses. Pearson was a long-standing Republican activist, had been a board member of the conservative Young Americans for Freedom foundation, and had served as a congressional aide. His most prominent role, though, was as executive director of the Conservative Victory Fund, which raised thousands of dollars for Republican candidates in Congress. In 1984, the fund contributed about $30,000 for 77 congressional races. When Pearson made his rounds in the capital to talk about South Africa, he found dozens of receptive ears.

In spite of hiring firms closely tied to the Republican Party, Pretoria didn't neglect the Democrats. Riley & Fox Inc. was a firm with close ties to the Democratic Party and had grown out of a lobbying company that had first been put on the South African payroll in 1980. It was paid about $400,000 a year by Pretoria. The firm also represented the South African Chamber of Mines at a rate of $39,000 per year. The firm gathered information on divestment and sanctions legislation, and helped arrange meetings between South African officials and members of the Democratic Party, which was less friendly to the apartheid government.

The US lobbying campaign was aided by a host of conservative US think-tanks mostly based in Washington, including the Heritage Foundation, the American Enterprise Institute, the Institute for Strategic and International Studies at Georgetown University, the Cato Institute and the Hoover Institution. Two other think-tanks, the Miami Institute for Policy Studies, which received $50,000 in funding from Pretoria, funnelled through a secret Swiss bank account, and the International Freedom Foundation, headed by the lobbyist Jack Abramoff, would also play a significant role in the lobbying campaign.

These idea shops churned out a steady stream of reports and policy papers, all of which reinforced the notion that South Africa was an important ally in the fight against the global expansion of communism.

The Miami Institute produced numerous reports on the country's vital role in defence of the West because of its important minerals, while the Heritage Foundation launched a campaign against the divestment movement. The foundations also sponsored a number of conferences and workshops where apartheid officials were able to rub shoulders with some of the most influential conservative policy-makers in Washington.

Despite the embarrassment of Muldergate and its revelations about South African interference in US elections, the apartheid government's American agents continued to try to influence and prevent the election of unsympathetic legislators. In 1982, the target was the Michigan congressman Howard Wolpe, chairman of the US House of Representatives Foreign Affairs Committee's subcommittee on Africa. Wolpe, a Democrat, was a vocal critic of the Reagan administration's constructive engagement policy, arguing that it was likely 'to increase the violence' in South Africa 'because the intransigent [white] elements have been led to believe they can engage in repression without any real cost or American response'. Wolpe would later co-sponsor a bill that sought to impose a trade embargo on South Africa and prohibit all US companies from conducting business there.

Leading the charge against Wolpe was John McGoff, long-time apartheid supporter. McGoff backed Wolpe's opponent, Richard Milliman, who had worked for one of his newspapers, providing thousands of dollars to his former employee's campaign. Wolpe was accused of being a 'free spending liberal' and 'social experimenter', but the attack steered clear of South Africa, perhaps to avoid an investigation by the US Justice Department. Other South African representatives were less restrained in their condemnation of Wolpe for his positions on South Africa. The US-Namibia Trade and Cultural Council, a lobby for the Pretoria-backed transitional government in South West Africa, denounced Wolpe in its newsletter for being 'blind to the Soviet threat' in southern Africa and being soft on communism. Copies of the newsletter were widely distributed in Michigan. The South Africa Foundation also joined in the attack on Wolpe. It began a series of speaking tours by its staffers leading up to the election, which included several cities in Wolpe's congressional district. All the same, Wolpe won with nearly 60 per cent of the vote. There would be no repeat of the 1978 Jepsen–Clark Iowa Senate race.

* * *

Even though it failed in its efforts to help defeat a prominent critic, the South Africa Foundation worked hard to prevent the US imposing punitive sanctions on South Africa in the 1980s.

From its modest beginnings nearly two decades earlier, the foundation, which received funding not only from South African companies, but from American members as well, had grown into an influential powerhouse. The man at the centre of this was John Chettle, who had become one of the most recognisable faces in the US capital and whom one South African business magazine described as 'the most effective foreign lobbyist in Washington'.

By 1985, with its US staff of four and a worldwide budget of $2.3 million a year—$350,000 in the US—plus the lobbying might and financial resources of its members, the foundation was sending its representatives to civic organisations, high schools and colleges, newspaper editorial board meetings, and radio and television talk shows. Chettle was a regular guest on Sunday morning political talk shows and public affairs broadcasting programmes such as 'NewsHour'.

The most effective work, though, was done in Congress. In congressional testimony, Chettle often won over law-makers with his frank criticism of apartheid and even earned the respect of those opposed to the South African government. Chettle counted several high-ranking policy-makers as friends, including Chester Crocker, architect of constructive engagement.

Together with the foundation staffer John Montgomery, who was also well known among American business leaders and civic organisations, Chettle argued before US audiences that sanctions would have no effect whatsoever on political developments in South Africa and would ultimately end up hurting black South Africans. The foundation was adamant that the ANC was influenced and led by communists. In 1986, in an appearance before the US Congress, Chettle told law-makers that South African Intelligence had estimated that up to 30 members of the ANC's national executive committee were communists. He accused the US media of underreporting the communist connection.

He added:

> None of this means, of course, that the ANC should be excluded from negotiations, but it should demonstrate what forces there are at work, and why radical elements do not want to see peaceful negotiations and reform. It is also clear that the sheer preponderance of members of the South African Communist Party on the National Executive of the ANC could be fatal to the hopes of democracy in any South Africa over which it had unfettered control.

While lobbying certainly helped, the most effective tool used by the foundation remained its offer of free trips for journalists, congressmen and business leaders to see South Africa for themselves. Chettle called the trips 'travelling fellowships'. Those who made the journey in the 1980s represented a who's who of American opinion-formers and high-ranking members of Congress. Chester Crocker had taken the trip before entering office. Zbigniew Brzezinski, national security adviser in the Carter administration, who remained a well-respected voice in US foreign policy, also travelled to South Africa at the foundation's expense. Members of Congress included prominent conservatives like South Dakota Republican senator Larry Pressler and his wife, and dozens of congressional aides. Gordon Jones, vice-president at the

Heritage Foundation, the conservative think-tank, was also a guest of the business group on one of its trips. In addition, state legislators were also invited, particularly those in states where divestment legislation was pending. Overtures were made to groups that traditionally filled the liberal wing of the Democratic Party, including blacks and Jews. Joseph C. Faulkner, a black American and executive director of the Congress of Racial Equality, a civil rights organisation, visited South Africa, as did Rabbi Israel Miller, president of Yeshiva University. In 1985 alone, the foundation 'awarded' 77 fellowships to law-makers, their aides, academics and religious leaders. 'It was better to send people over and let them see for themselves,' said Chettle, who would later leave the foundation to practise international law.

The trips weren't one-way affairs. The foundation also sponsored trips to the US for black pro-government or anti-divestment South Africans. The purpose was to show Americans that not all blacks in South Africa supported sanctions. However, one observer told the *New York Times* magazine, 'They are bringing over black people who are so utterly co-opted that it's pathetic.'

In a recent interview, Chettle, who now lives in the Washington DC area, said he has no regrets about his work with the South Africa Foundation. He continues to believe that the constructive engagement policies of the Reagan administrations were key in ending apartheid. Moreover, 'I thought then and I think now that South Africa was badly hurt by the sanctions and that it hurt blacks more than whites, because many businesses left and never came back.'

South African propaganda efforts weren't just limited to politics. In an all-out effort to win over Americans and refocus the debate away from sanctions and divestment, materials were sent to American universities, high schools and public libraries. According to records from the US Department of Justice, a company called Image Industries was one of the main PR firms paid to prepare and distribute educational materials about South Africa. In one case, within weeks of a new school's opening in Massachusetts, when the library shelves were still empty, the school librarian began receiving the magazine *Informa*. Jo Sullivan, the high school librarian, wrote about her surprise in getting the magazine unsolicited in a mailing:

> This publication of South Africa's Department of Foreign Affairs and Information is sent to schools all over the US free and unsolicited ... Many teachers do not realize that *Informa*, and other, similar materials, come from South Africa, nor do they always know that they come unsolicited. When I do workshops, librarians often tell me with pride that, 'Yes, we have one magazine in our library on Africa.' It is usually *Informa*.
>
> *Informa*, and its companion publication *Panorama*, are lavish, slick, glossy productions, always with Black people on the cover. They contain articles on development, family life, and industry in South Africa. The stress has always been on African activities, with frequent photos of blacks and whites working together. Recently, however, the emphasis has been on life in the bantustans, the so called 'homelands' where Africans have been forced to live by the South African government.
>
> Another widely circulated piece of propaganda is the filmstrip and cassette kit entitled 'Mosaic of Progress' from the South African Department of Information.
>
> All such materials should be used with considerable care, though one local teacher has a creative solution. After teaching a unit on South Africa, she distributes *Informa* and uses it as a lesson in propaganda.

* * *

While not as extensive as its Washington lobbying efforts, the South African propaganda campaign in London was strengthened in the 1980s as the regime came increasingly under internal and external threat. The main effort was handled by Strategy Network International (SNI), a lobbying firm set up specifically to counter calls for economic sanctions, promote the Angolan rebel group Unita, and support the 'transitional government' of South West Africa/Namibia, which had been established in defiance of a UN resolution on Namibian independence. The firm's two main clients were the South African Chamber of Mines and Eskom, the South African electricity-generating company. Campaigning to ward off sanctions, against cheap South African coal in particular, was a major preoccupation of SNI.

The firm also represented the homeland of Bophuthatswana, which was granted 'independence' by South Africa in December 1977. Moreover, the firm headed Pretoria's international propaganda campaign against the South West Africa People's Organisation (Swapo), which since Namibian independence in 1990 has been the ruling party in that country. SNI was paid and given its instructions through the company Transcontinental Consultancy, set up by Sean Cleary, a former South African diplomat, who was director of the administrator-general's office in Windhoek in the early 1980s. Cleary was later revealed as an agent of the South African intelligence services.

SNI operated out of plush offices in Storey's Gate, near Whitehall and the Houses of Parliament. The two men who ran the firm were Patrick Watson, a former captain in the Black Watch regiment of the British Army, and Steven Govier, a local government official. Govier initially denied in an interview with British newspapers that the firm was funded by the South African government, insisting that he was employed by the 'transitional government of national unity' in Windhoek, which had failed to win recognition from the United Nations after its establishment in 1985 by Pretoria.

The firm was later joined by Derek Laud, a black Briton and member of the conservative Monday Club. He would recommend recruiting sympathetic British MPs to work as consultants for the firm and travel to South Africa and Bophuthatswana. Many of the MPs were less than candid about their connection to the firm or about the trips they had taken. Neal Hamilton, a Conservative MP, recorded in the parliamentary register that he had gone to South Africa as a guest of the Chamber of Mines in February 1988, but neglected to mention that he had taken the trip as a paid agent of the lobbying firm SNI. When *The Independent* revealed this, Hamilton said he had not included it on his form because he was involved with the firm for less than a month before becoming a government whip and because MPs are allowed four weeks to make their entries in the disclosure documents.

Marion Roe, a Conservative MP for Broxbourne, in the annual register for 1989 disclosed a number of trips to southern Africa. Included were the following overseas visits: 'February 1989, to South Africa for three days, sponsored by the South African Coal Industry; 11–18 June 1989, to Angola, funded by Unita.' But Roe, too, neglected to mention that the trip had been paid for by SNI. This was later revealed when *The Guardian* obtained a letter in which the accounts manager at SNI wrote to Roe asking her to submit her receipts from the trip for reimbursement. The manager also enclosed a Unita badge for Roe to wear, which the MP said completed her 'guerrilla outfit'.

One of SNI's most prominent supporters was Michael Colvin, a member of the Conservative Party, who would become a vocal supporter of white South Africa. In 1986, he made two trips as a guest of the apartheid government, visiting South Africa and the Bophuthatswana homeland. Colvin visited Bophuthatswana again in 1989 and showed up in Angola as a guest of Jonas Savimbi. He also welcomed the visit of F. W. de Klerk to Britain in June 1989 and condemned a BBC broadcast that featured the anti-apartheid activist Peter Hain. According to *The Independent*, Colvin's job was to identify sympathetic MPs who might be interested in what came to be called the 'Bop run' – trips, generally with all expenses paid, for hand-picked Conservative MPs to the 'homeland' of Bophuthatswana.

In 1991 Colvin became a paid consultant for SNI. Later, he became a director, with Derek Laud, in another lobbying organisation called Laud Ludgate. Colvin would land in trouble for failing as an MP to report that he had been paid as a consultant by the South African lobbying firm. After the disclosures were made public, Colvin told the *Daily Mail*: 'It didn't last for long. I consider this was a trial as it were and therefore it was not registered. It was an error. I probably should have declared it, yes.'

Between 1987 and 1990, *The Independent* found that more than half a dozen MPs made the 'Bop' runs. They included Graham Riddick, one of the MPs investigated in the cash-for-questions scandal in the 1990s, when several MPs were charged with taking payments from lobbyists to ask parliamentary questions. Other MPs were John Watts, who later became a minister of transport, and Charles Goodson-Wickes, an MP from Wimbledon. In fact, records show that more than two dozen MPs, mostly Conservatives, took trips provided by the lobbying firm.

The 23-year-old David Cameron, the future British prime minister, was also a recipient of SNI's largesse. When his trip was revealed in a biography published in 2009, his office called it a fact-finding mission on which Cameron had met with a wide range of people, including Africans and labour leaders. But Francis Elliot and James Hanning, who wrote the book, reported that Cameron had described the trip as 'simply a jolly', adding: 'It was all terribly relaxed, just a little treat, a perk of the job. The Botha regime was attempting to make itself look less horrible, but I don't regard it as having been of the faintest political consequence.'

To the annoyance of the Bophuthatswana authorities and the lobbyists, most of the MPs would more often than not make a short one-day stop-over in Bophuthatswana before heading into South Africa for a vacation. The trips weren't cheap. In most cases the MPs were offered first-class travel, with the alternative of cashing in a single ticket for two club-class seats, enabling them to take their spouses. A number chose the second option, according to *The Independent*.

Patrick Watson, who today is the managing director at Montrose public affairs consultants, a London firm, refused to discuss his role in SNI or his lobbying on behalf of the former apartheid government. 'No, I'm not interested in speaking to you,' he said when contacted by phone. Asked why he did not want to talk about his lobbying for the apartheid government, Watson replied: 'The past is a foreign land. This is a very long time ago.'

In a recent interview, Steven Govier, who now runs a crime prevention programme in London, said that SNI was part of a global lobbying effort that also involved parallel operations in France, Germany and the US. 'The idea was to bolster the idea that Namibia was different from South Africa,' Govier said. All of the firms were paid about £500,000 annually through Cleary's Transcontinental Consultancy Ltd, which was in turn paid by the South African government.

The French operation was headed by Guy Ribeaud, who ran the L'Association des amis du Sud-Ouest africain (Association of the Friends of South West Africa). Ribeaud, according to Govier, focused on winning support for the Windhoek government in France and in French-speaking African countries. In Germany, the firm of Volker Stoltz led the pro-South African propaganda effort. Stoltz was well known as Pretoria's man in Bonn. He also ran the Namibian Information Office, which lobbied to win recognition in Bonn for the South African-backed transitional government in Windhoek. As part of his effort to win over German MPs, he arranged for selected members of the Bonn parliament and their wives to fly first-class to South West Africa/Namibia on fact-finding tours. In 1987, about 114 union representatives were also invited.

Statements from those who took the trip were written up in press releases by Stoltz and distributed to the media as proof that the puppet government in Windhoek had met the United Nations condition for the country's independence of being 'internationally recognised'. Stoltz was later the source of some controversy when he was given the Federal Cross of Merit, the highest civilian honour in Germany. The award apparently outraged the German foreign minister Hans-Dietrich Genscher.

In the US, the Cleary-led campaign was headed by the veteran Republican Party operatives Marion H. Smoak and Carl L. Shipley. The two had previously run the US-Namibia (South West Africa) Trade and Cultural Council, which they operated in the early 1980s on behalf of the South African-backed party, the Democratic Turnhalle Alliance (DTA), in South West Africa. For Cleary's American presence, Smoak and Shipley ran an organisation called the Namibia News Bureau, whose purpose was to lobby the US government to recognise the interim government in Namibia. It also promoted the Angolan group Unita and its leader, Jonas Savimbi. According to Govier, the various international lobbyists met on numerous occasions in Munich to plan strategy and to brief Cleary 'on what the line would be' in their respective countries. The SNI also worked with its German and French counterparts to lobby the European Union to exclude Namibia from the sanctions that had been imposed in 1986 on South Africa. 'We managed to get Namibia taken out of the sanctions package, which was quite important.' he said. In total, SNI received about £2 million for its work of 'spreading the message of the transitional government'. The overall object of the campaign was to discredit Swapo. Govier believes the campaign provided the South African government with a template for discrediting the ANC. The firm continued its work for a number of years before shutting down in 1992, two years before the ANC assumed power in South Africa.

* * *

In addition to the SNI, the South African government's major lobbying presence in London was the Bophuthatswana International Affairs Office, run by Ian Findlay and the PR consultant Anthony McCall-Judson. The purpose of the office was to promote Bophuthatswana as an 'independent' country, though it consisted of seven pieces of non-contiguous land, which are now situated in three different South African provinces. 'Bop', as it was commonly called, was the second tribal homeland to gain autonomy, in 1977, without actual freedom for its citizens. Although the homeland would later achieve some moderate economic success with revenues from casino resorts in the Sun City area and from its platinum mines, it survived largely on subsidies from South Africa, and apartheid control was evident to anyone who ventured into the homeland.

Findlay was the public face of the Bophuthatswana government; he was the chief executive of the Bophuthatswana National Commercial Corporation, a company set up in London in 1986 to serve as the unofficial diplomatic arm of the homeland. Its government had made several attempts over the years to gain diplomatic recognition from Britain and admission to the Commonwealth, but hadn't got very far. As a result a decision was made to have a permanent presence in London. It is unknown exactly how much the Bophuthatswana government (or its South African parent) spent to lobby in the UK. (British law does not require lobbyists to report how much they spend in trying to influence parliament.)

Findlay regularly appeared at Westminster, lobbying MPs, testifying before committees and recruiting friendly MPs to travel to the homeland. While a number of Conservative MPs appear to have taken the offer to travel on fact-finding missions to Bophuthatswana, Findlay, in an appearance before a foreign affairs committee, admitted he had had little success in getting members of other parties to go, particularly those from the Labour Party. Despite the cold shoulder, the Bophuthatswana office staff churned out a steady stream of materials for MPs, informing them about the would-be country.

While Findlay served as the face of Bophuthatswana and its chief spokesman, a large part of McCall-Judson's duties as a consultant with the Bophuthatswana International Affairs Office seems to have been firing off letters to the editors of newspapers complaining about poor coverage of the homeland. McCall-Judson also put out a steady stream of promotional materials and arranged for the press and others to visit the country. One visit seems to have backfired, when McCall-Judson arranged for Stephen Ellis, the independent-minded editor of the influential newsletter *Africa Confidential*, to visit the homeland. On his return Ellis wrote a long, scathing article denouncing the bantustan as a totalitarian cesspool. That assessment was later backed up by reports from Human Rights Watch and other NGOs. 'Since its independence in 1977, political life in Bophuthatswana has been characterized by continued torture, arbitrary dismissals, harassment and deportation of opponents of the regime,' said a 1991 Human Rights Watch report.

Nevertheless, the Bophuthatswana International Affairs Office managed to get a number of British MPs to travel to the country on ten-day junkets. The office considered most of the trips it sponsored for British MPs and the press a roaring success. The outings consisted of first-class airplane tickets, plus meals and hotel accommodation. Each trip cost about £26,000 for the group. The trips were popular and proved to be a major draw, especially for conservative law-makers.

Appearing before a House of Commons Select Committee on Members' Interests on 25 April 1989, Findlay was asked: 'Are you satisfied that your government is getting good value for money out of British members of Parliament?' He replied: 'Yes, very much so. There is not the slightest doubt in my mind that we get a tremendous return in the dedication of these people.' Findlay noted that in the previous two years, supportive MPs had organised two hearings to debate the recognition of Bophuthatswana, passed an early day motion—a formal motion that draws attention to an event or cause—signed by 117 members of the House congratulating the 'country' on the success of its development during its ten years of 'independence', and had dozens of questions submitted in parliament for written and oral replies. Findlay also noted that his office, with the support of friendly MPs, mostly from the Conservative Party, had succeeded in getting Bophuthatswana's president, minister of economic affairs and minister of foreign affairs to appear before a House of Commons committee on foreign affairs. While denying that he was part of a larger lobbying effort by the apartheid government, Findlay did acknowledge that Bophuthatswana received 'assistance from South Africa'. He also acknowledged that many of the MPs friendly to Bophuthatswana were also supporters of the apartheid government.

While Bophuthatswana International appears to have some limited successes in the UK at least in raising the profile of the homeland, there seems to have been little success from similar lobbying of the US government. The South African government and a number of lobbyists it hired in Washington had long pushed for recognition of the homeland in the US. In 1980, the lobbyist Ted Cobb, a black American, made an attempt to arrange a secret trip for several prominent black businessmen and women that was supposed to build support for the newly independent homeland among black Americans. The trip was exposed by several black American State Department officials, and the black anti-sanctions lobbying group TransAfrica persuaded the participants to withdraw. A *Washington Post* article was also instrumental in causing several people to cancel.

In addition, the Bophuthatswana government hired William Timmons, a leading Washington lobbyist, as its representative. Timmons was the consummate Washington insider, who had worked for every Republican president since Richard Nixon. Timmons's firm, Global USA, signed a three-year contract for an annual fee of $120,000 with the government of Bophuthatswana in 1983. According to the lobbying records, the company was supposed to distribute brochures to the American public about the homeland. Despite the money spent on Timmons and other lobbyists, there is little evidence that Bophuthatswana was ever on the foreign policy radar of most American citizens or politicians.

Bophuthatswana was never able to garner support for its recognition as an independent nation in either Britain or America. Neither Ronald Reagan nor Margaret Thatcher, despite their opposition to sanctions against South Africa, made any attempts to consider recognising Bophuthatswana. When Bophuthatswana disappeared off the map after it was reincorporated into the new democratic South Africa in 1994, the Bophuthatswana International Affairs Office was quietly shut down and the company was formally dissolved in 1996, two years after its funding was cut by the new ANC-led government. In the US lobbyists for the homeland simply moved on to other clients.

7

Free South Africa

'We knew that unless the government of South Africa felt the steel of some penalty for what they were doing, nothing would ever change.'

– Randall Robinson,
executive director of TransAfrica

All the new lobbying firms hired in the US during the early years of the Reagan administration provided the apartheid government with high-level access to the corridors of power in Washington. South African representatives had no trouble reaching top officials in the White House, cabinet members, diplomats at the State Department, senior Republican leaders, and even officials at the CIA and the American military. With a president less dependent on liberals and black American voters, who both supported stronger actions against the South African government, apartheid officials had less need to target America's increasing active, black-led anti-apartheid movement directly. As they had done in the 1960s and 1970s, Pretoria and its offices in Washington largely ignored the street-level protest in the US against apartheid. In fact, by the 1980s the images of Sharpeville and Soweto had long faded from the front pages of American newspapers and as topics on Sunday morning talk shows.

This would change on the morning of 21 November 1984, the day before Thanksgiving, when four African Americans—including Randall Robinson, executive director of the lobby group TransAfrica; Mary Frances Berry, a US civil rights commissioner; Eleanor Holmes Norton, a law professor at Georgetown University; and District of Columbia congressman Walter Fauntroy—visited the South African embassy in Washington to discuss the growing crisis in South Africa, in particular the eruption of the country's townships in insurrection, with the ambassador, Brand Fourie.

The conversation with the ambassador began cordially. Fourie, an accomplished diplomat who had also served as secretary for foreign affairs, launched into a talk in the hope of explaining his government's policies to the group. About 45 minutes into the discussion, Norton excused herself and left the embassy. The talk between the diplomat and the activists went on for another ten minutes or so until an embassy staffer entered the meeting room and asked the ambassador to step outside. Fourie excused himself and left the room. When he returned, the South African diplomat seemed disturbed, Robinson remembered.

'We are getting calls from the press,' Fourie told the activists. 'Ms Norton is outside telling the media that the three of you will not leave the embassy until your demands are met.'

'That's true,' Robinson said to a surprised Fourie, before launching into the group's prepared list of demands. The activists demanded that the South African government release all political prisoners, including Nelson Mandela, Walter Sisulu and Govan Mbeki. They also demanded that the government commit itself immediately and publicly to the speedy dismantling of the apartheid system. After listening to the activists read through their list for another few minutes, Fourie told them to leave or he would call the US Secret Service and the Washington DC police and have them removed. The group informed the ambassador that they would not leave until their demands were met. Fourie walked to his desk and called the police.

According to Robinson and the others, they never intended to leave the embassy and had staged the event to draw attention to the plight of black South Africans under apartheid rule. Before they entered the embassy that day, they had placed dozens of calls to supporters asking them to gather in protest outside the embassy. While Robinson, Fauntroy and Berry were in the embassy, Norton was outside holding a briefing for a large gathering of journalists from all the major American television networks, wire services and influential newspapers.

'Our own government is no recourse for us at this point,' Norton said in a prepared statement to the dozens of reporters. 'The Reagan policy of constructive engagement amounts to little more than letting the South African government go and do what it feels like doing ... We felt like we had to do something. If there was a government in Washington that looked like it was going to use its pressure, even diplomatically, on the government in Pretoria, we wouldn't be here tonight.'

The protest attracted international attention, especially as the activists were arrested, handcuffed and taken away by police. The arrest of activists protesting against segregation in the US had been an important tool for Martin Luther King Jr and the civil rights movement, a fact not lost on Robinson and his colleagues. 'You think about these things very strategically. What can move the needle and what will likely not,' said Robinson, in an interview of 2014 with the *Washington Post*. 'You can protest. But if you can make the wind move, you have to put a sail up. To make the wind move where there is no sail is useless.'

TransAfrica, the group that spearheaded the protest, had been formed in 1977 during a Black Leadership Conference organised by the Congressional Black Caucus, a group made up of black members of the US Congress. They felt that while they had made some inroads in Congress, what was needed was an organisation that would utilise the highly successful tactics of the civil rights movement, including hunger strikes, protest marches and other acts of civil disobedience, to bring the issues to the broad public and attract supporters. Randall Robinson, a civil rights attorney, was chosen to lead the new group. Robinson was steeped in the civil rights movement. He and his brother, Max, the first black American male to anchor a nightly news broadcast, had grown up in segregated Richmond, Virginia. 'I have been interested in Africa and the unity of the black world since I was a teenager,' Robinson told the *New York Times* in an interview in 1983. 'My parents left me with a positive impression of Africa and of myself. They made me aware that when we fought discrimination in the South, Africans were also struggling against discrimination and apartheid. All it required was a little reading to indicate that we were all part of a global struggle.'

Robinson had been a vocal critic of the involvement in South Africa of American corporations and the US government since his student days at Harvard Law School. He became active in the Southern African Relief Fund, which raised money for groups fighting the Pretoria government. After working in Tanzania as a Ford Foundation fellow, he returned to Boston for several years as a public interest lawyer and then went to Washington, where he worked for a number of years as a congressional aide to William Clay, a black congressman from Missouri, a sponsor of anti-apartheid legislation, and then to Charles Diggs, the black Democrat, who had long been a thorn in the side of the South African government. Robinson travelled to South Africa for the first time with Diggs in 1976, and worked on the report released by the Diggs subcommittee that revealed the conditions blacks endured under apartheid.

The trip to South Africa was an eye-opener. He remembered one incident where Diggs asked a liberal white businessman about voting rights for blacks. The businessman replied that giving black South Africans the right to vote 'would be like giving a five-year-old a gun'. Robinson said that he returned to the US with a 'fuller appreciation of what black South Africans had to endure' and a desire to help. He poured his efforts into helping Diggs organise his subcommittee on Africa hearings in which American government officials and business leaders were taken to task for their dealings with the apartheid government. The hearings, Robinson said, created 'what little Congressional interest there was in Congress on Africa' and were instrumental in giving anti-apartheid activists a voice in US foreign policy.

Moreover, Diggs cultivated several young activists who would later become involved in the movement for sanctions against South Africa. Robinson credited Diggs with paving the way for the later Free South Africa Movement, a coalition of church, labour and university activists. It was Diggs who suggested the need for an organisation that would 'remove Africa from the bottom of the American foreign policy agenda and bring it to the forefront'. This became known as TransAfrica, whose structure and mission Robinson outlined. He then embarked on a fundraising and informational tour with Richard Hatcher, former mayor of Gary, Indiana. Together, the two men began laying the groundwork for a grassroots movement against apartheid.

Robinson and TransAfrica first gained national attention in 1981 when he came into possession of a number of sensitive State Department documents indicating that the Reagan administration was seeking closer ties with the government of South Africa, despite its public condemnation of apartheid. One of the memorandums quoted Chester Crocker, the assistant secretary of state-designate for African affairs, as saying that after 20 years of worsening relations, 'the possibility may exist for a more positive and reciprocal relationship between the two countries based upon shared strategic concerns in southern Africa'. With regard to South Africa's policy of racial separation, the memorandum said, 'although we may continue to differ on apartheid, and cannot condone a system of institutionalized racial differentiation, we can cooperate with a society undergoing constructive change'. Robinson said the documents showed 'this State Department is the most pro-South African in post-World War II history'.

TransAfrica would stage a number of protests and campaigns leading up to the event at the South African embassy in 1984, but most had received little attention in the media. The arrests were just the catalyst the anti-apartheid movement needed.

The event was also just the beginning. For over a year protests and arrests at the South African embassy would take place daily, with the press coverage now including international media. In total, between 3,000 and 6,000 people were arrested at the embassy in Washington, including nearly two dozen members of Congress. Rosa Parks, who had helped spark the civil rights movement by refusing to give up her seat to a white man on a segregated bus in Montgomery in 1955, was arrested at the embassy a few weeks after the initial protest began. This was the anniversary of her arrest in Montgomery 29 years earlier. Others would follow. Among those arrested were clergymen, national labour and religious leaders, students, community leaders, teachers and celebrities, including the heavyweight boxer Larry Holmes; Amy Carter, daughter of President Jimmy Carter; and the entertainer Harry Belafonte. Singer and musician Stevie Wonder was also led away in handcuffs during a protest, as was Coretta Scott King, widow of the civil rights leader Martin Luther King Jr, who was also arrested, along with her children.

Five thousand people were reportedly arrested for protesting in front of South African consulates in other cities in the US. Those arrested weren't limited to liberal activists and celebrities. Lowell Weicker, a Republican from Connecticut, became the first member of the US Senate to be arrested in an act of civil disobedience when he joined protesters in front of the South African embassy in Washington and refused to leave when ordered by police. Weicker's arrest was significant as he was close to President Ronald Reagan. Reagan had campaigned for Weicker in an election contest against the son of his vice-president, George Bush.

Bishop Desmond Tutu, who had just been awarded the Nobel Peace Prize, showed up at one of the demonstrations and spoke against the 'sins' of Reagan's constructive engagement policy. Tutu's presence at the protest was especially galling for the Reagan administration, which had shown a dislike for the anti-apartheid leader. 'Black South

African attacks on CE [constructive engagement] become effective ammunition for our critics at home, especially when uttered by a Nobel laureate of charismatic talents who plays the US media like a violin,' read a secret memo written by Herman Nickel, the US ambassador to South Africa, shortly after Tutu's appearance at a protest. Before taking part in the protest Tutu had delivered a blistering speech on Capitol Hill, where he told law-makers that Reagan's 'constructive engagement is an abomination, an unmitigated disaster'. 'In my view, the Reagan administration's support and collaboration with it [apartheid] is equally immoral, evil, and totally un-Christian.'

The ongoing protests in Washington inspired other actions in the US and abroad. Universities in the US began to divest, followed by pension funds and some corporations. One of the many students who took part in protests on college campuses was the future president Barack Obama. As a sophomore at Occidental College, Los Angeles, in 1981 he helped to organise a rally supporting demands that the trustees of the school divest their stocks from companies doing business in South Africa. It was his first foray into politics. He also contacted representatives of the ANC, inviting them to speak on campus, drafted letters to the faculty asking them to oppose apartheid, printed flyers calling for sanctions and argued strategy with other students.

Anti-apartheid demonstrations following the Washington protests took place in London, Paris, Sydney and other cities around the world and also received widespread media attention. The intense media coverage of the protest unnerved the Reagan administration. Although it continued to oppose sanctions, Reagan invited Bishop Tutu to the White House, though Tutu said it was little more than a photo opportunity for the president. Entries from Reagan's diary show how much he disliked Tutu and his repeated criticisms of his administration.

Under pressure from the protesters and Congress, Reagan gave a televised speech that criticised the Pretoria government and called on it to 'reach out to its black majority by ending the forced removal of blacks from their communities and the detention without trial and lengthy imprisonment of black leaders'. His administration also placed South Africa on the State Department's list of countries where human rights were regularly violated. At the same time Reagan reiterated his position that engagement with South Africa was working. He noted that President Botha had initiated constitutional changes in 1983 that granted political rights to Indians and Coloureds in a system of racially segregated chambers of parliament. These reforms did not address the central problem of the disenfranchisement of black Africans. Although Botha did add that he would consider giving blacks who lived in the homelands—Bophuthatswana, Ciskei, Transkei and Venda—dual citizenship, the proposal was rejected by South African anti-apartheid groups, including the ANC, which called it 'lame'.

In the US, neither Reagan's nor Botha's actions did much to stem the anti-apartheid protest, which was also leading to a renewed push in Congress for sanctions legislation. Even some conservative members of Congress, normally supporters of the South African government, began to change their views. In a letter addressed to the South African ambassador, Brand Fourie, 35 conservative law-makers, including the future speaker of the House of Representatives Newt Gingrich, wrote that unless South Africa worked quickly to dismantle racial segregation and end the denial of rights for blacks, they would not stand in the way of the sanctions legislation moving through Congress.

From Pretoria, government officials watched the growing black-led protest with alarm. The daily protests and calls for economic sanctions were quickly turning American public opinion around. More and more Americans now believed that the US needed to take stronger action against the apartheid government. South African officials determined to try to turn the tide.

8

Stopping the
Anti-Apartheid Movement

'It's important that we recognize in the US the reality of the ANC as a terrorist outlaw organization which has perpetrated violence primarily against innocent black people.'

— *William Keyes, black American lobbyist*

The man chosen for the task of blunting the grassroots campaign against South Africa was a then little-known Republican operative named William Keyes. Born in a small, rural North Carolina town, Keyes had hitchhiked to Washington DC in 1978 with almost no money in his pocket, hoping to make his mark in politics. Lacking a college degree, Keyes found a number of small jobs in and around Washington. Eager to get involved in politics, he took a pay cut to accept a position with a Republican study group. Eventually he would rise through the conservative political ranks as an aide in Congress, and then landed a job as a low-ranking domestic policy adviser working in the White House for President Reagan. He quit the job after a few years, frustrated because he was treated 'shabbily' and ignored by his colleagues, who only saw a 'black face'.

Unemployed for a while, Keyes tried his hand at a number of ventures: he started a conservative black-oriented newspaper and then ran a committee that raised money for conservative and right-wing American politicians. When neither of the projects proved to be fruitful, Keyes signed up for a free trip to South Africa sponsored by the South Africa Foundation. Despite having left the White House, he still supported the Reagan administration's position on South Africa. More importantly, he was a black man, exactly the kind the South African government was looking for when they began thinking of ways to counter the budding US sanctions and divestment movement.

In an interview with the *Washington Post* in 1985, Keyes said that during his trip to South Africa he met Louis Nel, the deputy minister of foreign affairs, in Pretoria. Nel was also director of the South African Bureau of Information, the government's new propaganda arm set up after the Muldergate scandal and given responsibility for improving the country's image at home and abroad. During a second meeting with Nel over dinner, Keyes discussed the role of black Americans in the growing anti-apartheid movement. Nel was well aware of the importance of American blacks to the anti-apartheid protest. He and other government officials closely monitored the activities of the Congressional Black Caucus. Keyes said that he later met with the foreign minister, Pik Botha.

Reached at his law office in Pretoria, Nel, who has retired from politics, said that neither he nor Botha, whom he had asked, remembered Keyes specifically and also had no recollection of Keyes being on the government's payroll. Nel said the former lobbyist must have been representing the South Africa Foundation. But he did recall having met several black Americans who had come to South Africa during that time. 'We were trying to show them things from our point of view; that things were changing in South Africa; that we were moving away from apartheid.'

Records at the US Justice Department reveal that a month after his meeting with government officials, the South African embassy hired Keyes as a lobbyist. His salary was nearly $400,000, making him the second highest-paid lobbyist for Pretoria. Keyes joined South Africa's other long-time black lobbyist, Jay Parker, to create the public relations firm International Public Affairs Consultants, which handled the South African account. The Justice Department records show that Keyes's contract called for him to be the South African government's liaison with the black community in the US as part of a broader propaganda campaign, headed by Nel, to sell the government's new policy of gradual reform.

Part of Keyes's job was also to arrange fact-finding trips to South Africa for key black journalists, set up meetings with black media for visiting South African diplomats, and establish exchange programmes at American universities for black South Africans. As the *Washington Post* noted at the time, 'Like the little Dutch boy with his finger in the dyke, Keyes's job was to "stop a rising tide of black American opposition to the South African government".'

Keyes's contract drew widespread criticism from blacks, especially those in the anti-apartheid movement. 'I find it incredible,' Randall Robinson told the *Washington Post*. 'It's this kind of thing that is a shock to your system to see a black American lobbying for the South African government.'

Keyes dismissed the criticism: 'The question I ask people is: "Does getting arrested in front of the South African embassy help solve any of those people's problems, or are there any programmes we should put into effect if we really want to benefit those people?"' he argued in response. Keyes said he believed the calls for majority rule were largely being punted by those with little understanding of blacks in South Africa. 'One-man, one-vote is the principal question only for those outside of South Africa,' he told the *Washington Post*. 'The principal question for men and women inside of South Africa is whether they will be able to provide for themselves and their families. After that political participation comes into play.'

As Pretoria's point man with the US black community, Keyes arranged a television appearance for the South African ambassador,

Herbert Beukes, on a black-oriented television programme called 'America's Black Forum'; he also assisted black American businessmen and reporters to travel to South Africa, and reportedly organised scholarships for a few black South African students. In addition, Keyes enabled Nel, the deputy foreign minister, to meet with black reporters and tried to recruit black businessmen to invest in South Africa. In media reports at the time, Keyes said he had hundreds of black businessmen interested in travelling to South Africa and engaging in business ventures. But it is unclear just how many people took up his offer. Keyes also wrote editorials in key conservative newspapers, including the *Washington Times*, attacking the ANC for being communist-led. The editorials did not identify him as a lobbyist for South Africa.

Despite his high profile and salary, Keyes appears to have accomplished little for the apartheid government. Few if any blacks beyond conservative circles were persuaded by his arguments against sanctions nor were they convinced that the South African government was changing its apartheid policies and reforming towards a more equitable society. There is scant evidence that he attracted any investments from black businessmen in the South African economy or that under his direction large numbers of black South African students were brought to the US on scholarships.

The reason for Keyes's inability to bring a large number of black Americans around to his message was that, despite his colour, Keyes had very few ties within the wider black community and was little known outside right-wing conservative circles. It didn't help that he had worked for the Reagan administration, which was hardly popular with blacks in the US. It also didn't help that he had accused the ANC and other anti-apartheid groups of being agents of Moscow. 'It's important that we recognise in the US the reality of the ANC as a terrorist outlaw organization which has perpetrated violence primarily against innocent black people,' he said in an interview with CNN in 1985.

These comments did not go down well with the black community, the majority of whom supported the ANC, PAC or the Black Consciousness Movement. Keyes had also alienated many blacks with his support of arch-conservative politicians like Senator Jesse Helms, a Republican from North Carolina, who was a key opponent of sanctions against apartheid. Keyes's political fundraising group, BlackPac, supported a number of right-wing and conservative politicians like Texas Republican senator Phil Gramm and conservative California congressman Robert Dornan. BlackPac declared that its mission was to oppose the 'terrorist outlaw' ANC and 'extremists' such as Jesse Jackson and the Congressional Black Caucus. The group's treasurer was Jay Parker, Keyes's lobbying partner and a long-time public relations consultant for the South African government and several homelands.

When approached recently, Keyes refused to discuss his role as lobbyist for the South African government and turned down several requests for an interview. Today he runs the Institute for Responsible Citizenship, a Washington-based leadership development programme for college-age black American men.

* * *

Despite the insistence of lobbyists like Keyes that things were improving in South Africa, news reports from the country revealed escalating violence as the government continued to try to contain the growing civil insurrection in the country during the 1980s. In 1985 and 1986 alone, nearly 2,100 people died in riots, internecine battles and clashes with police and soldiers. The government declared a limited state of emergency that granted security forces virtually unlimited powers of search and arrest and imposed strict censorship on the media.

In an address of 15 August 1985 that became known as the 'Rubicon speech', President Botha refused to back down, telling the world that he would not give in to black demands for a political system based on one man one vote or for the release of Nelson Mandela.

Building on the momentum of the street protests that were now occurring daily in the US, black members of Congress and their allies moved ahead with a South African sanctions bill, first introduced in 1972 by Ronald V. Dellums. The Congressional Black Caucus worked hard to win the support of their white counterparts to sign the bill. In the Senate, the Republican-led body, over significant opposition from some of its more conservative members, worked on its own version of a sanctions law. Reagan tried to pre-empt the bill by signing an executive order that imposed limited sanctions on South Africa. The order called for restrictions on bank loans to South Africa and a ban on exports of computers and nuclear technology. Another executive order by the president banned the importation of Krugerrands. But all this failed to move the opposition.

Democrats called the executive order a 'watered down and less effective version of the Congressional measure' that was being scheduled for a vote. In reply, Reagan and some Republican leaders argued that his executive orders should be given time to work. As part of his efforts to show that the administration was taking the situation in South Africa seriously, Reagan also undertook to appoint the first black ambassador to South Africa, though it later admitted that the unsuccessful attempt to appoint a black businessman with no diplomatic experience was a stalling tactic meant to buy time in the face of growing congressional pressure.

In the lead-up to the sanctions vote, the administration also dispatched William B. Robertson, a black American who was the deputy assistant secretary of state for African affairs, to address a gathering of black leaders at the International Conference Against Apartheid in Atlanta, Georgia. This was held at Ebenezer Baptist Church, where Martin Luther King Jr had served as minister. In front of a crowd of civil rights leaders and anti-apartheid activists, including Coretta Scott King and Desmond Tutu, Robertson assured the mostly black congregation that the Reagan administration was strongly opposed to apartheid. 'This administration has gone on record indicating its disdain for a policy which relegates approximately 23 million people, a majority, basically to a status of serfdom,' Robertson said. But the diplomat argued that sanctions were not the way to achieve the goal of abolishing apartheid. Instead, he insisted that business and education for black South Africans were more appropriate ways to deal with the problem. 'Economically, we cannot leave South Africa in shambles. We must stay but always prod for change. We must see that the environment constantly signals change,' he said. 'Our aim must always be that of bringing South Africa to its senses, not to its knees. It must function on the world market when apartheid is dismantled. We must see that it enters this arena with strength.'

Robertson received a polite but muted round of applause after his speech, but failed to move the pro-sanctions gathering. Many of those in the audience had been arrested while protesting in front of the South African embassy and would do so again.

Other White House officials were also sent on public outreach missions to 'those states and cities where we can influence impending divestment decisions', according to secret White House documents that were declassified in 1995. One official was sent to Indianapolis, Indiana, to convince the city council there to vote against a ban on companies doing business in South Africa. Charles Bray, the recently returned ambassador from Senegal, was dispatched on a three-week speaking tour to several states including Michigan, California, Pennsylvania and Ohio—states that play a major role in presidential elections and the control of Congress.

When these efforts failed to halt the push for stronger sanctions in Congress, the White House launched a charm offensive with Republicans and Democrats. The president, who was known to win over even his strident critics with his trademark chuckle and tilt of the head, personally called senators and representatives to make the case that his policy be given time to work. In a letter to Congress, he toughened his language towards the South African government.

In Britain around the same time, Reagan's closest international ally, Margaret Thatcher, was facing her own problems for supporting South Africa. In the streets of London and elsewhere, the Anti-Apartheid Movement (AAM) had launched a series of protests against the apartheid government and the effects were beginning to be felt. Activists secured support from local government councils, which passed resolutions condemning the South African government or took other actions. The Trades Union Congress, which had long rebuffed efforts by the AAM to become involved in its campaigns, came out in support of sanctions. They were joined by several churches in the UK. But the biggest impact came from the movement's campaign targeting British companies operating in South Africa. In a dramatic step Barclays Bank decided to pull out of South Africa after repeated boycotts by activists and students across the country. One official at the bank admitted, 'Our customer base was beginning to be adversely affected.'

Throughout it all, Thatcher remained unmoved. Even a plea from Queen Elizabeth failed to change her mind. According to a *Sunday Times* article of 20 July 1986, the queen had become dismayed by Thatcher's policies, and royal advisers took the unusual step of leaking to the newspaper the monarch's political views and the growing distance between her and the prime minister over South Africa. The queen was particularly worried that Mrs Thatcher's firm opposition to sanctions threatened to break up the Commonwealth.

In 1985, in a meeting in the Bahamas of the Commonwealth nations, four leaders, including Thatcher and Zambia's Kenneth Kaunda, met to try to reach agreement on a set of policies to end apartheid. The plan would include a statement on the Commonwealth's abhorrence of apartheid and its determination to see the system of racial discrimination brought to an end as soon as possible. It would also have required South Africa to take certain steps, such as ending the state of emergency, freeing detainees and political prisoners such as Nelson Mandela, and lifting the ban on the ANC. Thatcher had agreed on most of the terms, but adamantly opposed any measure that included sanctions. An exasperated Kenneth Kaunda, who was one of the primary negotiators for the Commonwealth's action plan on South Africa, asked that Thatcher be excluded from the planning of sanctions.

Still, Thatcher held firm, and Conservative members of the British parliament, who had supported the apartheid government in the past, refused to rebuke their leader. Unlike Reagan's Republican colleagues in the US, the Tories held fast even in the face of enormous support for sanctions from the British public and opposition political parties. In the end the Commonwealth agreed to a limited set of proposals that it required the South African government to accept, including political dialogue with banned organisations like the ANC; but sanctions would remain off the table, for the moment. Pretoria had avoided a major disaster.

But even with Commonwealth actions weakened by the resistance of Britain, government officials in Pretoria still felt their back was against the wall. A sanctions bill passed by the US could cause other countries to follow suit. The South African government began to redouble its efforts to prevent the sanctions legislation from being passed. A month before the vote on the bill, the government gathered its army of lobbyists and public relations consultants in a conference room in Pretoria for a planning session. The participants included William Keyes; John Sears, the former Reagan campaign manager; Michael Hathaway of United International Consultants; Robert Pipkin of Pearson & Pipkin; and Stephen F. Riley, another lobbyist. For days, in a series of meetings and strategy sessions, the lobbyists and government officials mapped out their game plan. Key members of Congress would be targeted, particularly those in the US Senate leadership who could stop or, at the very least, postpone a vote. A media campaign to encourage a more moderate approach would also be launched in concert with the lobbying in the capital. Newspaper editors and publishers and television news executives would need to be visited and persuaded that sanctions weren't the answer to the escalating problems in South Africa.

Returning to Washington, the lobbyists spread throughout the corridors of Capitol Hill to present the case against sanctions and deal with what seemed like a tidal wave of public opinion against apartheid. Sears's job was to reach out to Republicans. He arranged for the South African ambassador to meet the chairman of the Senate Foreign Relations Committee, White House staffers and the Senate majority leader, Bob Dole of Kansas, who had the power to stop the sanctions bill from coming up for a vote.

Keyes reached out to the black media, approaching a number of publications including the *Chicago Defender*, a prominent and widely read black-owned newspaper. He also tried to schedule meetings for the South African ambassador with black congressional and civil rights leaders. He wrote letters to black church leaders warning them about the effects that sanctions would have on black South Africans. But owing in large part to the counter-lobbying of TransAfrica and other anti-apartheid groups, most black leaders and organisations refused to meet with Keyes.

Hathaway, the former congressional staffer, worked his sources on Capitol Hill and reported back the political intelligence to the embassy and government officials in Pretoria about which law-makers might be sympathetic to South Africa. He found there were few, even among Republicans. Riley worked the diplomats at the US State Department, urging them to put more pressure on Congress to resist sanctions.

While the lobbyists were making their rounds in the US Congress on the sanctions bill, American business leaders also added their voices to the debate. In late 1985, more than 80 chief executives of American companies with investments in South Africa formed a group called the United States Corporate Council on South Africa. The council, which included General Motors, Citicorp, Mobil Oil and the Burroughs Corporation, ran full-page advertisements in dozens of American newspapers, including the *New York Times* and *Washington Post*, calling for an end to apartheid. Many of these companies had poured millions into lobbying to try to prevent sanctions legislation by the federal, state and local governments.

The council, which was chaired by the CEO of General Motors, Roger B. Smith, and by Michael Blumenthal, chairman of Burroughs, also called for negotiations between the South African government and 'acknowledged black leaders about power sharing'. While voicing their opposition to apartheid, business leaders did not necessarily endorse majority black rule or sanctions, and none of the companies favoured divesting their holdings in South Africa. 'The decisive arena of this historic struggle is inside South Africa itself, and US corporate resources can be most effectively brought to bear there,' said the steering committee of the council in a statement at the time.

The Corporate Council on South Africa received widespread coverage for its willingness to criticise the racial policies of the South African government. 'Business Protest on Apartheid Grows,' read a headline in the *New York Times* of 2 December 1985. Other papers ran similar articles, noting that the American business community, which, after years of sitting on the sidelines, had become more vocal in the South Africa debate. But secret State Department documents show that the corporate council, rather than being a business-led effort to try to solve the South African racial problems, was in fact part of a secret domestic and international public relations campaign led by the Reagan White House. Hoping to head off calls in Congress for more action on South Africa, the administration had gathered corporate executives for a strategy session in 1985. This would lead to the creation of a corporate council that would 'coordinate its efforts with the State Department's public diplomacy program on South Africa'.

According to a memo of 24 October 1985, White House and State Department staffers came up with the idea for the group a month earlier; its main purpose was to 'resist divestment and promote reform'.

Corporate leaders offered to spend $100 million over a two- to three-year period on community outreach efforts in South Africa and to increase job opportunities for blacks.

The corporate leaders also agreed to renew their commitment to the so-called Sullivan Principles, a corporate code of conduct drawn up in 1977 by the Reverend Leon Sullivan, a black minister, for companies operating in South Africa. The code called for non-segregated workplaces and equal pay among races in US-owned South African businesses. Sullivan would later renounce his code, saying it had failed to make US companies take on the apartheid government over its racial policies. He would also endorse sanctions as a remedy for making the government negotiate with banned political parties like the ANC. According to Sullivan, during an interview on 7 June 1987, even though American business had a 'notable record' against segregation, 'the main pillars of apartheid still remain, and blacks are still denied basic human rights in their own country and are denied the right to vote'.

Anti-apartheid activists hailed the move by Sullivan, declaring that businesses could no longer find observance of the Sullivan Principles an effective shield against pressures to divest their business operations in South Africa. But the companies vowed to push on even after Sullivan's change of heart. 'We owe a great debt to Leon Sullivan, but we will now have to carry out the Sullivan Principles without him,' Allen Murray, the senior executive of the Mobil Corporation and co-chairman of the United States Corporate Council on South Africa, said at the time.

The companies that made up the secret lobbying campaign were supposed to coordinate their efforts with South African business leaders, according to State Department documents. The records reveal that the American corporate leaders did have at least one meeting with their South African counterparts in Europe, though they do not say what was discussed. The memos disclose that the corporate effort was supposed to be augmented by conservative groups and the recruitment of 'public figures—academics, former government officials, politicians—who are prepared to take part in a process of public education on the South African issue and encourage them to write op-ed pieces and letters to the editors, appear on TV and other discussion panels'.

One of the conservatives tasked to help the Reagan White House in its efforts to stall sanctions was Carl 'Spitz' Channell, a conservative fundraiser, who ran a network of organisations that raised millions of dollars from wealthy Republican donors. Much of Channell's fundraising was carried out through the National Endowment for the Preservation of Liberty, a tax-exempt foundation formed in 1984, to 'educate members of the general public on American political systems and societal institutions'. But the group functioned more as a lobbying and fundraising organisation.

Channell would later gain notoriety for his involvement in the Iran-Contra scandal, in which the US government secretly sold weapons through intermediaries to Iran and used the money to fund a guerrilla movement in the Central American country of Nicaragua, ostensibly to counter the influence of Soviet-backed political parties. But little of Channell's role in the anti-sanctions campaign of the Reagan White House has ever been disclosed. A number of documents declassified in 2006 show that he played a significant role in trying to keep Congress from imposing sanctions on South Africa.

In the fall of 1986, shortly before the US Senate voted on sanctions, Channell, as records demonstrate, was recruited by the Reagan admini-stration to assist the White House in its efforts to stop the legislation. Channell was given high-level national security briefings and immediately launched an advertising campaign targeting Congress and the American media. 'When you ask us to help, we try the best we can,' Channell wrote to Marl Maseng, an assistant to the president and director of public liaison at the White House, the office that coordinated the administration's policy with outside interest groups. 'Within an hour of the briefing we began to gear up on the issue of South African sanctions.'

Channell told the White House that he had sent lobbyists from one of his group, the Sentinel Corp, to Congress to build support for Reagan's South African agenda, mailed telegrams to key Senators and secured political advertisements warning about the consequences of sanctions in the conservative *Washington Times*. Channell's attempts to delay the sanctions vote appear to have caused some Republicans to rethink their vote.

Corporations with operations in South Africa and conservative Congressmen were just one part of the White House plan to stop the movement for sanctions. Another memo dated 28 September 1985 shows that a senior State Department official suggested bringing in a task force, which included representatives from the CIA, the FBI and the Department of Defense, which had worked on countering Soviet propaganda in Africa, to offer suggestions on counteracting the sanctions movement.

It was a remarkable commitment of resources by the Reagan administration to halt the anti-apartheid movement, which was itself run largely on a shoestring budget. In effect, US taxpayers paid for free lobbying to aid the apartheid government's efforts to resist sanctions. But they weren't enough to turn the tide.

Despite the fierce lobbying, the sanctions bill was finally passed in the fall of 1986, dismaying not only the Reagan administration, but also the South African government, which had poured at least $5 million into defeating the legislation. The Comprehensive Anti-Apartheid Act of 1986 imposed economic sanctions on South Africa, and listed five conditions for ending them, including the release of Nelson Mandela and all political prisoners, and agreement by the South African government to enter 'good-faith negotiations' with the black majority. The legislation banned all new investment by Americans in South African businesses; prohibited the importation of such products as steel and coal from South Africa; and cancelled landing rights in the US for South African airlines. It was a serious defeat for Pretoria.

The sanctions, indeed, went further than those which had been enacted a few weeks earlier by the European Community. These banned new investment and the import of gold coins, iron and steel from South Africa, but did not include a ban on coal imports, as did the American legislation. The European Community had already banned military and police cooperation, as well as oil sales and cooperation in nuclear development. On top of the ban on military and police cooperation with South Africa, six members of the Commonwealth adopted more stringent sanctions between August and September 1986. These were India, Canada, Australia, Zambia, Zimbabwe and the Bahamas.

Thatcher had again refused to go along with the proposed sanctions, saying they would harden the attitudes of South Africa's white rulers and hurt blacks, not to mention British investments. The new Commonwealth sanctions came about as a result of lobbying by the prime minister of Canada, Brian Mulroney. Although Canada had significantly fewer investments in South Africa than Britain, Mulroney said this was not a factor. 'I viewed apartheid with the same degree of disgust that I attached to the Nazis,' he wrote in his memoirs. 'I was resolved from the moment I became prime minister that any government I headed would speak and act in the finest traditions of Canada.'

This put Mulroney at odds with Thatcher, and the two would engage in fierce debates about the best way to deal with the South African government. In a letter to the Canadian prime minister, Thatcher wrote that while she 'loathed apartheid' she thought sanctions would be 'counterproductive'. Mulroney also reached out to Ronald Reagan, but the American president rebuffed his calls for sanctions.

All the same, the Canadian leader's lobbying would pay off. In a meeting in August 1986 in London, over the objections of a furious Margaret Thatcher, who reportedly greeted Mulroney with a cold stare for raising the issue of apartheid, 11 other members of the Commonwealth voted to impose sanctions, leaving Britain isolated.

In Washington, Reagan tried to stop the US sanctions law by refusing to sign it, saying it undermined his ability to conduct US foreign policy.

But Congress, in an almost unprecedented move, voted to override his veto. The Democratic-controlled House of Representatives voted 313 to 83 to override the presidential veto, with 81 Republicans voting in favour of the measure. Reagan hoped for a better result in the Republican-controlled Senate, where several of his long-time supporters were in key leadership roles. Leading up to the Senate vote, Reagan again tried to persuade law-makers that a veto would weaken him in the eyes of the leaders of the Soviet Union, with whom he was scheduled to hold talks just a few weeks later.

Ironically, what may have helped many Republicans decide to vote to override the presidential veto was the actions of the South African government itself during the critical debates over the bill. Angered by the passage of the sanctions bill, Pik Botha, the foreign minister, put in a call to two senators from big farming states and threatened to cut off the South African purchase of American grain if the bill became law. Botha had reached out to the senators through his long-time friend and apartheid government supporter, the Republican senator Jesse Helms. But the call backfired. Instead of feeling pressured, the law-makers were angered by the boldness of the call and the implied threat.

With Coretta Scott King watching from the galleries, the Senate voted 78 to 21 to override Reagan's veto and impose stricter sanctions on the apartheid government. More than half of the 53 Republicans voted for the legislation. The vote was a stinging defeat for the president's policy of constructive engagement. More importantly, it marked the most serious defeat Reagan had suffered on a foreign policy issue and one of the most serious blows of his presidency, according to James Baker, Reagan's former chief of staff, who also served as US Treasury secretary. In an interview with the CBS News 'Face the Nation' programme, shortly after Mandela's death in December 2013, Baker said that Reagan later regretted his decision to veto sanctions against South Africa, although nothing in the president's diaries indicates that he had had second thoughts. In fact, the entries seem to show that Reagan believed he had done the right thing in his conduct of policy towards South Africa.

In a statement after Congress voted, Reagan called the sanctions legislation misguided. 'I deeply regret that Congress has seen fit to override my veto of the Comprehensive Anti-Apartheid Act of 1986. Punitive sanctions, I believe, are not the best course of action; they hurt the very people they are intended to help,' Reagan said. 'My hope is that these punitive sanctions do not lead to more violence and more repression.'

The passage of the Act emboldened the anti-apartheid movement, which began to push for even stronger sanctions and called for American corporations to withdraw from South Africa. Dozens of American cities passed laws pulling their investments in companies that did business in South Africa. A number of American universities did the same. Other countries followed suit. Japan passed legislation that renewed sanctions against South Africa, including prohibiting the import and purchase of Krugerrands and steel and iron. The legislation also barred South African Airways from landing in Japan and suspended the issuing of visas for South African tourists.

The passage of the US sanctions law proved that the grassroots campaign that had started with the arrest of four black American activists at the South African embassy had grown into a potent political force. It signalled too that black Americans, both as activists and as members of Congress, had emerged as a force in US foreign policy, particularly towards Africa.

It also proved something else: that the South African campaign to influence black Americans wasn't working. Keyes's and Parker's conservative talking points and anti-ANC rhetoric hadn't won the day but had, in fact, alienated blacks and their allies in the anti-apartheid movement. 'The fact that the South African government was spending millions on these black lobbyists to try and derail the movement for sanctions and divestments only served to remind us that we needed to struggle harder,' said Sylvia Hill, a professor at the University of the District of Columbia and board member of TransAfrica, who was active in the 1980s anti-apartheid struggles. 'The effect that Keyes and Parker had on the black-led protests was minor in the grand scheme of things.'

What Pretoria needed was a more sophisticated and subtle approach – one that did not publicly try to defend the apartheid system. The South African government needed a message that would resonate with law-makers and leaders of the black American anti-apartheid movement. It would come from an unlikely source.

9

Sanctions Only Hurt Blacks

'As an organization we are convinced that divestment by American companies has been a failed tactic and practical disaster.'

— *The Coalition on Southern Africa*

The passage of the Comprehensive Anti-Apartheid Act was a significant political victory for the Free South Africa Movement. But the Reagan administration did its best to delay implementing its provisions. One of the law's requirements was that the administration work with international partners to pressure the South African government to bring a speedy end to apartheid. Reagan, however, voted against further sanctions provisions sponsored by the UN Security Council. A study by the independent research arm of the US Congress, the Government Accountability Office, found that the administration also created various loopholes in the sanctions law and did not provide adequate funding to the government agencies responsible for overseeing the prohibitions. Consequently, momentum began to build in the streets and in Congress to add a new round of sanctions.

In September 1987, a year after Congress approved the first sanctions law, the Pretoria government and the Reagan administration received unexpected support from a group calling itself the Coalition on Southern Africa. This coalition, composed of black ministers from several religious denominations, black businessmen and academics, outlined what they claimed was a new strategy in the ongoing fight against apartheid. The marches and sanctions, they said, were starting to achieve the desired effect, forcing the white-led government to make changes. What was needed now, the group said, was not further sanctions, but help from American business to provide jobs and assist black South Africans to prepare for a post-apartheid society. The group announced it would develop business links between black Americans and black South Africans, promote the education and training of South African blacks, and press for an end to apartheid by seeking other alternatives. 'As an organization we are convinced that divestment by American companies has been a failed tactic and practical disaster,' the group wrote in a letter to President Reagan in September 1987.

It was hard to dismiss the group as another front for South African government interests. Many of the ministers were from religious denominations that had actively supported the anti-apartheid movement and opposed many of Reagan's domestic and international policies. One member of the coalition, the Reverend Gilbert Caldwell, a United Methodist minister, had been arrested two years earlier while protesting outside the South African embassy. Caldwell had a long history of social activism. Growing up during the turbulent 1940s and 1950s, he was inspired by Martin Luther King Jr to work for social justice for blacks. Caldwell first heard King speak at a 'prayer pilgrimage' rally in 1957, celebrating the Supreme Court's decision to strike down the 'separate but equal' notion of public schooling. While in seminary in 1958, Caldwell invited King to speak to several classes at King's alma mater, Boston University School of Theology. In 1964 Caldwell joined in the Mississippi Summer Project, an effort to help African American residents in the state of Mississippi to register as voters. He also participated in the famous 1965 march from Selma to Montgomery.

At the launch of the Coalition on Southern Africa, Caldwell and other members declared that they had created the organisation to push for social change in South Africa in the same way that black churches had taken a leading role in the American civil rights struggles. Clyde Williams, a Christian Methodist Episcopal minister, who served as general secretary of the new group, said that members had not consulted other anti-apartheid organisations about their plans. 'We need no endorsement,' said Williams, who was also president of a small black college in Alabama. 'We get our endorsement from God.'

The coalition lobbied the US Congress against further sanctions. Much later the group travelled to South Africa and held an event in Alexandra Township, where members gave out food, clothes and books. It also presented a $7,500 cheque from TV personality Oprah Winfrey, who had taken an interest in South Africa after reading the book *Kaffir Boy*, by Mark Mathabane. Winfrey's fiancé, Stedman Graham, worked for one of the founders of the coalition, Robert Brown, a black PR executive.

Most importantly, the coalition tried to steer the debate about South Africa away from sanctions and divestment towards preparing blacks for eventual rule. 'The plight of the black South African workers has been disregarded in the public debate about what to do to end apartheid,' said Richard Fisher, a bishop in the Episcopal Church and senior member of the group.

The coalition received favourable coverage in the American media, though many reported that the group's anti-sanctions stance ran counter to that of other anti-apartheid organisations. The influential *Washington Post* columnist William Raspberry, a black American who won the Pulitzer Prize in 1994, wrote a column noting that the coalition's position was likely to be unpopular, but added: 'It does make sense to begin thinking about helping the victims of apartheid and not merely hurting those who perpetuate it.'

Major US companies with South African operations began invoking the work of the coalition as they lobbied Congress not to impose additional sanctions, arguing that the new organisation demonstrated that not all US church groups backed sanctions.

Just weeks after the formation of the group, a parcel appeared on the doorstep of the Interfaith Center on Corporate Responsibility, a small shareholder advocacy organisation based in New York City. The centre had been in the forefront of the push for US companies to divest from South Africa until blacks were allowed to participate fully in all facets of society. Inside the package researchers at the centre found a 265-page secret document that Pagan International, an American PR firm hired by Shell Oil, had developed to undercut the anti-apartheid movement's calls for American companies to withdraw from South Africa.

The release of the document, widely reported in the media, caused an immediate backlash against the coalition and against Shell. Codenamed the 'Neptune Strategy', the plan suggested that instead of giving up its South African holdings, Shell should 'develop a task force' of South Africans, church leaders, US activists and executives, and get them to issue a statement about the company's role in helping South Africans prepare for life after apartheid. The activists would then say the company was assisting to devise 'post-apartheid plans' for black rule. This, the plan advised, 'will ensure the continuation and growth of the Shell companies in the United States and South Africa'.

The ambitious plan called for other measures the company could take. Among the ideas were two university-based projects: at the University of Notre Dame the document recommended the establishment of an 'Institute for the Study of Post-Apartheid Problems'; at Georgia University of Technology, a centre for the training of potential black South African leaders. The strategy document also discussed setting up a programme to gather intelligence on supporters of boycotts against the company. The operation was to be led by Arion Pattakos, a staffer at Pagan International and former US Defense Department intelligence analyst. Staff members on this programme were to pose as reporters and tape interviews with boycott activists, which would be sent to Pagan and mined for intelligence on how to counter the groups. Labour unions were also targeted, with special instructions to discourage members of the National Education Association and the American Federation of Teachers from participating in boycotts in their communities.

But the main focus of the oil company, as the Neptune plan made clear, was religious organisations. 'The churches represent the "critical mass" of opposition,' the plan argued. 'If they join the boycott and pressure for divestment, it will become a radically and far most costly problem than it is.'

To give the plan legitimacy, Pagan had hired James Armstrong, a former United Methodist Church bishop and one-time president of the National Council of Churches, which was a long-time supporter of US economic withdrawal from South Africa. Armstrong was a noted peace activist in the church and a strong advocate of human rights. Because of his ties with the US religious community, he was also hired as an executive vice-president at Pagan International. Armstrong was to meet with international and US church leaders and, according to the plan, 'deflect their attention away from boycott and divestment efforts' and 'give churches and religious agencies sufficient reasons not to join the boycott'.

The overall purpose of the plan was 'designed to attain the company goals', which meant staying in South Africa. Shell, which had begun operations in South Africa in 1902, was a major supplier of fuel to the South African government, particularly its military and police forces. Company records, news accounts and reports by anti-apartheid groups revealed that the company supplied 18 per cent of the oil used by the South African Defence Force in the 1980s. According to a 1989 report by the American Committee on Africa, an activist group that supported sanctions against South Africa, the oil giant also provided raw materials for napalm, defoliation agents and nerve gas for the South African Defence Force's biological and chemical weapons unit. Shell's total investment in South Africa in 1988 was about $2 billion, including holdings in mining, forestry and chemicals among other things.

Shell also had long-standing ties with the government of South Africa. In 1984 the London *Observer* revealed that the company had met with South African government officials to help break oil sanctions imposed on the country. Shell was paid almost $200 million in secret incentives for supplying the apartheid regime with oil. According to the report, company officials asked for higher prices to compensate them for the risk of supplying crude oil to the country. The South African government created an Equalisation Fund to 'compensate' oil companies for the higher cost of securing its oil supplies. At one point oil firms were being paid $39 a barrel, far more than the going price of oil at that time. A year after the fund was created, the companies pushed for an even higher rate because of the risks involved.

The Observer's findings were partly based on a confidential document presented to the South African parliament that laid out details of the secret arrangements. Prior to 1979, South Africa had bought most of its oil requirements from Iran, then under the Shah, Reza Pahlavi, a close US ally. But when the Shah fell in 1979, the country was forced to look elsewhere because all the major oil-producing countries had boycotted South Africa. Consequently, according to the government report, South Africa was forced to engage in 'unconventional means' to secure oil supplies.

'So both Shell and the South African government had a lot to lose if the company was forced to withdraw,' says Donna Katzin, a former staffer at the Interfaith Center. 'South Africa is rich in natural resources, but the one thing it doesn't have is oil.'

After the leak of the Neptune document, both Shell and Pagan claimed that the plan was just a strategy document given to Shell as one of many ways to handle organised protest against the oil giant. None of the actions had actually been taken, they insisted, even though most of the people identified in the document as key black activists were working for the Coalition on Southern Africa. The president of Pagan

International admitted that the coalition had been provided with free office space, phones and funds for travel. But Pagan's president claimed the company was only assisting because it wanted to help 'folks out there who are concerned with what will happen to the black population' once apartheid had ended.

More revelations would follow the release of the Neptune document. Additional records showed that the coalition of black clergy had also received funding from other major American companies that were trying to maintain their operations in South Africa. Mobil, for instance, led a fundraising drive among other major US firms with South African ties. These included Control Data, Combustion Engineering, Johnson & Johnson, Pfizer and Caltex. The companies combined to raise $1.2 million to put the coalition on its feet.

'They almost got away with it,' says Timothy Smith, former executive director of the Interfaith Center. 'Shell's goal was to obscure the ways in which it had supported the white minority government rule and the system of apartheid by diverting the debate to "post-apartheid South Africa". If the documents hadn't been delivered to us, no one ever would have known that the group was just a front.'

After the leak, Shell denied responsibility for the document and for the creation of the coalition, saying that Pagan International had come up with the plan but the company had never acted on the advice. Some of the participants in the coalition tried to deflect the growing criticism, arguing that while business corporations had provided funding, none of this had come from the South African government. The fact that nothing tied the coalition directly to Pretoria failed to quell criticism from other groups in the anti-apartheid movement, who charged that the ministers had allowed themselves to be used for money.

The fact that the money to start the coalition hadn't come directly from the South African government wasn't the point, said Smith in an interview in May 2013. 'By taking money from these companies and allowing themselves to be used by them, the ministers were, in essence, helping the South African regime tighten its system of institutionalised racism and discrimination. However they want to justify what they did, they helped support apartheid.' The Truth and Reconciliation Commission would come to the same general conclusion, stating that 'business was central to the economy that sustained the South African state during the apartheid years'.

Following the revelations about corporate funding, several members of the coalition, including Caldwell, resigned. He told reporters that he believed corporations could work with churches to help South Africa achieve racial equality. But 'that unique role is accomplished best when the corporate and other sectors respond to our agenda rather than use us to achieve their agenda'.

In fact, records and interviews show that Caldwell had known all along that the coalition was a front for US companies with operations in South Africa. He said he had been recruited to the organisation by Pagan International's vice-president, James Armstrong, the former Methodist bishop. According to Caldwell, he had met Armstrong during a visit to Denver, Colorado, for a Methodist Church event. 'He was telling me about this effort that Pagan was putting together and asked if I would join up,' Caldwell said in an interview in April 2013. 'I guess they needed someone like me, with my background and history, to make it seem legitimate.'

After his meeting with Armstrong, Caldwell was hired by Pagan International as a consultant, to liaise with civil rights leaders and organisations. Caldwell did not say what religious organisations he met with during his time as a PR consultant. Nor did he reveal what he said to the groups in his discussions about South Africa or divestment by American companies. He disclosed that he received a stipend from Pagan and went on several trips to South Africa at the company's expense, attending the enthronement of Desmond Tutu as archbishop. He would not disclose how much the stipend was. 'I firmly believe that I was trying to change things from the inside. I'd really like to think that's what I was doing. I was trying to do the right thing.'

Today, Caldwell, who has become a leading voice calling for the acceptance of gays and lesbians in the Methodist Church, says he has mixed feelings about his work with the coalition. In 2007 he was honoured by the Church Within a Church Movement, an association of religious groups that combat racism and sexual discrimination in churches, for what organisers declared was his lifelong work for racial, gender, sexual orientation, economic and peace issues, including his work as an activist against apartheid. The award, the Reverend Gilbert H. Caldwell Justice Ministry Award, honoured him as the first recipient at a ceremony attended by dignitaries from around the world, including the Reverend Mpho Tutu, daughter of Archbishop Desmond Tutu and executive director of the Desmond Tutu Institute. Caldwell's work with the Coalition on Southern Africa was never mentioned.

10

The Fixer

*'It's fine to talk about ending apartheid, but people needed
to have jobs and eat, even ANC members.'*
– Robert Brown,
co-founder of the Coalition on Southern Africa

Robert Brown offers no apologies for his work with the Coalition on Southern Africa. Nor does he deny that he had close ties with individuals within the apartheid government. He believes his work as a representative for companies opposing sanctions was good for black people in South Africa.

Brown is the owner and president of B&C International, a public relations firm he founded in 1960 to provide crisis communications consultations for corporate clients. An associate of Martin Luther King Jr, Brown said that he advised, travelled with and raised money for King and the civil rights movement. 'I was beaten up many times and was put in jail on occasion,' Brown recalled of his experiences while working with King during an interview in May 2013.

After a four-year career in law enforcement, Brown set up his own public relations firm, taking on Woolworth and S.C. Johnson as corporate clients. In politics, Brown started out as a Democrat, supporting Robert F. Kennedy in the 1968 presidential election, before the latter's assassination. Brown then worked on the campaign of Richard Nixon and served as a press aide after Nixon won the presidency. Later, as a conservative black Republican, Brown enjoyed a broad range of support from both liberals such as Andrew Young, the black United Nations ambassador during the Carter administration, and from conservatives like Senator Jesse Helms.

Brown made his first trips to South Africa after Sara Lee, one of his firm's clients, bought the South African subsidiary of a shoe polish company in 1984. Brown's firm also represented the Nabisco food company, then owned by the tobacco giant R.J. Reynolds. During this visit, Brown became aware of the appalling circumstances in which black South Africans were living. 'I was seeing kids with no shoes, people just living in horrible conditions.' But rather than supporting sanctions, Brown urged Sara Lee, Nabisco and other businesses to do more to help blacks, by adding them to corporate boards and placing them in supervisory positions. Brown thought American companies should invest more in the South African economy to help the black population, a stand that put him at odds with the leaders of the US anti-apartheid movement and liberation movements like the ANC.

But Brown's position made him a perfect choice for Reagan as the first black US ambassador to South Africa. Brown had come to the attention of the White House because of his participation in a State Department working group set up to promote the Reagan administration's conservative engagement policy with South Africa and to strengthen ties between American and South African interests. Secret documents, later declassified, show that the 'working group' had been responsible for creating a 'diplomatic counter-offensive' against the anti-apartheid movement.

Many black Americans, including Jesse Jackson, cautioned Brown against accepting the position because of Reagan's opposition to sanctions. Jackson and others called the appointment a 'suicide mission'. Brown's appointment was even opposed by the secretary of state, George Shultz, who thought a more seasoned diplomat would be a better choice for the job. But the White House believed the fact that he was black would send a message to the South African government and help bridge the gap with black South Africans.

Before Brown could be formally nominated, reports emerged about his close ties to Umaru Dikko, a Nigerian politician who had fled the country after a military coup and who was accused of stealing hundreds of millions of dollars in oil money from the state's coffers. Brown had served as a public relations consultant to the Nigerian government when he met Dikko, who was then acting as transport minister. Brown also had a business relationship with Dikko, but denied that he was involved in the alleged embezzlement.

There were other accusations, vehemently denied by Brown, that he had engaged in anti-union activities at a textile company which his firm represented. The resulting public outcry proved too much for the Reagan administration. A planned public announcement of the appointment as part of a State of the Union address by Reagan was scuttled, and the nomination did not go forward.

Despite having his ambassadorship aborted, Brown continued to work in South Africa, cultivating ties with South African government and corporate leaders. He announced the formation of the International Concern Foundation, which he claimed provided clothes, food, financial assistance and scholarships to black South Africans. (Tax documents do not show if the organisation ever operated in South Africa.)

Brown also sought out and established a relationship with Winnie Madikizela Mandela, wife of the imprisoned leader of the ANC. This relationship would later spark controversy when Brown, with help from South Africa's ambassador to the US, Piet Koornhof, gained the right to visit the imprisoned Nelson Mandela in July 1988. Brown said he had met Koornhof at a prayer breakfast in the US and the two had struck up a friendship.

After the meeting, a smiling Brown and Mrs Mandela announced at a press conference that he had been given power of attorney to represent the Mandela family interests and prevent the 'rip-off' of the imprisoned leader's name. Brown would be given control over the disbursement of proceeds from concerts, movies, T-shirts and buttons that used Nelson Mandela's name. Following the announcement, the ANC denounced the move. 'Mandela is a public figure. His name does not belong to the family but to the movement,' the ANC said in a statement.

Nelson Mandela confirmed that position when he quickly summoned his attorney, Ismail Ayob, to Pollsmoor Prison in Cape Town and issued a statement denying that Brown, or anyone else besides the ANC, had been given the authority to speak on his behalf. According to the letter, Nelson Mandela said his wife had told him that Brown had been misquoted as saying he had been given power of attorney for the Mandela family. Brown's claim was one of the first public disputes between the ANC and Winnie Mandela over who had authority to speak on the imprisoned leader's behalf.

The controversy grew when it was revealed that Brown had solicited hundreds of thousands of dollars from individuals in the US to build a luxury home for Winnie Mandela in Soweto. After the funding for the house was made public, Mrs Mandela decided not to move into the mansion 'until Nelson Mandela is released from prison'. Brown would later pay for two of the Mandela children to attend college in the US.

Brown also raised eyebrows when the Coalition on Southern Africa held a food and clothes giveaway in Alexandra Township. The group had enlisted the help of the South African government to publicise the event. The South African Bureau of Information sent a telex to the media, 'on behalf of Robert J. Brown', announcing the event. A spokesperson for Brown, Armstrong Williams, now a conservative radio talkshow host, said that he requested the government's help because 'I didn't have a list of news agencies ... and we are guests in this country and we wanted to go through the channels'. The government connection would prove embarrassing both for the Coalition and for Winnie Mandela, who did not attend the event.

While Brown later admitted he was a member of the Coalition on Southern Africa, he insisted that he played no role in the day-to-day operations of the group and refused to say whether he was one of its founders, as an investigative reporter, Jack Anderson, claimed in an article in 1987. Brown would also not disclose if he was behind the creation of the group, as Anderson alleged.

The purpose of the group, Brown declared, was not to mislead the public about its origins but to work to bring churches and business corporations together to find a solution to apartheid. 'No one was trying to hide anything,' he said. 'We were trying to find a solution that would hasten the end of apartheid, but didn't leave blacks worse off than they were under the race-based apartheid system.'

Brown later quit the coalition, not because it was revealed to be funded by corporations with business interests in South Africa, many of whom were his clients, but because the group 'was being perceived as being pro-apartheid and pro-apartheid government'. 'That's not what I was about.'

Donna Katzin, a former anti-apartheid activist, says that Brown's position was clear to those fighting for an end to apartheid. 'Robert Brown was serving the corporations that he worked for,' Katzin said. 'He can talk all he wants about wanting to help black people in South Africa and not serving the apartheid government, but his actions say otherwise.'

Despite the criticism of his stance on South Africa during the apartheid years, Brown said in a recent interview that he has no regrets about his work there. 'I challenge anybody to put their work up against mine,' he said. 'It's fine to talk about ending apartheid, but people needed to have jobs and eat, even ANC members.' Asked whether he believed sanctions against South Africa worked, Brown said he did. But he added: 'I think my way worked too.'

Today, Brown continues to work in South Africa. He started the South African BookSmart Foundation in 1993, which provides thousands of books to needy South African children. The organisation is now called the International BookSmart Foundation.

Following the death of Mandela in 2013, Brown would speak fondly, at a Republican Party convention, of his meeting with the anti-apartheid leader and his work with the Mandela family. He never mentioned the role he played in trying to stop the very sanctions that Mandela himself would praise for paving the way for his release from prison.

'All I want people to do with me is to judge me for what I did. I did a lot of good and I did not lobby for the South African government.'

11

Operation Heartbreak

*'The worst thing in South Africa you can be today is not a
white racist, but a black teacher, a black doctor or lawyer—
any person of colour who is using the South African system
to create for himself and his family the trappings of an
abundant life.'*

*– Kenneth Frazier,
director of the Wake Up America Coalition*

Few people in Washington had ever heard of the Reverend Kenneth
Frazier when he stepped behind a podium at the National Press
Club building to announce the launch of his 'Operation Heartbreak'
campaign in June 1988. Speaking in the booming cadences common to
many black preachers, Frazier denounced members of Congress who,
he said, were preparing to vote for imposing further sanctions on South
Africa, which would push millions of the country's children into a life
of greater hardship and poverty by taking away the jobs of their parents.
'Many congressmen are so gun-shy of being labelled "white racist" that
they are on the verge of being manipulated to perform the most hateful
and repugnant act—that of abandoning black South African children to
more hunger, misery and disillusionment,' he declared to the assembled
reporters.

Describing himself as someone who was a civil rights leader in the 1960s, Frazier said that he had fought for the political and economic rights of blacks in America and that by taking on sanctions he was fighting to do the same for black South Africans.

Frazier denied that his campaign was a response to the upcoming vote in Congress on the Comprehensive Anti-Apartheid Act, scheduled for the end of June. He said his position was based on his own visits to South Africa and his concerns about the country's black population. 'They are caught between apartheid and US sanctions, which represent another form of hostility and oppression. We are tired of seeing black and brown children the world over always carrying the political burdens and consequences of these irrational struggles for power among politicians.'

Little is known about Frazier's past, and there are no records or news accounts that show him participating in civil rights struggles. It seems that he was a former minister in the Methodist Church. According to a press release issued at the time of the Operation Heartbreak campaign, Frazier was a consultant to several US government agencies, including the Department of Housing and Urban Development and the Mental Health Services Administration. He also claimed to have been appointed to the staff of President Lyndon Johnson's task force on discrimination against women. He ran unsuccessfully for Congress in 1986 in California as a Republican.

In 1985, a year before he ran for Congress, Frazier received some local attention in the *Los Angeles Times* when he told students at a college that the anti-apartheid movement was communist-led and would put all of Africa under communist rule and allow the Soviet Union to control most of the strategic minerals needed by the US 'to sustain our military and our way of life'. 'We have but to look at the millions dead, the economic chaos and human misery in Afghanistan, in Ethiopia, in the killing fields of Cambodia and Vietnam to understand how the communists liberate people of colour,' he said, according to the *Times*. 'In South Africa, the saga continues as blacks themselves, inspired by the wild rhetoric of Marxism, murder and mutilate their own black teachers, doctors, lawyers, businessmen and women. The worst thing in South Africa you can be today is not a white racist, but a black teacher, a black doctor or lawyer—any person of colour who is using the South African system to create for himself and his family the trappings of an abundant life.'

To illustrate his point about ANC violence, Frazier presented a gruesome videotape in which a mob of black South Africans pounded the mutilated body of a black man with bricks, then set him on fire. The man had attracted the group's wrath because he was a teacher, Frazier said, although there was little on the tape to indicate the reason for the violence or that it had anything to do with the ANC. The refusal of American television stations to air the tape, Frazier said, was evidence of the media's distortion of the truth about what was occurring in South Africa.

None of this was known when Frazier showed up three years later in Washington, weeks before Congress was set to vote on another sanctions bill.

As chairman of a group called the Wake Up America Coalition, which was supposedly made up of several prominent black American leaders concerned about the impact of sanctions on black children in South Africa, he reached out to several schools, which were told that the intention of the campaign was to convince Congress to sponsor food and clothing for the children in South Africa. The coalition's plan was to distribute 858 black dolls to congressional offices and the White House to raise awareness about the plight of South Africa's children, he told the schools, and asked whether their students could go on a field trip to the capital to help raise awareness. Moved by his description of the condition of South African children, the schools were eager to join his awareness campaign.

But at the press conference announcing the campaign, many in attendance thought the effort was more about stopping the sanctions bill than about helping South African children. In his opening remarks Frazier launched into an attack on the ANC and declared that white members of Congress who supported the sanctions bill did so because they were afraid of being labelled racists. He called on members to resist efforts to impose sanctions: 'If you are prepared to vote for another round of more restrictive sanctions and disinvestment against South Africa, understanding the consequences for its black children, let us establish for the record that you are not hypocritical, that you will lead our nation in a show of compassion for South Africa's black children,' Frazier said.

Mervyn Dymally, a black Democrat from California, denounced Frazier and his campaign, calling it a 'front for one of the many South African-supported and -funded groups'. 'There is no doubt in my mind that this is designed to develop opposition to the sanctions bill.'

Frazier would not confirm or deny that his group was lobbying for the South African government against the sanctions bill, deflecting questions when asked about the source of its funding. 'No matter what political side you are on, anti-sanctions, pro-sanctions, it doesn't matter,' he said in response.

Frazier's Operation Heartbreak failed to sway the House of Representatives. Two months later, by a vote of 244 to 132, the lower legislative chamber approved the bill and the Wake Up America Coalition was never heard of again.

Contacted afterward, many of the schools said that they felt duped by Frazier. School administrators, who supported the anti-apartheid movement, declared they had no idea that their children had been used in an anti-sanctions lobbying campaign. Although anti-apartheid activists were never able to tie the campaign directly to the South African government, they had no doubt that the Wake Up America Coalition was one of many groups funded behind the scenes that sprang up as calls for sanctions grew.

The US Department of Justice has no records listing Frazier or the coalition as lobbyists for the South African government or, indeed, that a group called the Wake Up America Coalition has ever existed. Lobbying for a foreign government without registering with the US Department of Justice is illegal and the group could have faced criminal charges. Likewise, the US Senate Office of Public Records, where domestic lobbyists are meant to register, did not have a registration for Frazier or the coalition. Frazier did, however, meet several times with William Keyes, the black American lobbyist hired by the apartheid government to stop the push for sanctions, according to records from the US Department of Justice. One of the meetings occurred just months before he launched Operation Heartbreak.

It is also unclear how Frazier was able to travel to South Africa, as he claimed, or whether he went there at all. Many anti-apartheid activists suspect that he was one of dozens of people who were taken on trips by the South Africa Foundation.

What is known is that after leaving the Methodist Church, Frazier became one of the leaders of the Church Universal and Triumphant, a religious group founded in 1975 by Elizabeth Clare Prophet. This controversial New Age sect is fiercely anti-communist. In 1979, after the Soviet invasion of Afghanistan, several high-ranking members of the group joined the Committee for Free Afghanistan, a group that had ties to the World Anti-Communist League and that raised money and lobbied for US support for the mujahideen. Involvement in the Afghan Committee brought church leaders in touch with people who had ties to a number of right-wing groups, including supporters of the apartheid government, which they saw as the next target of the Soviet Union.

Elizabeth Prophet, the leader of the sect, often praised South Africa in her writings, seeing it as a bulwark against Soviet expansion. In her book *Pearls of Wisdom*, published in 1980, Prophet wrote that the 'nations of South Africa and Rhodesia themselves have carried a great light in the African continent'. Though she said she did not approve of apartheid policies, Prophet nevertheless called on followers to support the 'light' (the governments of South Africa and Rhodesia), warning that their fall would be a blow to the 'cause of world freedom' and allow the 'Soviet Union to take control of the Indian Ocean, the ports, the waterways, the minerals, the resources, the tremendous wealth of South Africa, and to use the excuse of racial division to cause a bloodbath that would be beyond compare in the history of Africa should it come to pass'.

Nothing ties the Church Universal and Triumphant directly to the South African government. A search of South African and US government records did not reveal financial links between the church and the apartheid regime, but it is clear that the sect was an active supporter of South Africa. In addition to Prophet's proclamation of South Africa as the 'light' of Africa, the sect hosted a number of seminars on South Africa and communism, which drew government officials, lobbyists and individuals who supported Pretoria.

On 3 July 1987, a year before Frazier's Operation Heartbreak brought school children to the Capitol, the Church Universal and Triumphant invited Uys Viljoen, a political counsellor at the South African embassy in Washington, to a panel to discuss the political situation in South Africa. The event was held at the sect's own Summit University. No anti-apartheid activists were invited to participate.

Viljoen was joined on the panel by James W. Kendricks, a conservative black American, who had worked with William Keyes and Jay Parker, both lobbyists for South Africa, and who was listed as an expert on South African affairs. Also on the panel were Frazier and the Reverend Gene Vosseler. Previously a Lutheran and Unitarian minister, Vosseler, who is white, was ordained in the sect as a minister in 1985. He was chairman of Citizens for a Strong America and High Frontier, both conservative political groups that advocated a strong American national defence force. He was also a close associate of David W. Balsiger, whom he joined to form an organisation protesting against Soviet participation in the 1984 Olympics. Balsiger, who is also white, was a long-time supporter of the white South African regime and frequent traveller to the country. He confirmed that at least one of his trips was funded by the South African Department of Foreign Affairs.

Balsiger defended the apartheid government through a number of organisations that he established, including the Biblical News Service. In 1987, the Biblical News Service published a special issue of its magazine, *Biblical Scorecard*, entitled 'South Africa: A Nation on Trial'. In it Balsiger wrote in support of apartheid and also suggested several ways in which Americans could respond to the 'South African bashing' by liberal activists and the media. The suggestions included taking tours of South Africa; subscribing to the *South African Digest*, a publication of the South African Bureau of Information; distributing films about the 'real situation' in South Africa, including at least five produced by the South African government; and disseminating copies of the *Biblical Scorecard* magazine to public leaders in areas where 'sanctions, divestment or disinvestment are being debated'.

In all, 525,000 copies of *Biblical Scorecard* were sent to numerous federal and state law-makers, including black elected officials. The articles in the magazine described the ANC, the United Democratic Front and the South African Council of Churches as supporters of communism and terrorism. The South African Tourism Corporation provided the only advertising for the special issue. The total amount of the advertising was $300,000, a significant amount for a magazine that had a small circulation and about which few people had ever heard. The South African embassy also helped distribute the special issue of the magazine.

In addition, the Biblical News Service was responsible for the distribution of a videotape called *The ANC: A Time for Candor*. In the video, viewers were shown the 'necklacing' (burning by a petrol-soaked tyre) of a young black woman and the killing of a black soldier from the Ciskei, another of the black 'independent' homelands. The killings were carried out by angry crowds, which the voice-over narrator identified as members of the ANC. The video also featured an interview with Craig Williamson, a former government spy who had been responsible for the death by parcel-bomb of the anti-apartheid activist Ruth First, wife of the Communist Party leader Joe Slovo. Viewers were asked to write to their senators, representatives and local newspaper editors to protest against the meeting in January 1987 between the ANC president, Oliver Tambo, and George Shultz, the US secretary of state. Some 10,000 copies of the videotape were distributed.

Balsiger's National Citizens Action Network launched a lobbying campaign in June 1998, at the same time as Frazier's Operation Heartbreak, opposing a second sanctions bill against South Africa. In mailings to members of Congress, the network, which was allegedly made up of 300 organisations, including Frazier's, argued that sanctions would hurt only blacks, especially children. The mailing included a 12-minute video called *Listen to Our Voices*, which featured black South Africans who declared they were opposed to sanctions.

Balsiger was also the exclusive American distributor of the *Aida Parker Newsletter*, a pro-apartheid magazine produced in South Africa. Gordon Winter, a former South African government agent, later identified Aida Parker, a reporter with *The Citizen*, which initially had been secretly funded by the government, as an agent of the notorious Bureau of State Security (BOSS). The South African Truth and Reconciliation Commission would confirm that the newsletter, codenamed 'Project Villa Marie', was one of the many secret propaganda projects funded by the Defence Force in order to discredit the ANC.

Several calls were made to Frazier, who now lives in the Washington DC area, for comment on his work in relation to sanctions, his Operation Heartbreak campaign, his work with the Church Universal and Triumphant, and his association with David Balsiger. None of the calls seeking comment was returned. In an interview Louis Nel, the former deputy foreign minister, said he could not remember having met anyone fitting Frazier's description or a group like the Church Universal and Triumphant lobbying on behalf of the South African government. But he didn't rule out the possibility.

12

The Anti-Sanctions Videos

'These black South Africans don't want paternalism, they don't want others to decide how their battles should be fought.'

— *J. Morgan Hodges,*
member of the National Religious Broadcasters

At about the same time as Frazier was delivering dolls to members of Congress, two videos made by the black American J. Morgan Hodges appeared in the mail boxes at congressional offices. The videos urged members of Congress to oppose the sanctions bill. In a letter accompanying them, Hodges said he was a lifelong Democrat who had recently travelled to South Africa to see the country for himself and had come away with the conclusion that sanctions would not be in the best interest of black South Africans.

A stocky man with a round face and booming voice, Hodges had registered as a lobbyist with Congress in 1986. Records show he was paid $9,500 for his efforts, which were expressly directed at defeating the sanctions bill. They do not list the source of the funding. The records also show that Hodges had never lobbied Congress on any issue previously.

The records do not indicate whom he represented. Hodges listed

Chris/Mor Productions as his employer, but a search of business records failed to show that a company with that name ever existed in Washington DC.

In meetings with members of Congress and their staff, Hodges denied he was part of any organised effort to defeat sanctions, saying that during his travels in South Africa he had found that most blacks opposed sanctions and thought they would do more harm than good. But a number of congressional staff interviewed at the time recalled that Hodges claimed he was an associate of a conservative pro-government black South African religious leader.

The first video Hodges sent to Congress was called *South Africa: A Closer Look*. This well-produced work of 12 minutes, which featured African drums beating in the background, consisted of interviews conducted with several black South Africans opposed to sanctions, including the businessman Mohale Mahanyele, chairman and founder of National Sorghum Breweries.

Instead of hearing from 'international spokesmen and political activists', Hodges said in his narration, he had gone to South Africa to hear the voices of ordinary people and publicise their concerns. 'These black Africans don't want paternalism, they don't want others to decide how their battles should be fought,' Hodges declared, as images of South Africans flashed across the screen. 'As a black American I understand and endorse their decision.'

A second video, called *Listen to Our Voices*, featured interviews with other black South Africans opposed to sanctions, most notably Mangosuthu Buthelezi, founder of the Inkatha Freedom Party and prime minister of the KwaZulu homeland. American conservatives often held Buthelezi up as an example of a black South African opposed to sanctions.

It is unclear how Hodges was able to finance the production of the videos or his trip to South Africa, and it is also unclear from the videos whether he is the person who is asking the questions or merely the narrator.

Public records show that Hodges was minister of the Universal Holiness Church, a small church in Washington DC. He was also a board member of the conservative National Religious Broadcasters, or NRB, a group of mostly white broadcasters with a long history of support for the apartheid government. Members of the group went on a number of fact-finding tours to South Africa in 1986 and 1987 and later produced programmes favourable to the South African government. It is not known whether Hodges went with them. The trips were ostensibly paid for by an 'anonymous group of South African businessmen', who asked the NRB to form a South African affiliate. Tom Wallace, a member of the NRB's executive board, said the South African businessmen had approached the religious broadcasters and paid for the tours because 'they perceived their future depends on getting a different view across in this country'. But, in later interviews, Ben Armstrong, then executive director of the NRB, admitted that some of the funding for the trips might have come directly from the South African government.

Ronn Haus, a board member of the NRB, and owner of the Family Christian Broadcasting Network, confirmed that the apartheid government provided funding for the trip. Haus said he was invited on one of the South African tours but cancelled at the last minute after learning that the trip was 'at the invitation of and underwritten by the South African government, and I finally decided that I didn't want to be wrongly interpreted as a pawn'. Other religious leaders on the broadcaster felt differently.

The South African Tourism Corporation had a regular presence at the NRB's annual conventions. Officials of the tourism corporation manned booths and distributed literature encouraging evangelicals to travel to the country to 'get a proper understanding of the South African situation'. As a further sign of its ties with the South African government, in 1987 the NRB awarded the South African foreign minister, Pik Botha, its international award, for his 'outstanding leadership in justice, freedom and democracy'.

At their 1986 and 1987 annual conventions, the NRB hosted the pro-government Bishop Isaac Mokoena, founder of a conservative alliance of independent black churches in South Africa. The bishop was promoted by the South African government as a viable alternative to more radical black leaders, such as Nelson Mandela and Archbishop Desmond Tutu. President P.W. Botha later awarded the Decoration for Meritorious Services to Mokoena, who had once called the awarding of the Nobel Peace Prize to Tutu 'an insult to black Christians in South Africa'.

Introduced at the broadcasters' convention in 1986 as a man who represented the views of 4.5 million black South Africans, Mokoena criticised the efforts of American anti-apartheid campaigners and members of Congress who wanted to impose sanctions on South Africa. 'I have come to appeal to you to speak to your congressman, speak to your senator, ask him to offer some words of encouragement to the President of the United States to step up investments, not only with the present areas of South Africa but also in the homelands,' Mokoena told his audience.

The NRB had other ties to the South African government through its members. Trinity Broadcasting Network, a member of the broadcasters' group, flew officials from the Ciskei homeland to America for interviews. The South African government had earlier helped the network build a television station in Ciskei. Paul F. Crouch, president and owner of Trinity, also enlisted help from the South African government in facilitating an introduction to General Bantu Holomisa, the leader of Transkei from 1988, so that he could establish television stations there, and signed an agreement for another station in Bophuthatswana. During one of his many trips to South Africa, Crouch met with President P.W. Botha to discuss the establishment of a nationwide Christian broadcasting network.

Anti-apartheid activists criticised the decision by Crouch to set up his broadcasting operations in the 'homelands' and condemned its affiliations with the apartheid government. 'I don't think you can more grievously and more measurably support apartheid than he has,' TransAfrica's Randall Robinson told the *Los Angeles Times* in an interview in 1989. 'To lend massive television technology to the legitimizing of this forceful warehousing on these remote parcels [the homelands] amounts to the most important, significant support for the apartheid system that one can give, particularly the United States.'

Other members of the NRB who gave unstinting support to the South African government were the well-known American televangelists Jimmy Swaggart, Jerry Falwell and Pat Robertson. These evangelists repeatedly called on their followers to lobby congressmen and officials in the US to resist imposing sanctions on the apartheid government.

In 1985, following his return from a trip to South Africa where he met with President Botha, Falwell encouraged 'millions of Christians to buy Krugerrands' to help the South African economy, and at the same time expressed his opposition to economic sanctions against South Africa. While Falwell declared he opposed apartheid, he said that his main worry was the influence of the Soviet Union in southern Africa, in particular on groups like the ANC.

In a separate mailing sent to thousands of followers in September 1985, Falwell urged them to write to their congressmen and senators and ask them to oppose sanctions, again raising the spectre of a communist take-over of South Africa by 'Marxist leaning organizations [that] are constantly creating violence and bloodshed among the blacks of the country'. He urged his followers to 'pray for the leadership in South Africa' in their reforming efforts to move the country away from apartheid. In his letter he also attacked Desmond Tutu and the Reverend Allan Boesak, a leader of the United Democratic Front, and accused the 'liberal media' of telling just one side of the South African story.

Falwell's defence of the South African government prompted a backlash, even in his conservative home town of Lynchburg, Virginia. Donations to his ministries also dropped as the controversy drew more and more media attention. Falwell, for his part, turned the backlash into a personal fundraising appeal. In a mailing sent to his followers he wrote: 'Communist terrorists are openly threatening to kill me because of my campaign to prevent the Soviet Union from taking over the vital minerals, strategic sea lanes, and naval bases of South Africa,' he wrote in the fundraising appeal, urging supporters to 'please send your $100, $25 gift now'.

Jimmy Swaggart, before his downfall in a sex scandal involving several prostitutes, was one of the most influential American evangelical ministers in South Africa. He had a large office and spiritual centre in downtown Johannesburg, which provided tapes, books and pamphlets to whites and blacks. He also constantly sided with the apartheid government. In one sermon during a rally in South Africa, Swaggart declared that 'apartheid was dead', much to the surprise of the nation's black inhabitants. In another sermon, widely broadcast by the South African Broadcasting Corporation, he said that the country was being targeted by a 'communist onslaught'. This brought a rebuke from a group of black South African evangelicals. 'We as concerned Evangelicals have been outraged by the way in which American evangelicals like Jimmy Swaggart came here to South Africa in the midst of our pain and suffering, even death, and pronounced that apartheid is dead,' the group wrote.

Of the three televangelists, it was Pat Robertson who was the biggest supporter of the South African government. His Christian Broadcasting Network ran several pro-government features during the 1980s, including the video that allegedly showed supporters of the ANC necklacing a young woman and beating a man to death. The host of the network's flagship programme, 'The 700 Club', was Ben Kinchlow, a black American, who travelled to South Africa, where he was feted by government officials. Returning to the US, Kinchlow gave the country glowing reviews on his programme, telling viewers that he had personally experienced no racism during his time there. Pro-apartheid South African blacks were also given airtime on 'The 700 Club'. In 1985, two of the guests were evangelical ministers while a third was a young woman who said she had previously been in the ANC but had abandoned the organisation when she was 'born again'. Of the three, the person who would receive the most press during his visit to the US was the Reverend Barney Mabaso. During his appearance on 'The 700 Club', Mabaso called the ANC ungodly, saying the spirit of the ANC was the spirit of the anti-Christ. Later, in a trip to the US capital to meet with members of the Republican Study Committee, Mabaso attacked both Desmond Tutu and the ANC, telling the congressmen that religious leaders like Tutu were 'wolves in sheep's clothing'. Conservatives used the speech to support their contention that not all blacks in South Africa supported Tutu or the ANC.

Robertson owned a TV station in Bophuthatswana that was also broadcast into nearby Namibia. The network also produced an Afrikaans version of 'The 700 Club'.

The efforts of the Reverend Morgan Hodges and other conservative religious evangelists would ultimately fail to sway the members of the House of Representatives, which in August 1988 voted to pass tougher sanctions laws against South Africa. For its part, the Senate did not pass the bill, ending the chance to impose additional sanctions; a minor victory for Hodges and other South African lobbyists. They were, however, unable to stop another piece of legislation, removing tax breaks for US companies that operated in South Africa, a provision introduced by the congressman Charles Rangel, a black Democrat from New York. The legislation prohibited American companies from deducting taxes paid to the South African government from the taxes they paid to the US Inland Revenue. This made it more costly for companies to operate in South Africa and several firms, including Mobil Oil, which had operated in South Africa for 92 years until then, withdrew from the country as a result. A report in the South African newspaper *Business Day* said that Rangel's tax legislation cost Mobil about $5 billion in lost profits.

There are no records indicating that Hodges showed any further interest in South Africa. When he died in 2012, he was praised for his work as a minister, a civic leader, a religious broadcaster and crusader for the rights of blacks worldwide. As in the case of the Reverend Gilbert Caldwell, no one mentioned his anti-sanctions lobbying efforts on behalf of apartheid.

13

Apartheid's Man in Angola

'They didn't care that black people were dying in Angola, they were focused on sanctions. That was the thing to do, a fad to go and get arrested in front of the South African embassy.'

Clarence McKee, lobbyist for Unita

On 30 June 1988 a smiling Jonas Savimbi, the leader of the Angolan movement Unita, stood before flashing cameras at the National Press Club in Washington DC, addressing reporters. Savimbi had just come from a meeting with President Reagan, who had promised to continue supporting the rebel leader, then engaged in a brutal civil war with the ruling party in Angola, the MPLA—a war that had been raging since Angola gained its independence from Portugal in 1975.

On his visit to the US in June 1988, Savimbi had won additional concessions from the Reagan administration, which agreed to provide Unita with new weapons, including Stinger missiles to take out Soviet-made MPLA aircraft. The rebel leader, dressed in his trademark camouflage uniform and Che Guevara-style black beret, was given a hero's welcome by American conservatives. After his personal meeting with Reagan and speech at the Press Club, he was whisked to an engagement at the conservative Heritage Foundation, where he participated in a panel on communist intrusion into Africa. According to a State Department memo, Savimbi was transported to Heritage in the personal car of George Shultz, the US secretary of state.

Savimbi would receive similar welcomes in other countries. At the request of conservative French MPs, Savimbi made several speeches before the French parliament. Britain, despite its support of South Africa, kept Savimbi and Unita at arm's length, not wanting to jeopardise its trade with the MPLA-led Angolan government. Records show that despite behind-the-scenes lobbying by executives at Lonrho, a British company with operations throughout southern Africa, the government of Margaret Thatcher refused to meet with the Angolan rebel. But the British government aside, Savimbi was widely hailed in almost every Western capital he visited.

American and South African support for Unita went back to the mid-1970s, to the very origins of the Angolan civil war. In late 1975, as Portugal prepared to turn over control of its former colony to a local government, hostilities broke out between rival factions. One faction, the Popular Movement for the Liberation of Angola (MPLA), which was Marxist in ideology and aligned with the Soviet Union, immediately named its leader, Agostinho Neto, president of the newly independent country. One of Neto's first acts as president was to offer sanctuary to the South West Africa People's Organisation (Swapo), then engaged in a struggle for an independent Namibia against the occupying power of South Africa.

Pretoria, alarmed at the thought of Angola falling into the orbit of the Soviet Union, appealed to the US for help. Prime Minister Vorster warned that 'only a bigger western presence' could prevent Angola from being 'hounded into the communist fold'.

The apartheid government, which had the most powerful army on the African continent, felt that it could not take on the combined might of the MPLA and the Soviet Union. The US agreed to help and approved covert funding to another of the Angolan factions, the FNLA, which was an ally of the CIA-backed Congolese dictator, Mobutu Sese Seko. The FNLA received US aid totalling $32 million in addition to military equipment, and Unita, then a minor player, was asked to align itself with the FNLA. South Africa then threw its support behind the FNLA and Unita. In late 1975, South African troops entered Angola, fighting alongside the two rebel groups.

This was the beginning of one of the longest and deadliest proxy conflicts of the Cold War era. It was a war that would consume millions of lives and last 27 years, finally ending in 2002 after the old Soviet Union had collapsed. The South African government and the US would provide millions of dollars both covertly and overtly for weapons and a global propaganda effort to turn Savimbi into an authentic African leader, while demonising the MPLA as puppets of the Soviet Union.

Records acquired by the Truth and Reconciliation Commission show that Pretoria created dozens of secret projects to support Savimbi and Unita, with money flowing through front companies and friendly NGOs. One of them, called 'Project Byronic', funded through the South African Defence Force, involved the transport of goods and weapons to Unita via front companies to hide the involvement of the apartheid government. Estimates of South Africa's support for the group were as high as R108 million in 1991/92 alone, with an additional R98 million allocated for the following two years.

To promote its leader as Washington's best chance against the Soviet Union in Africa, Unita hired several high-powered lobbyists to make its case in the US capital, often coordinating their efforts with South African lobbying groups. The top lobbyist for the group was the firm of Black, Manafort, Stone & Kelly. In 1987 Unita paid it $600,000 to represent the group in Washington DC, although it is likely that the money actually came from Pretoria. Several of the key partners in the lobbying firm had been prominent figures in the Reagan and Bush presidential campaigns. Lee Atwater, a controversial political operative known for his race-baiting political advertisements, was the campaign manager for George H.W. Bush's 1988 campaign and later served as the head of the Republican National Committee.

The money paid to Black, Manafort, Stone & Kelly was well spent and proved to be a political boon for Unita. The firm was responsible for arranging Savimbi's trip to meet with Reagan in 1988 and would secure another visit the following year. It reported more than 500 meetings with members of Congress, which undoubtedly played a role in the rebel group's getting its covert funding restored by the Reagan government, after it had been cut off in the late 1970s thanks to the work of Senator Dick Clark of Iowa. The firm did more than just set up meetings with the administration and Congress. Savimbi was also given a crash course in how to speak to members of Congress, what issues he should raise and how he should address an American television audience.

Black, Manafort, Stone & Kelly provided crucial help in bringing Unita close to the seat of power in Washington. In addition, Unita made a concerted effort to win the support of black Americans and focused much of its lobbying on trying to win over key black leaders. Over the years Unita would wage a public relations battle with its rival, the MPLA, for the backing of black Americans. In an effort to win their support, Savimbi even named one his fighting units the Black Panthers, in a reference to the California-based group that had promoted black self-defence (rather than the non-violence of Martin Luther King Jr).

Many US civil rights leaders and anti-apartheid groups opposed Savimbi, and considered him to be little more than an extension of the apartheid government. Black leaders such as Jesse Jackson and members of the Congressional Black Caucus refused to meet him, despite repeated requests by the Angolan rebel and his lobbyists. TransAfrica, the anti-apartheid lobbying group, called the group an attempt to 'beautify apartheid' under a black mask. Many African countries also denounced the rebel leader and the Organisation of African Unity referred to Unita as a 'known agent of apartheid South Africa'.

According to Sylvia Hill, an anti-apartheid activist, Unita presented a special challenge for blacks in the US and caused a split among black Americans between those who supported the group because of its professed black nationalism and those who backed the MPLA.

The courting of black Americans by Unita started in the 1970s, as Congress was preparing to cut off covert aid to the group. Charles Simmons, a reporter for *Muhammad Speaks*, the newspaper of the Nation of Islam, said that Savimbi was skilled in telling black Americans what they wanted to hear. 'Savimbi was a chameleon of a character who would say different things to different audiences and was able to capture lots of support within the African American community [among those] who did not have access to international perspectives,' Simmons wrote. According to Simmons, Savimbi would on suitable occasions casually drop the name of the black leader Malcolm X, and implied he had met Malcolm X during an Organisation of African Unity meeting which both men attended in 1964. 'That was heaven' to some US black nationalists, said Simmons. Among those who supported Savimbi was Edward Vaughn, founder of the Pan-African Congress USA and later a state senator in Michigan. 'We were convinced that any African leader who exposed the concept of pan-Africanism was our friend,' Vaughn said at the time.

The black filmmaker Nana Akpan was also a supporter of Unita and Savimbi in the 1970s. Akpan had made a film called *Kwacha* about the Portuguese colonisation of Angola and became friends with Savimbi during the filming. Akpan would remain steadfast in his support of Unita. During the Reagan years, he would serve as executive director of the Angola Peace Fund, a group that distributed information about Savimbi and the Angolan war.

In its drive to win African American support, Unita hired Florence Tate, a black American woman who described herself as someone who for '20 years had played an active role in the civil rights, black power and pan African socialist movements in the United States'. Tate had been a pioneering black woman journalist at the *Dayton Daily News* and a member of the more militant black power groups, the Student Nonviolent Coordinating Committee and the Congress of Racial Equality. Records show that Tate represented the rebel group as a lobbyist until 1982. According to Tate, failure to support Unita would have left the US supporting an unpopular regime in Angola.

Tate's appeal failed to resonate with civil rights leaders at the time or with the wider black community. The Congressional Black Caucus also steered clear of Unita because of its suspected ties to the apartheid government. The subsequent exposure and confirmation of Savimbi's South African support would cause many of his black American allies to distance themselves from the Angolan guerrilla leader.

Despite this widespread opposition, Savimbi was able to gain a small following among black Americans, which was enough for him to claim that he had significant black American support. On the day he met Reagan in 1988, Savimbi was accompanied to the White House by Ralph David Abernathy of the Southern Christian Leadership Conference as well as several prominent black Republicans, who all vouched for Savimbi's long-standing opposition to apartheid.

Abernathy's appearance with Savimbi was a shock to many civil rights leaders and was a major public relations coup for Unita. Abernathy was one of the most well-known and respected civil rights leaders in the US. He and Martin Luther King Jr had been instrumental in organising the Montgomery bus boycott in 1957, which helped launch the modern struggle for black political rights in the US. After King's death Abernathy had taken over leadership of the Southern Christian Leadership Conference, the organisation the two men had founded. While Coretta Scott King, widow of the civil rights leader, called Unita a 'puppet army controlled by the repressive apartheid regime', Abernathy argued that Savimbi deserved support from 'the black people of America and the world, and white people of goodwill and all mankind' for his efforts to bring peace to Angola. It is unclear how Unita was able to enlist the aid of the civil rights leader. Abernathy did exchange letters with the Reagan administration urging the president to work to bring the warring factions in Angola together, though the letter did not specifically mention Unita.

Clarence McKee, an attorney and former official in the Reagan administration and a supporter of Unita, who was also present at the meeting with Abernathy and Savimbi, dismissed criticisms of the rebel leader. McKee was a long-time associate of Jay Parker, the black lobbyist who had represented South Africa for over a decade. In the 1970s McKee had written an article for Parker's conservative magazine, *Lincoln Review*, opposing sanctions. McKee wasn't at the White House meeting in June 1988 solely as an observer: he was paid about $20,000 a year as a lobbyist whose job was to sell Savimbi to a sceptical black community.

Another black conservative, Maurice Dawkins, a minister and candidate for the Senate in Virginia, was also retained as a lobbyist. Dawkins's firm, Government Relations International, was paid about $200,000 a year by Unita. When Savimbi visited the US, Dawkins's job was to arrange for Savimbi to speak in black churches in Texas, South Carolina, Oklahoma, Alabama and other states. Meetings were also set up with local black politicians, although few signed up in support of Unita. This did not stop Dawkins and McKee, who set up a front organisation in Washington called Black Americans for a Free Angola, to showcase the broad base of support among blacks for the Angolan rebel. In reality, it consisted of little more than a post office box and letterhead used to send out press releases. Dawkins and McKee appeared to be the only members.

Before coming to Washington to meet Reagan, Savimbi carried out a two-day tour of the Southern US, with stops in Mississippi and Alabama, in an effort to build support in predominantly black churches and meet local black elected officials. Dawkins organised the arrangements.

During his stop-over in Mississippi, Savimbi was met with protest, but he did manage to win some support from conservative black ministers such as C.A. McKinney of Ocean Springs. McKinney said he supported Savimbi because 'I hate communism more than I hate apartheid'. Despite Unita's record of human rights abuses, Savimbi was given the Medgar Evers Humanitarian Award by Charles Evers, mayor of Fayette, a small town in Mississippi, and older brother of the civil rights martyr Medgar Evers, who was killed in 1963 while trying to register black voters. Medgar Evers's widow, Merlie Evers, called the award a 'travesty'.

In an interview in 2014, Evers, who is today a radio talkshow host in Jackson, the capital of Mississippi, said that he had met Savimbi when he travelled to Angola on a fact-finding mission with some people he 'knew from New York'. He declined to say who these people were. While touring Savimbi's guerrilla base, Evers recalled that he had been impressed by the Angolan leader's dedication to keeping his people free from communist control. Evers said he extended an invitation to Savimbi to visit Mississippi so that blacks there could see the guerrilla leader for themselves and make up their own minds whether or not to support him. Evers denies that Unita or anyone else ever paid him for his efforts. According to Evers, Savimbi was given the humanitarian award because 'he has done the same thing Medgar Evers did. We fought to free Mississippi; he's fighting to free Angola.'

As for Savimbi's alliance with the apartheid government, Evers said he was unaware of any ties between the two. When told that Unita had long been a client of Pretoria, Evers replied: 'If he was, then he certainly fooled me, but I still haven't seen any evidence with my own eyes to suggest that he was getting money from South Africa.'

In Alabama, Savimbi spoke before 900 people at a black church. He asked the supporters to soften the heart of P.W. Botha, the South African president and his military backer, 'so we can free Africa'. During the trip Savimbi also managed to win the support of John Smith, the black mayor of Prichard, a small town in Alabama.

During his tour of the US, when speaking before black audiences,

Savimbi played up Unita as an 'authentically black African movement', as opposed to the MPLA, with its 'mulatto leadership'. Savimbi's ties to South Africa were ignored or denied during the appearances before black audiences, while to white American conservatives he boasted of such connections. In these circles he often referred to P.W. Botha, president of South Africa, as a friend.

South Africa's policy of apartheid was also denounced in front of blacks, even though Savimbi and Unita continued to cooperate with the South African government in military operations and received financial backing from it. According to diplomatic records from the British government, both Savimbi and the South African government had agreed to criticise each other publicly so as to downplay their military and financial ties.

Through the efforts of Dawkins and McKee, Unita did manage to win some press coverage for Savimbi in black newspapers and arrange meetings with black journalists, but there is little evidence that the movement gained significant support among black Americans despite Savimbi's boast about 'our developing black American support'. Ultimately, most blacks, including black congressmen, would support ending aid to Savimbi's rebel group.

Today, McKee blames the lack of black support for Unita on the biased American media and on anti-apartheid activists like Randall Robinson. 'The liberal black left bought into the idea that Unita was a puppet of the apartheid government, which was not true,' he said. McKee called Robinson and other anti-apartheid leaders hypocrites for supporting African liberation movements that opposed apartheid while ignoring Unita and its fight against (white) Soviet and Cuban troops. 'They didn't care that black people were dying in Angola, they were focused on sanctions. That was the thing to do, a fad to go and get arrested in front of the South African embassy,' McKee said in an interview in July 2013. 'Condemning South Africa was easy. But no one said anything when it was blacks killing blacks, like Rwanda.'

McKee continues to maintain that Unita and Savimbi were freedom fighters, battling against the MPLA and the Soviets, who were trying to gain a foothold in Africa. Asked about Unita's dependence for its military support on apartheid South Africa, McKee responded: 'So what! He was trying to do what he needed to do to survive. As Savimbi was fond of saying, "if you are getting your teeth kicked in you don't care who comes along to help you".'

Unita would continue to fight for at least five more years after Savimbi's meeting with President Reagan before both the US and South Africa eventually cut off military aid. In 1993 President Bill Clinton finally recognised the Angolan MPLA government. This was after Unita resumed fighting following an election in which Savimbi failed to win the presidency, and despite the fact that a peace accord had been reached. Savimbi had even been offered the vice-presidency in the newly elected government. Several of his closest allies in Unita, tired of the ongoing war, sued for peace and eventually joined the MPLA-led government. But Savimbi refused to give up.

The US government later joined the UN in condemning Unita for its human rights abuses. Savimbi died in a battle with Angolan troops on 22 February 2002. When news of his death reached the Angolan capital city, it was reported that war-weary residents rushed out into the streets in celebration.

14

Apartheid's Last Gasp

'We decided that the only level we were going to be accepted was when it came to the Soviets and their surrogates, so our strategy was to paint the ANC as communist surrogates.'
   – Craig Williamson, apartheid spy

In 1990, shortly after his release from prison, Nelson Mandela made a triumphant visit to the US. Americans laid out the welcome mat for the 71-year-old icon. The highlight of the trip was a visit to New York City, where Mandela was greeted by more than 200,000 admirers at an event held in the historic Yankee stadium, home to the New York Yankees. As an enthusiastic crowd chanted 'Amandla! Amandla!'—the Zulu word for 'power'—the mayor, David N. Dinkins, placed a Yankee jacket around Mandela's shoulders and a Yankee hat on his head. Mandela smiled and declared: 'You now know who I am. I am a Yankee.' The crowd roared in laughter.

The low point of the trip would come in a stop-over in the city of Miami. Civic leaders had planned to present Mandela with keys to the city and provide a tour like those offered by nearly every other American city he visited. But just days before the event was to take place, adverts began appearing in local newspapers linking Mandela with Fidel Castro, the president of Cuba, which lies about 90 miles off the coast of Miami.

Many Cubans living in Miami who had fled the Caribbean country after Castro took power were incensed. One advert in the *Miami Herald* portrayed Mandela as an ally and defender of Castro, who it said had done to Cubans what the apartheid government had done to blacks. The city's large Cuban community was so agitated that they threatened to protest against any event that honoured Mandela.

Miami's mayor, Xavier Suarez, in a move that was condemned by black leaders in the city, publicly released a statement that criticised Mandela's support of Castro. 'We, Cuban Americans, find it beyond reasonable comprehension that Mr Nelson Mandela, a victim of oppression by his own government, not only fails to condemn the Cuban government for its human rights violations, but rather praises the virtues of the tyrannical Castro regime,' Suarez wrote.

Bowing to pressure from the Cuban community, which constitutes about 60 per cent of the city's population, civic leaders cancelled the official Mandela event. Instead, a smaller affair was conducted at the city's convention centre, where Mandela spoke to a crowd of about 3,000 mostly black supporters. Small planes flew over the event with protest banners as a large crowd of Cubans demonstrated outside. Later, blacks outraged by the treatment of Mandela staged their own protests

The adverts that led to the scrapping of plans to honour Mandela had been placed in local newspapers by the International Freedom Foundation (IFF), a conservative Washington-based body, which had been set up ostensibly to promote press freedom, free markets and opposition to communism. It wasn't the first time the foundation had targeted Mandela or his supporters. In 1988, when anti-apartheid organisers in London staged a music concert at Wembley Stadium to honour the imprisoned ANC leader on the occasion of his seventieth birthday, the IFF circulated flyers and fake programmes that claimed the money being raised at the event would fund black terrorists in South Africa.

The foundation's US advisory board comprised a who's who of American conservatives, including leading right-wing figures like

Senator Jesse Helms, who served as chairman of the editorial advisory board for the foundation's publications, and Dan Burton, who was the ranking Republican on the House of Representatives Foreign Affairs Committee's subcommittee on Africa. Alan Keyes, a black American conservative who had sought the Republican presidential nomination in 1996, 2000 and 2008, worked as an adviser; and Jack Abramoff, the Washington lobbyist, who would later serve time in prison for his part in one of America's biggest lobbying scandals, was president until he left in the late 1980s.

At its height the IFF employed a staff of about 30 mostly young conservatives, in offices in Washington, who churned out policy papers on such issues as keeping the Panama Canal as US property and warning of the dangers of Soviet expansion in Latin America and Africa. Power-brokers like the former secretary of state and national security adviser Henry Kissinger were invited to IFF seminars to deliver keynote speeches. In 1991 the foundation brought together the world's leading intelligence experts at a conference in Potsdam, Germany, to mull over the changing uses of intelligence in the post-Cold War world.

On the surface, the IFF was just one of many policy bodies that dominate the landscape in Washington DC. But behind the scenes, the foundation served another purpose: it was a front organisation for the South African government, bankrolled as a last-gasp attempt to prolong its existence, according to investigations by *Newsday* and the London *Observer*. Later reports by the South African Truth and Reconciliation Commission would validate the investigations of the two newspapers.

The foundation's operations recalled some of the secret projects that had been exposed during the Muldergate scandal. But during its existence from 1986 to 1993, the foundation would exceed anything conceived by Eschel Rhoodie in the 1970s. The reports by the TRC would show that the IFF was one of the South African government's most costly propaganda programmes. 'Operation Pacman', which was the codename for the IFF, had offices in Johannesburg, Washington,

London, Brussels and Bonn, according to the TRC report. Its main purpose was to combat international sanctions and provide support to other apartheid initiatives through publications, lobbying, conferences and a speakers' bureau. IFF support was also extended to Jonas Savimbi and his Angolan rebel group, Unita. Many of the principals on the IFF's board had known Savimbi for years, and had lobbied the Reagan administration to restore US support to Unita, which had been cut off in the 1970s by Congress. But the main purpose of the group seems to have been to target the ANC and its allies. The attempt to portray the ANC as a tool of Soviet communism was intended to undercut the movement's growing international acceptance as government-in-waiting of a future democratic South Africa.

The campaign against Mandela during his trip to Miami was just one of the dirty tricks carried out by the IFF. The group also targeted Oliver Tambo, the exiled leader of the ANC. When Tambo met with George Shultz in Washington in 1987, the IFF arranged for demonstrators to drape tyres around their necks in protest against the 'necklace' killings of suspected government informers in black townships in South Africa, thereby linking the ANC to these gruesome murders.

The IFF also led the charge against TransAfrica, the black lobbying group heading the fight for sanctions, and in a 1987 publication accused its leaders of being communist agents. 'All the facts point to TransAfrica being very useful to revolutionary causes, if not, indeed, a communist front.'

In addition, the IFF worked to counter the activities of other US anti-apartheid activists and politicians. When Senator Edward Kennedy chaired an investigation in 1987 into the treatment of children in apartheid's prisons, the foundation prompted its advisory board member Dan Burton to launch a counter-investigation into alleged human rights abuses during the 1980s at ANC guerrilla camps in Angola. The information gathered by Burton's investigation would be shared with the IFF office in London and used as part of a special commission whose report forced the ANC to acknowledge that some abuses had occurred in its Angolan camps.

More than half of the IFF's funds came from a secret South African military account, according to TRC documents. Its entire annual budget for the years 1991 and 1992 exceeded R10 million. After Mandela had been let out of prison and the ANC was no longer banned, in late September 1991 the South African minister of finance agreed to a one-off payment of R7 million to the IFF, approved by the minister of defence, 'to enable the country to withdraw from the enterprise'.

The IFF had been founded in 1986, against the backdrop of increasing international pressure on Western governments to take action against the apartheid regime. Pretoria faced the biggest threat yet, both international and domestic, to its very survival. In the government's thinking, the IFF represented a far more subtle approach to defeating the anti-apartheid movement than more overt attempts such as hiring lobbying firms. According to Craig Williamson, the South African spy who helped set up the IFF, the idea was to move away from the traditional allies of Pretoria, the fringe right in the US and Europe, 'some of whom were to the right of Genghis Khan'.

The approach taken was that the foundation could not be used to defend the system of apartheid. Instead it would focus on trying to discredit the ANC and the anti-apartheid movement by linking them to communism. 'We couldn't convince Americans that apartheid was right. The only chance of manipulating things to survive just a little bit longer was to paint the ANC as a project of the international department of the Soviet Communist Party,' he told *The Observer*. 'The more we could present ourselves as anti-communists, the more people looked at us with respect. People you could hardly believe cooperated with us politically when it came to the Soviets,' Williamson added. 'The advantage of the IFF was that it pilloried the ANC. The sort of general Western view of the ANC up until 1990 was a box of matches [a reference to a statement by Winnie Mandela in support of the use of violence] and Soviet-supporting—slavishly was the word we latched on. That was backed up with writings, intellectual inputs. It was a matter of undercutting ANC credibility.'

The foundation would provide the perfect cover for a political intelligence operation. It was an elaborate intelligence-gathering operation designed to collect information on apartheid enemies that could be used as an instrument for 'political warfare', Craig Williamson told *Newsday* in 1995. Even some of the people who worked for the IFF or served on its advisory board were unaware of its funding by the South African government. According to Williamson, the operation was deliberately constructed so that many of the people involved would not know of its backing by a foreign government. 'That was the beauty of the whole thing: guys pushing what they believed,' he told *Newsday*.

Not everyone seems to have been fooled by the foundation fronting for Pretoria. 'We knew that the IFF was funded by the South African government,' Herman Cohen, who ran African operations for the National Security Council, told *Salon* magazine in an interview in 2005. 'It was one of a number of front organizations.' Although the IFF may have violated federal law by not reporting its lobbying to the US government, the Justice Department never pursued a case of illegal lobbying against the group.

Williamson, who was finally exposed as a spy in 1980, had been involved in a series of state-sponsored bombings, burglaries, kid-nappings, assassinations, sabotage and propaganda during the apartheid era. In 1971 he became a member of the security police, and informed on students at the University of the Witwatersrand, where he enrolled in 1972. Williamson's first undercover assignment abroad was in Geneva, where he worked for and eventually became deputy director of the International University Exchange Fund (IUEF), set up with Swedish money to provide scholarships to African students. The Swedish investigative reporter Anders Hasselbohm, who investigated Williamson's time as an employee at the IUEF, said that the fund operated as a front for the Swedish government to channel money to the anti-apartheid movement in South Africa and elsewhere. Hasselbohm told the *Los Angeles Times* in 1996 that he had evidence that Williamson diverted at least some of the money to the South African security police. This was then used to start another front operation called Long Reach, supposedly a British-based company, whose job was to gather data on the ANC for South Africa's Military Intelligence.

The IFF would later pass on information it collected in Washington to Long Reach, which in turn passed it on to South African intelligence officials. Williamson told *The Observer* that both organisations, the IFF and Long Reach, were 'false flags' and that the IFF had traded on the names and anti-communist sensibilities of leading conservative political figures in the Reagan–Thatcher era in the 1980s.

Williamson also established another front for the South African government in an attempt to undermine the ANC. This was a South African office of the GRM Group, a company started by the reputed Italian mobster Giovanni Marco Ricci, who was based in Seychelles. Through a GRM office in Switzerland, Williamson funded and paid for the distribution of several videotapes of alleged atrocities committed by the ANC, in an effort to discredit the movement. Apparently the tapes were mailed to public officials, universities and libraries in the US. They were also broadcast in a number of US cities, but strangely not in New York or Washington DC, the economic and political capitals of the US. The tapes were distributed through various conservative religious organisations, including, as we have seen, the Biblical News Service.

Another US distributor of the videotape *ANC: A Time for Candor* was a ministry called About My Father's Business, based in Kentucky. According to US lobbying records, About My Father's Business listed GMR as a client. In describing GMR, Richard Schmidt, president of the ministry and video narrator, said, 'To the best of our knowledge they are engaged in international free enterprise such as banking, manufacturing and trade.' About My Father's Business was paid $177,000 to distribute the videotape.

In an interview in 2014 Schmidt disputed lobbying records, which he had signed, showing that his group was paid to distribute the tape. 'I did this on my own.' Asked why, he replied: 'The ANC was considered the number one terrorist threat according to our own CIA and I wanted to shine some light on this group that was getting so much positive press in the American media.' According to Schmidt, the videotape was strategically planned to be released around the time that the secretary of state, George Shultz, met the ANC leader Oliver Tambo in early 1987. 'We got really good coverage and exposed the ANC for what it was, a communist-inspired terrorist group,' he said. Schmidt added that Nelson Mandela was a convicted bank robber and terrorist. 'He was judged by a jury of his peers and found guilty,' he said. (South Africa did not have jury trials when Mandela was tried.)

In the interview Schmidt didn't deny that funding for his anti-ANC videotapes had come from South Africa, but said it was from a group of businessmen he had met when he first visited South Africa in 1980 to set up a ministry. US lobbying records tell a different story. In an amended filing with the US Justice Department one year after the original application, a document signed by Schmidt shows that GMR 'was the largest single contributor to the project of disseminating "ANC: A Time for Candor"', according to the 1989 document.

In testimony to the TRC, Craig Williamson confirmed that the videotapes allegedly showing violence against blacks by the ANC were paid for by the South African government with money channelled through the Defence Force.

* * *

The IFF's operations weren't limited to the US, although the activities there seem to have formed the hub of the group's global propaganda efforts. Leading figures in government circles in Europe, in particular conservative politicians in Britain, were also involved in the foundation's work on behalf of the South African government. One of those was David Hoile, who was listed as a co-founder of the IFF's UK office. As vice-chairman of the Federation of Conservative Students, the student organisation of the British Conservative Party, during the 1980s Hoile had once worn a 'Hang Nelson Mandela' T-shirt. When *The Guardian* newspaper in 2001 published an investigation detailing Hoile's involvement in the anti-Mandela student campaign, he demanded that the publication retract its story, but the paper refused.

The South African-born Hoile wrote a book, *Understanding Sanctions*, that was published by the IFF's UK office in 1988. In it, Hoile called sanctions against South Africa immoral and argued that they would have little effect on the South African economy. The book was one of a series published by the IFF that would question the use of sanctions to end apartheid.

Marc Gordon, a conservative activist who worked with Hoile, was also involved in the IFF. Gordon gained notoriety when he led an IFF campaign against the anti-poverty charity Oxfam, accusing the group of using its tax-exempt status for political purposes because of its criticism of the Pol Pot regime in Cambodia. As a result of Gordon's efforts, Oxfam was censured by the British Charities Commission, which said that the group had 'prosecuted their campaign with too much vigour'.

There may have been other reasons for the IFF to target Oxfam. Oxfam had a long history of involvement in South Africa. The group had provided aid to black townships in South Africa and the so-called homelands where poverty was endemic. Although the group's aid was based on humanitarian reasons, in the early 1980s Oxfam began to link the existence of poverty in South Africa to the system of apartheid. Having long been a supporter of the anti-apartheid and sanctions movements, Oxfam then went further. In 1985 it withdrew its business from Barclays Bank, which was heavily involved in South Africa, as a sign of solidary with the global divestment movement. Both actions would make it a target of the South African-backed IFF.

The Observer's investigation also revealed that the IFF office in London had access to several key politicians who were close to Prime Minister Margaret Thatcher. They included Sir George Gardiner, a right-wing politician who was a bitter critic of the ANC and an opponent of economic sanctions against South Africa. Gardiner served on the IFF's advisory board. He was also a leading member of the Monday Club, which had long ties to South Africa. Gardiner's zealous support of the South African government earned him the nickname 'Botha boy' from Labour Party opponents.

Another MP involved in the IFF was Andrew Hunter, a Conservative MP. Like Gardiner, Hunter had a long history of relations with South Africa and was an advocate for the recognition of the Bophuthatswana homeland. Financial disclosure documents from the British parliament show that Hunter made numerous trips to South Africa paid for by that country's government.

A former South African security police officer told *The Observer* that his division had supplied information to Hunter that had led to the expulsion from Britain of the ANC's representative, Solly Smith. (Smith, who died in 1993 and whose real name was Samuel Khanyile, was later revealed as a spy for the apartheid government.) Hunter admitted to *The Observer* in an interview in 1995 that he regularly met with and received intelligence from the South African security police as well as the National Intelligence Service. He said that the prime purpose of the meetings was to obtain information on ANC 'terrorists', and that he and the South African agencies shared a common interest on this front. 'Everything they told me was in the hands of MI5 and MI6 as soon as possible.'

Hunter produced reports for Prime Minister Margaret Thatcher that sought to establish links between the ANC and the IRA—a subject he wrote about for IFF publications—and document the ANC's support for 'terrorist' operations in South Africa. This information reinforced

Thatcher's belief that the ANC was a 'terrorist group' and a front for communists. Moreover, the South African security police helped him to gain access to three ANC members detained without trial—Susan Westcott, Ian Robertson and Hugh Lugg—to question them about ANC activities in London and its links with the IRA.

The newspaper found that Hunter's key contact in the South African security police was Colonel Vic McPherson, who was a suspect in the South African police bombing of the ANC's headquarters in London in 1982. McPherson was one of seven police officers who were awarded the Police Star, the highest police commendation by the South African government, for their part in the bombing.

Just before the IFF was effectively shut down, it made one final last-gasp attempt to embarrass the ANC. In 1992 the IFF appointed a commission chaired by the British barrister R.S. Douglas to investigate human rights abuses in the ANC camps in Angola, in an effort to inflict political damage on the organisation in the same way that exposure of Swapo atrocities had caused damage for that liberation movement in Namibia's first elections. The commission chaired by Douglas issued a report that found that high-ranking officials in the ANC had engaged in gross human rights abuses in the camps. The findings helped to put pressure on the ANC to conduct its own investigation into the matter, the Motsuenyane Commission, which confirmed many of the Douglas Commission's findings. Not long after the release of the commission's report, the IFF quietly closed its doors.

* * *

Jack Abramoff, one-time president of the IFF, did agree to an interview about his role in the organisation. Abramoff, who served 43 months in prison after pleading guilty for his role in one of the biggest lobbying scandals in US history, now spends his days as a proponent of lobbying reform. Since being released from prison he has turned his experience of exploiting lobbying loopholes into insights on how to close them.

Abramoff said the idea for the IFF began when he visited South Africa as part of a delegation of conservative students in the mid-1980s. He corroborates news accounts that during the trip he met with Russel Crystal, a pugnacious anti-communist 'libertarian' who had as a student set up and run the conservative National Students' Federation in Johannesburg, and established links with the student right in the US and UK. Crystal claimed to have come up with the idea for a secret lobbying organisation. The IFF was the result of his and Abramoff's discussions. Although it continued to oppose the ANC because the liberation group was Marxist-led, Abramoff said that the IFF did support the release of Nelson Mandela from prison as part of its efforts to help end apartheid. 'I actually caught a lot of flak from other American conservatives about that. I was even called a communist by a conservative during a dinner I attended in Washington because I was saying that Mandela needed to be released from prison.'

Abramoff told me that to the best of his knowledge the South African government never funded the IFF, despite media reports and documents from the TRC exposing the organisation's link to Pretoria. Rather, it was bankrolled by a network of corporate, progressive donors who were not affiliated with the government. 'I mean, how could we talk about free markets and no government control and take money from the government?' he asked. If the IFF had taken money from the government, it would have been after he left the organisation in the late 1980s.

As far as Crystal's and Williamson's connections with South African intelligence were concerned, Abramoff said he had no knowledge of this while he was president of the IFF. 'If any of these things happened it would have been after I left. When it all came out in the 1990s about the government funding, I was as surprised as anyone else.'

Abramoff confirmed that the IFF was behind the adverts targeting Mandela's trip to Miami. 'I supported releasing the guy; it didn't mean that I supported giving him the keys to an American city. So, yes, I would have supported the ads, although I wasn't at the foundation when they were made.'

The bottom line, Abramoff said, was that the IFF was an anti-apartheid body which opposed sanctions because their imposition would have made the racial problems worse. 'We, and certainly I, never lobbied for the apartheid government,' he said. 'That is just not true. I never had anything to do with the government and anyone who says otherwise is not telling the truth.'

Ken Silverstein, a US-based reporter, who has written extensively about Abramoff, has disputed the former lobbyist's denials. 'According to my source, Abramoff was briefed by South African representatives about the nature and importance of the foundation's work. Yes, some people were duped by the IFF, but Jack was not one of them. As chairman [of the IFF], he understood where the money was coming from. He knew exactly who he was playing with.'

* * *

The formation of bodies like the IFF showed that the white minority government in South Africa would not go down without a fight. While President F.W. de Klerk freed Nelson Mandela and lifted the ban on the ANC and other anti-apartheid movements in February 1990, his government also continued to fund secret propaganda projects aimed at undermining the ANC and Mandela. Many of these projects were operated by the South African military under the direction of the State Security Council, which was responsible for counter-insurgency and operations against the liberation movements.

The South African foreign ministry also had its share of secret projects, including Radar, a Paris-based group that focused on a psychological warfare programme to boost South Africa's case in Europe and the European Parliament, and to counter pro-liberation movement support from the United Nations and the Organisation of African Unity. Radar was a front group for the Association for the Development of Exchanges and International Relations (ADERI), an important base for the international right wing, which was headed by Léon Delbecque. Delbecque, a master of propaganda and psychological warfare, had been an intelligence officer in the French resistance during the Nazi occupation of France but later turned to the right after the French withdrew from their colony of Algeria, where Delbecque had fought against the rebel FNL. He began lobbying for the South African government in the late 1970s as part of a group calling itself the French Friends of South African Communities, or ACFA. This was one of several front groups supported by Pretoria to shore up its image in French-speaking countries. According to documents produced during the Muldergate scandal, the South African Department of Information under Rhoodie provided about 120,000 francs to start ACFA.

ADERI also organised a number of fact-finding trips to South Africa by French politicians. As was the case in the US and UK, many of the French legislators would return home and speak favourably about South Africa and its importance to Western interests. ADERI was one of several projects that survived the public disclosure of South Africa's secret propaganda campaigns during the Muldergate scandal.

In Germany, too, the South African government ran secret projects aimed at countering the ANC and the growing worldwide movement against apartheid. These French and German projects would continue even as the apartheid government was publicly committed to a negotiated settlement with the ANC. One of the most prominent schemes during this time was devoted to finding a way to bypass the sanctions that had been imposed against the country.

Shortly before the end of apartheid, an organisation calling itself the International Association for Co-operation and Development in Southern Africa, or Acoda, after the French version of its name, began holding a series of conferences and seminars on investment in southern

Africa, particularly South Africa. At the centre of the group was Guy Guermeur, president of the French office and the face of the organisation. Guermeur was a French politician and member of Rassemblement Pour la République, or Rally for the Republic, a right-wing political party. He was also a member of the European Parliament.

Beginning with its founding in 1990, Acoda attracted a number of respected politicians and academics in Europe. They included Vasco Garcia, a former official in the Portuguese colonial government in Angola, who was a vice-president of Acoda and member of the European Parliament; the former Belgian prime minister Leo Tindemans; and Heinz Schwarz, who was chairman of Acoda in Germany and a member of that country's parliament.

Acoda was particularly active in the UK where it quickly established a high-profile presence in the British parliament, sponsoring trips to southern Africa for MPs, arranging seminars and hosting expensive dinners. At the invitation of Patrick Watson, the South African lobbyist, several conservative MPs joined Acoda's international advisory board, including John Biffen, who served as leader of the House of Commons from 1982 to 1987; Timothy Raison, the former UK minister for overseas development; and Baroness Judith Hart, a Labour MP and fierce opponent of apartheid. Other members of the advisory board were Conservative MP Baroness Diana Elles, a former vice-president of the European Parliament and British representative to the UN; Professor John Fyfe, an economic development specialist; Professor Jack Spence, director of studies at the Royal Institute of International Affairs (Chatham House); and Lord Henry Plumb of Coleshill, a Conservative MP and former European Parliament president.

In 1990, three members of the group made a widely publicised trip to southern Africa to discuss economic investment in the region. While on the visit the members called on the international community to drop sanctions against the South African government. 'Sanctions are counterproductive to the whole of southern Africa and therefore it should be lifted,' Leo Tindemans told reporters before a photo op at the Union Buildings in Pretoria with Pik Botha, the South African foreign minister. The Acoda members were also in South Africa to open a local office of the organisation.

Guermeur and Baroness Elles accompanied Tindemans on the trip. Tindemans said that sanctions hurt the country's black population and the economies of neighbouring countries. The group declared they were convinced that the topic would be discussed when the heads of state of the 12 European Community countries met for a conference that December in Rome. They vowed to be an active voice for lifting sanctions against the country. Baroness Elles told reporters that Acoda in Europe would help change the attitudes of European policy-makers towards South Africa. 'There will definitely be a forward movement in the direction of a better understanding and an agreement with South Africa.'

A year later, a German delegation visited South Africa under the auspices of Acoda. The participants included two German MPs, including Acoda's German chairman, Heinz Schwarz, Ulrich Heinrich and Dr Joachim Worthmann, foreign editor of the influential German newspaper *Stuttgarter Zeitung*. Like his British, French and Portuguese counterparts, Schwarz urged investment in South Africa despite the sanctions that were in place. 'There is a misconception that investors have to wait until the political situation in the region has stabilized,' Schwarz told reporters during his four-day visit. 'However, we believe that investors should now participate and help the situation stabilize.'

Members of Acoda also visited other southern African countries, including Zambia, Angola, Namibia and Mozambique, to promote practical and effective economic cooperation between Europe and southern Africa. The delegation sought information about political reforms in those countries, the impact of the peace process in Angola and the reaction of other countries to the political changes in South Africa.

But while many MPs were happy to join the new group, other members of the European Parliament had their suspicions about Acoda and stayed away. Many of them had heard rumours and suspected that Acoda was part of Pretoria's broader diplomatic initiative to ensure that the South African economy—most of which would remain in white hands for the foreseeable future—received the lion's share of regional foreign investment and aid in the post-apartheid era.

When questioned about a possible connection to the apartheid regime, British Conservative MPs Biffen and Raison said they did not know of any links. 'I was not aware of Acoda having any covert ambitions,' Biffen told British newspapers. Raison, when questioned, also denied South African involvement, telling reporters that he had resigned from the group because he had become less involved in southern Africa and 'I didn't feel on the same wavelength'.

Guy Guermeur, the French president of Acoda, also denied that the South African government was involved in creating or funding the group, even though he had a long history of defending apartheid leaders. Even in 2011, few people who were listed as members of the group seemed to know much about its origins. Professor Jack Spence, who has since retired from Chatham House, said he didn't know who had started the group and assumed that it was formed to deal with the economic development of post-apartheid South Africa. Spence said he couldn't remember who had invited him to join the advisory board. As far as funding was concerned, Spence said, 'I assumed that it was funded by the EU since it was based in Brussels.'

But records released by the Truth and Reconciliation Commission appear to show that the group was part of a last-ditch clandestine effort by the apartheid government to position itself in anticipation of the post-apartheid era. Documents made public by the TRC would later confirm that the group was one of many sanctions-busting secret projects funded by the Department of Foreign Affairs.

South African government documents show that the purpose of the group was to build support for overturning sanctions legislation in various countries by organising fact-finding visits to South Africa by prominent Europeans, American businessmen and members of the US Congress. While the group appears to have been active in cities such as Paris, Bonn and London, there is no evidence that it operated in Washington, a curious omission.

At the centre of the Acoda project was Sean Leary, a former South African diplomat who masterminded Pretoria's international propaganda campaign to discredit the South West Africa People's Organisation (Swapo) in Namibia. In London, Acoda shared the same offices in Westminster that housed SNI, the company set up by Cleary and paid through his company, Transcontinental Consultancy. SNI also acted as Acoda's public relations representatives. The same office also housed the International Freedom Foundation, the global front group that had been set up by other South African operatives.

The same pattern was repeated in Acoda's offices in Johannesburg, Windhoek, Bonn and Paris, with companies representing the transitional government in Namibia also housing and lobbying on behalf of Acoda. In Bonn, Acoda's German arm was run out of the public relations firm of Volker Stoltz, the same man who ran the Namibian Information Office. Acoda not only shared an office, but the same phone number as Stoltz's firm. A company called Interaction International, which was later shown to be a front for the South African government, shared Acoda's Paris office. A former South African Military Intelligence officer, Nick Basson, who defected in 1991, claimed that the South African foreign ministry and the Defence Force controlled the company. The man he fingered as the point person for the company was Cleary.

The Acoda project appears to have worked in tandem with another secret project funded by the South African government, called Operation Agree. The project was first revealed by Basson, who said the military-funded programme was an effort to discredit Swapo in the Namibian independence elections of 1989 for a constituent assembly. Basson argued that the plan was not just intended for Namibia, but was also to be used in South Africa similarly to discredit the ANC, while building up the rival Inkatha Freedom Party of Mangosuthu Buthelezi.

But as negotiations for a settlement in South Africa advanced, the National Party would be forced to wind down its secret projects. In response to pressure from Mandela and the ANC to demonstrate that he was not complicit in intelligence and propaganda activities targeting the ANC, President F.W. de Klerk put an end to the global campaign. The process had begun when De Klerk dismantled the powerful and secretive National Security Management System, taking power away from the bureaucrats whose job was to gather intelligence on 'subversive' elements, detain activists and issue pro-government propaganda. After the release of Mandela and as negotiations between the National Party and ANC progressed, the president cut funding to many of the government's overseas lobbying and propaganda operations whose campaigns had painted the ANC as 'terrorist'. Records from the Truth and Reconciliation Commission reports and from lobbying documents in the US show that by 1992 most of the apartheid government's propaganda projects had wound down. The worldwide campaign to sell apartheid was at an end.

15

The End of Apartheid

'They didn't succeed, but they did manage to create confusion and allow the government in South Africa to survive a little bit longer than it should have. But in the end, they couldn't stop the inevitable.'

— Sylvia Hill, US anti-apartheid activist

The International Freedom Foundation, the black dolls of Operation Heartbreak, and Acoda were last-gasp attempts by the apartheid government to influence political opinion in America and Europe. Faced with massive dissent at home and sanctions campaigns around the world that had cut it off from financial markets, military aid and technology, the apartheid government realised the game was up and that a deal had to be sought with its enemies. On 2 February 1990 President F.W. de Klerk lifted the ban on the ANC, the PAC and the South African Communist Party and later released Nelson Mandela from prison after 27 years, thus laying the groundwork for the dismantling of the apartheid system. As one of his last acts as president, De Klerk would dismantle the propaganda apparatuses that had helped the apartheid government resist diplomatic and grassroots pressure for change for nearly 50 years.

On 27 April 1994 the first democratic elections were held in South Africa, with people of all races casting their vote for a new president and a new parliament. After the vote was counted, the once-outlawed ANC won 62.65 per cent of the poll, taking most of the seats in parliament, and a triumphant Nelson Mandela was elected the country's first black president, with De Klerk and Thabo Mbeki as deputy presidents.

The election of Mandela and the accession of the ANC as the leading party were the culmination of decades of struggle by the liberation movements and by ordinary people across the length and breadth of South Africa. Yet there is no doubt that the anti-apartheid coalition in America and similar campaigns in Canada, Europe and the rest of the world played a role in the demise of the white regime, not least by helping to pressure the US government—the world superpower and a major trading partner of South Africa for much of the apartheid period—and its allies to impose economic and military sanctions, which hastened the end of apartheid. (Britain was a key exception in that it never imposed sanctions on South Africa.)

In 2007 Mandela himself praised this work: 'On occasion the work of our American colleagues was indispensable. The economic sanctions bill passed by the US Congress in 1986 is a case in point. Without the decades-long divestment campaign undertaken by university students, churches, civil rights organisations, trade unions and state and local governments to cut economic ties to South Africa, the US Congress would not have acted, even to the extent of overriding a presidential veto. International sanctions were a key factor in the eventual victory of the African National Congress over South Africa's white minority regime.' Mandela would give similar thanks to activists in other countries he visited.

Much remains unknown about the apartheid government's global propaganda efforts to maintain allies and the vital economic links it needed to stay afloat. During the course of writing this book, I have asked many people just how successful the efforts of the South African government were to try to influence world policy-makers and ward off the inevitable. In other words, what did Pretoria accomplish by spending hundreds of millions of dollars over nearly five decades on its campaigns to win hearts and minds overseas? Neither the commissions set up by the South African government to investigate secret funding nor the Truth and Reconciliation Commission ever attempted to answer the question of what the apartheid government received for the billions it spent on lobbying, setting up front groups and companies, and buying off politicians and journalists.

Part of the problem lies with the absence of records. It is common knowledge that the apartheid government deliberately and systematically destroyed thousands of pages of records related to its propaganda activities before the handover of power to the ANC in 1994. By some estimates, about 44 tonnes of documents were burnt in the purge. According to the TRC, the destruction of records started in 1978 during the Muldergate scandal. The Botha administration also ordered the destruction of classified police, intelligence and defence records. Well into the 1990s, the obliteration of records continued in an effort to keep the apartheid state's secrets hidden.

President De Klerk told the TRC that an agreement had been reached by the Government of National Unity, which came to power after the 1994 elections, that many of the apartheid-era covert operations would not be publicly disclosed. These mainly consisted of programmes that were set up for information gathering or disinformation campaigns and those that provided assistance to groups opposed to liberation movements such as the ANC.

Indeed, in response to a request for apartheid government records from the author, the Department of Justice and Constitutional Development denied a request under the Promotion of Access to Information Act to see documents provided to the TRC about the secret projects that are mentioned in its reports. In its denial, the department said the records were 'confidential correspondence between functionaries in the performance of their duties'. Furthermore, the department wrote, 'The documents contain information that was supplied in strict confidence by various third parties. The information was supplied after their confidentiality was guaranteed, so we are unable to break out undertaking.' It is a curious stance taken by a government run by a political party that was the target of many of these secret projects.

Records from the US and European countries shed some light on the global lobbying effort by Pretoria. But even these records are incomplete, and numerous projects in the US, which has perhaps the best record-keeping system in tracking foreign lobbyists, have evaded scrutiny. For example, just a few of the Muldergate secret projects or later ones were found in US lobbying records.

Lobbyists in the US are obliged to self-report their spending and propaganda, and many failed to report at all. The attempt by John McGoff to buy the *Washington Star* on behalf of the South African government is a glaring example. The Justice Department office in charge of keeping track of the lobbying disclosures is short-staffed and unable to go after violators, even when there is clear evidence that organisations may have failed to register and report their lobbying.

Britain lacks a similar reporting requirement for foreign lobbyists. While British MPs are required to report trips they take that are paid for by foreign organisations or governments, many have failed to record these trips properly as well. The cash-for-questions scandal in the UK in the 1990s exposed widespread problems in reporting on the MPs' interest forms, indicating that members probably hadn't always reported that they had taken trips paid for by the apartheid government or public relations consultants in the pay of Pretoria.

In addition to questions about the magnitude of the projects, there is also the issue of just how effective the propaganda efforts were. Answers about the efficacy of lobbying from those who participated in various ways vary. For some, like Stephen Bisenius, the Iowa state senator and founder of a business group to fight divestment by American companies, the lobbying was essential in stopping what they say were overly harsh sanctions against South Africa. For others, the lobbying itself was only a minor distraction, and the survival of the apartheid government had much more to do with the fact that American administrations and European leaders felt a kinship with white South Africans and needed little convincing from lobbyists.

The truth is, it is hard to tell what the lobbying ultimately accomplished. For all the money spent, as time went on public opinion in the US towards South Africa during the apartheid era began to change. As a result, paid lobbyists and front groups weren't enough to stop the passage of the sanctions bill through Congress in 1986 or the 1987 Rangel amendment. Nor were South Africa's lobbying efforts able to stop sanctions imposed by Canada or other Commonwealth nations.

Nevertheless, other, more stringent sanctions laws never saw the light of day. Was this due to the impact of lobbyists or to the long-held beliefs of law-makers like Senator Jesse Helms, who needed little prodding to see a communist behind every black South African?

Karen Rothmyer, writing in *The Nation*, found that there was little clear evidence that the attempts to buy or influence newspapers and journalists were effective long-term propaganda tools for putting across the South African government's message, even though John McGoff, for instance, tried to get his editors to publish more positive stories about the country. Reporters and editors at the papers McGoff owned were too professional to print articles that were clearly propaganda. In fact, the clumsy effort to 'buy' favourable coverage outright resulted instead in embarrassment and condemnation for both McGoff and Pretoria, Rothmyer said in an interview.

Sylvia Hill, an anti-apartheid activist and scholar, has argued that Pretoria's attempts to enlist American blacks in its effort to stall sanctions or win support in the black community in the US were also ineffective, although she adds: 'Such paid lobbyists who claimed to represent "moderate" black opinion in South Africa caused considerable confusion when they spoke to black [American] communities. But their effect on national opinion was minimal, as the Free South Africa Movement successfully presented the anti-apartheid movement as representative of black opinion.' At the same time, conservative black leaders such as Jonas Savimbi and Mangosuthu Buthelezi were 'far more effective in presenting contrary views sympathetic to Pretoria's anti-sanctions, anti-communist messages.' Still, it wasn't enough.

Ultimately, as Garth Jowett and Victoria O'Donnell write in their book *Propaganda and Persuasion*, 'What South Africa could not prevent was the constant pressure of world opinion against an increasingly unwieldy political apparatus and repugnant racial policies.' The simmering township unrest that began to be seen nightly on American and European television sets in the 1980s meant that 'no amount of golf or free trips to what is one of the most beautiful countries on the globe could prevent increased pressure from special interest groups who now countered with their own propaganda'.

While it is easy to dismiss the lobbying and propaganda efforts as ineffectual, it is important to note that after the South African government increased its armoury by hiring more lobbyists and getting support from corporate and religious organisations fronted by blacks, no additional sanctions legislation was passed by the US Congress, and anti-apartheid activists were unable to keep the Reagan administration from taking a lax approach to the enforcement of sanctions. Still, by this time the tide had turned and the apartheid government knew that its days were numbered. Thereafter, efforts were focused more on trying to ensure that the white minority would remain a force in the country even if blacks were granted the vote.

Perhaps the greatest impact of the worldwide propaganda campaign, as Sylvia Hill has said, is that it allowed the government to stall for time for several decades while it continued to keep the lid down on the aspirations of black South Africans. 'In the end, there is no doubt that they were able to delay things,' said Sylvia Hill. 'They didn't succeed, but they did manage to create confusion and allow the government in South Africa to survive a little bit longer than it should have. But in the end, they couldn't stop the inevitable.'

Notes on Sources

Introduction

Kenneth Frazier and Operation Heartbreak: 'Motives of South African Children Lobby Questioned', Associated Press, 8 June 1988; press release from the Wake Up America Coalition dated the same day; and the Africa Fund's 1989 report 'Apartheid's Whitewash: South African Propaganda in the United States' by Richard Leonard, http://africanactivist.msu.edu/document_metadata.php?objectid=32-130-F6B. Mwiza Munthali, an information specialist with TransAfrica, also provided information about Frazier, in an interview with the author on 25 June 2013.

Eschel Rhoodie, *The Paper Curtain* (Voortrekkerpers, 1969) outlined South Africa's global propaganda war.

Estimates of the apartheid government's spending on lobbying: Department of Justice, Foreign Agents Registration Office's Reports of the Attorney General to the Congress of the United States for the Administration of the Foreign Agents Registration Act, 1950 through 1991; various interviews with Rhoodie, including an article in the *Sydney Morning Herald*, 28 September 1978; Mervyn Rees and Chris Day, *Muldergate: The Story of the Info Scandal* (Macmillan South Africa, 1980); and the Truth and Reconciliation Commission Report, Volume 2, Chapter 6, released on 29 October 1998.

Comparison of Rhoodie with Goebbels: James Sanders, *South Africa and the International Media 1972–1979* (Frank Cass, 2000).

1

Apartheid Is Good For Blacks

The election of the National Party government in 1948 and its subsequent political activities: Freda Troup, *South Africa: An Historical Introduction* (Penguin Books,

1972) and Leonard Thompson, *A History of South Africa* (Yale Nota Bene, 2000).

Early lobbying operations by the apartheid government: Professor Vernon McKay, Johns Hopkins University, School of International Studies, testimony before the Subcommittee on Africa, House Foreign Affairs Committee, entitled 'South Africa Propaganda', 3 March 1966.

D.F. Malan's relationship with the United States and Great Britain: Linda Koorts, *D.F. Malan and the Rise of Afrikaner Nationalism* (Tafelberg, 2014).

Relationship of the Truman administration and South Africa: Thomas Borstelmann, *Apartheid's Reluctant Uncle: The United States and Southern Africa in the Early Cold War* (Oxford University Press, 1993).

Max Yergan: surveillance files of the American Federal Bureau of Investigation and documents from the US State Department's Office of the Historian.

On Yergan and his stay in South Africa: David Anthony III, *Max Yergan: Race Man, Internationalist and Cold Warrior* (New York University Press, 2006), widely considered to be the definitive biography of Yergan.

US surveillance of Yergan and the Council on African Affairs: FBI files on Dr Max Yergan, Federal Bureau of Investigation, Department of Justice Files 71-1978 and 100-26011. These files were obtained by the author under the US Freedom of Information Act.

Fight between Yergan and Paul Robeson supporters over the Council on African Affairs: Penny M. Von Eschen, *Race Against Empire: Black Americans and Anticolonialism 1937–1957* (Cornell University Press, 1997); Martin B. Duberman, *Paul Robeson: A Biography* (Ballantine Books, 1989); Glenda Elizabeth Gilmore, *Defying Dixie: The Radical Roots of Civil Rights* (WW Norton, 2008); *New York Times*, 3 February 1948; Max Yergan papers, Moorland-Spingarn Research Center at Howard University, Washington DC.

Yergan's blackmail attempts: David Levering Lewis, *W.E.B. Du Bois: The Fight for Equality and the American Century, 1919–1963* (Henry Holt, 2000).

Yergan's letter to the South African government requesting a visa and subsequent correspondence between South Africa's secretary for external affairs and the American government: memo of 4 June 1949, State Department files, US National Archives in College Park, Maryland. The American response by Dean Acheson: memo of 8 August 1949.

Yergan's visit to the Bantu Men's Social Centre: Anthony Sampson, *Mandela: The Authorized Biography* (Vintage, 2000).

Walter Sisulu's claims that Yergan tried to talk organisers out of the Defiance Campaign: David Anthony III, *Max Yergan*.

Yergan and communists in South Africa: 'Africa: Next Goal of Communists',

US News and World Report, 1 May 1953.

Responses to Yergan's claims of communism: David Anthony III, *Max Yergan* and Glenda Elizabeth Gilmore, *Defying Dixie*.

Yergan naming ANC members as communists: Gerald Horne, *Black and Red: W.E.B. DuBois and the Afro-American Response to the Cold War, 1944–1963* (State University of New York Press, 1986).

President George W. Bush removing the ANC and Nelson Mandela from the terrorist list: 'Mandela Off Terrorism Watch List', CNN.com, 2 June 2008.

The United Nation's position on apartheid and South Africa: J.P. Brits, 'Tiptoeing along the Apartheid Tightrope: The United States, South Africa and the United Nations in 1952', *International History Review* 27, 4 (December 2005).

The United States worrying about its relationship with South Africa: State Department cable of 29 September 1952, accessed from US State Department Office of the Historian, https://history.state.gov/historicaldocuments.

The appointment of Eric Louw as foreign minister and his subsequent work: James Barber and John Barratt, *South Africa's Foreign Policy: The Search for Status and Security, 1945–1988* (Cambridge University Press, 1990)

The South African government's 1950 lobbying information: US Department of Justice, Foreign Agents Registration Office's Reports to Congress, 1950–1954, published June 1955, www.fara.gov/annualrpts.html.

The South African government's attempts to gather information on racial problems in the US: Nicholas Grant, 'The Racial Politics of the Cold War: South African Apartheid and the United States, 1948–1960' , presented on 6 December 2010 at the Institute for the Study of the Americas, https://coldwaramericas. wordpress.com/conference-papers/#_ftn13.

The formation of the South Africa Foundation: William Minter, *King Solomon's Mines Revisited: Western Interests and the Burdened History of Southern Africa* (Basic Books, 1986).

?

In Defence of Apartheid

Sharpeville massacre: Tom Lodge, *Sharpeville: An Apartheid Massacre and Its Consequences* (Oxford University Press, 2011) and various media accounts including 'South Africa Put in State of Alert: Opponents Jailed', *New York Times*, 31 March 1960.

US State Department's statement on the Sharpeville shootings: briefing of 22 March 1960 by Lincoln White, director of the Office of News, in response to questions from reporters, State Department's Central Files 745A.00/ 3-2160.

Responses of President Eisenhower and the secretary of state, Christian A. Herter, to the press statement: memo of 24 March 1960, by Andrew Goodpaster, staff secretary and defense liaison officer to President Eisenhower, Eisenhower Presidential Library, Abilene, Kansas.

United Nations Security Council resolution: www.un.org/en/ga/search/view_doc.asp?symbol=S/RES/134(1960).

The reaction of Martin Luther King Jr to the Sharpeville massacre: telegram of 24 March 1960 from King to Claude Burnett of the Associated Negro Press, a black-owned wire service, published on 28 March 1960.

Billy Graham's reaction and the South African government's response to the US reaction: E. Nathaniel Gates (ed.), *Race and US Foreign Policy during the Cold War* (Routledge, 1998).

The hiring of the Hamilton Wright Organization by the South African government: US Department of Justice, Foreign Agents Registration Office's Report to Congress for the year 1961, published in October 1962.

The Hamilton Wright Organization's work for the South African government: US Senate investigation into foreign lobbying entitled *Activities of Nondiplomatic Representatives of Foreign Principals in the United States*, by the Senate Committee on Foreign Relations, 88th Congress. The committee held dozens of hearings from 4 February through 6 May 1963. Senator James William Fulbright headed the investigation.

Hamilton Wright Organization's suspension from the Public Relations Society of America: 'Publicity Group Suspends Wright', *New York Times*, 4 March 1964.

Hamilton Wright's claim that it had been wronged by the Fulbright hearings: Scott M. Cutlip, *Unseen Power: Public Relations, A History* (Lawrence Erlbaum Associates, 1994).

US trade with South Africa and President Kennedy's speech on 'an extraordinary group of African leaders': 'US View of Mandela Changed from Cold War Communist to Anti-Apartheid Hero', Voice of America, 5 December 2013.

Mandela as a communist: from several sources, most notably the Central Intelligence Agency's now declassified 21 May 1961 *Current Intelligence Weekly Summary*.

The Kennedy administration's arms sanctions against South Africa: Alex Thomson, *U.S. Foreign Policy Towards Apartheid South Africa, 1948–1994* (Palgrave Macmillan, 2008) and Y.G.M. Lulat, *United States Relations with South Africa* (Peter Lang, 2008).

Charles W. Engelhard: Geoffrey G. Jones and Elliot R. Benton, 'Goldfinger: Charles W. Engelhard Jr and Apartheid-era South Africa', *Harvard Business*

Review, 3 June 2013. See also the group's 1965 annual report, Max Yergan papers, Moorland-Spingarn Research Center, Howard University; and William Minter, *King Solomon's Mines Revisited*.

Engelhard as a power-broker in South Africa: *Time* magazine, 27 January 1961.

Engelhard's presence in lobbying the Johnson administration: State Department memo of conversation, 23 March 1965, obtained from the National Security Archives at George Washington University, Washington DC.

Max Yergan's 1964 appearance in South Africa: 'US Negro Sociologist Praises South Africa's Apartheid Policy', *New York Times*, 30 November 1964. Yergan and his interracial marriage on a prior visit to South Africa: Penny M. Von Eschen, *Race Against Empire*. Yergan's speech in London: 'Leading American Negro Supports Apartheid', draft speech, Max Yergan papers, Moorland-Spingarn Research Center, Howard University.

Max Yergan and the formation of the American African Affairs Association: Sara Diamond, *Roads to Dominion: Right-wing Movements and Political Power in the United States* (Guilford Press, 1995).

Carl Rowan's criticism of Max Yergan and his support for apartheid South Africa and other white-led African governments: 'Group Boosting Ian Smith Called Racist, Dangerous', *Spokane Daily Chronicle*, 23 February 1966.

The work of the American African Affairs Association: Elsie and Frank S. Meyer (eds.), *Some Americans Comment on Southern Africa* (American Affairs Association, 1967); and Anthony Lake, *The Tar Baby Option: American Policy Toward Southern Africa* (Columbia University Press, 1976).

The A A A A's 1971 fact-finding trip led by Dr Alvin J. Cottrell: David Anthony III, *Max Yergan*.

The American African Affairs Association's lobbying for South Africa: interview with Louis Gerber by the authors of *The Power Peddlers*, Russell Warren Howe and Sara Hays Trott (Doubleday, 1977).

Yergan's letter of regret to Paul Robeson: Martin Duberman, *Paul Robeson*.

Martin Luther King Jr's early exposure to South Africa and Martin Luther King Sr's communication with the ANC and Albert Luthuli: Francis Njubi Nesbitt, *Race for Sanctions* (Indiana University Press, 2004).

King's involvement in the Declaration of Conscience on South Africa: *Declaration of Conscience: An Appeal to South Africa*, drafted by the American Committee on Africa (New York, 1957). The pamphlet can be found at the King Center Library and Archives, Atlanta, and is also discussed in George Houser, *No One Can Stop the Rain* (The Pilgrim Press, 1989).

Eric Louw's criticism of the Declaration of Conscience campaign: transcript

'Radio Address by the Minister of External Affairs (The Hon. Eric H. Louw) on Thursday Evening, 12 December, 1957', Max Yergan papers, Moorland-Spingarn Research Center, Howard University.

Communications between Martin Luther King Jr and Albert Luthuli: King Center Library and Archives. One of the earliest communications is a letter King wrote to Luthuli on 8 December 1959. Lewis V. Baldwin, *To Make the Wounded Whole* (Fortress Press, 1992) further discusses the communications between King and Luthuli.

The 1962 joint letter from Martin Luther King Jr and Albert Luthuli: from documents posted as part of the film *RFK in the Land of Apartheid*; see www. rfksafilm.org/html/doc_pdfs/luthuli_king.pdf. The film chronicles Senator Robert F. Kennedy's 1966 trip to South Africa where he gave his 'Ripple of Hope' speech at the University of Cape Town and met with anti-apartheid leaders like Albert Luthuli. The film is directed by Tami Gold and Larry Shore.

King's visit to the White House to meet Kennedy and discuss South African sanctions: Tom Lodge, *Sharpeville*.

Martin Luther King's 1964 speech invoking Nelson Mandela and Robert Sobukwe: address of 7 December 1964 in London at City Temple; see www. democracynow.org/2015/1/19/exclusive_newly_discovered_1964_mlk_speech.

King's 1965 speech in criticism of South Africa, given on 10 December 1965 at Hunter College in New York City: transcript at www.rfksafilm.org/html/speeches/ pdfspeeches/14.pdf.

King's application for a visa to visit South Africa: letters at the King Center Library and Archives. King's letter is at http://thekingcenter.org/archive/ document/letter-mlk-south-african-embassy, and the response from the South African consulate in New Orleans is at http://thekingcenter.org/archive/document/ letter-n-m-nel-mlk.

For a full treatment of Martin Luther King and South Africa, see Lewis V. Baldwin, *Towards the Beloved Community: Martin Luther King Jr and South Africa* (The Pilgrim Press, 1995).

Malcolm X's speech at the University of Ghana about South Africa: Francis Njubi Nesbitt, *Race for Sanctions*.

The formation of the American Committee on Africa and its role in the early divestment movement: George Houser, *No One Can Stop the Rain*.

Black American influence on US foreign policy: Raymond W. Copson, *The Congressional Black Caucus and Foreign Policy* (Nova Publishers, 2003).

The US government's backlash against the black liberation struggle: Kenneth O'Reilly, *Racial Matters: The FBI Secret File on Black America 1960–1972* (Free

Press; reprint edition, 1991) and Kenneth O'Reilly (ed.), *Black Americans: The FBI Files* (Carroll & Graf Publishers, 1994).

William F. Buckley Jr's trip to South Africa and subsequent article about his travels and reflections: 'Apologists without Remorse', *American Prospect*, 19 December 2001. Russell Kirk's comments about votes for black South Africans bringing anarchy and 'the collapse of civilization' are from the same article.

George S. Schuyler and his support of South Africa and other white-minority African governments: Oscar R. Williams, *George S. Schuyler: Portrait of a Black Conservative* (University of Tennessee Press, 2007).

The FBI's monitoring of Schuyler: William Maxwell, *F.B. Eyes: How J. Edgar Hoover's Ghostreaders Framed African American Literature* (Princeton University Press, 2015).

George S. Schuyler's comment on apartheid: from an October 1968 interview with conservative radio talkshow host Marilyn Manion. See Manion, 'Race and Foreign Policy', *Hawkins County Post*, 31 October 1968.

Connections between white South Africa and white conservatives in the American South: Zoë Hyman, 'American Segregationist Ideology and White Southern Africa, 1948–1975', University of Sussex thesis, September 2011.

Senator James Eastland's trip to South Africa: James O. Eastland Collection, University of Mississippi, File series 1, subseries 14: Trips, Folder 1-3. 1969 – Africa, Public Relations.

President Richard Nixon's policy toward southern Africa: Anthony Lake, *The Tar Baby Option* and William Minter, Gail Hovey and Charles Cobb Jr, *No Easy Victories: African Liberation and American Activists over a Half Century, 1950-2000* (Africa World Press, 2007).

Nixon's 1957 trip to Ghana's independence celebration with black American leaders: Mark Ledwidge, *Race and US Foreign Policy: The African-American Foreign Affairs Network* (Routledge, 2011). Eric J. Morgan, 'The Sins of Omission: The United States and South Africa in the Nixon Years', Miami University MA thesis, 2003, was also a valuable source.

3

Taking the Offensive

The origins of the apartheid South African government's launch of secret projects to influence world opinion: Mervyn Rees and Chris Day, *Muldergate*; Eschel Rhoodie, *The Real Information Scandal*; Eschel Rhoodie, *The Paper Curtain;* and Les de Villiers, *Secret Information* (Tafelberg, 1980).

The Anti-Apartheid Movement in the United Kingdom: communication with

Peter Hain (17 September 2014) and his book *Outsiders In* (Biteback, 2013).

The founding of the Interfaith Committee on Corporate Responsibility: various documents at the African Activist Archive Project, Michigan State University.

The rise of black law-makers in the United States and their attempts to impose sanctions against South Africa: Raymond W. Copson, *The Congressional Black Caucus and Foreign Policy* and Francis Njubi Nesbitt, *Race for Sanctions*.

Ronald Farrar: 'A Memorandum on Some Current Public Relations Efforts by South Africa in the US', published by the American Committee on Africa, 2 July 1976.

Donald E. de Kieffer: lobbying records filed by Collier, Shannon, Rill & Edwards and the South African Department of Information with the Department of Justice, Foreign Agents Registration Office's Reports of the Attorney General to the Congress of the United States for the Administration of the Foreign Agents Registration Act, 1974 through 1978. See also Les de Villiers, *Secret Information*; Mervyn Rees and Chris Day, *Muldergate*; and Julian Burgess, *The Great White Hoax: South Africa's International Propaganda Machine* (Africa Bureau [London], 1977).

Donald E. de Kieffer's secret lobbying effort with Lester Kinsolving: 'South Africa Is Waging Extensive Publicity Drive', *Washington Post*, 27 January 1977.

South Africa Foundation lobbying: Julian Burgess, *The Great White Hoax*; Department of Justice, Foreign Agents Registration Office's Reports of the Attorney General to the Congress of the United States for the Administration of the Foreign Agents Registration Act, 1974 through 1978; the foundation's annual reports for 1974 through 1979; and interview with John Chettle, former director of the South Africa Foundation, 3 March 2014.

The South Africa Foundation as a front for the South African government: Russell Warren Howe and Sara Hays Trott, *The Power Peddlers*.

Mulder and Rhoodie's praise of the foundation: Julian Burgess, *The Great White Hoax* and Eschel Rhoodie, *The Real Information Scandal*.

South African government spending on lobbying: Department of Justice, Foreign Agents Registration Office's Reports of the Attorney General to the Congress of the United States for the Administration of the Foreign Agents Registration Act, 1973 through 1978.

US Department of Justice's legal action against the South Africa Foundation: Department of Justice, Foreign Agents Registration Office's Report of the Attorney General to the Congress of the United States for the Administration of the Foreign Agents Registration Act, 1978. See *Attorney General* v. *Casey, Lane & Mittendorf* (Civil Action No. 77-1272) in the United States District Court for the District of Columbia, July 1977.

4

Operation Blackwash

The Soweto uprising: P.L. Bonner, *Soweto: A History* (Maskew Miller Longman, 1998); and '6 Killed in South Africa as Blacks Protest on Language' and 'South Africa Toll at Least 54 as Rioting Goes On', *New York Times*, 17 and 18 June 1976.

Meeting between Henry Kissinger and John Vorster: memo of conversation at the Hotel Sonnenhof, Grafenau, West Germany, 24 June 1976, Library of Congress, Manuscript Division, Kissinger Papers, Box CL 344, Department of State, Memoranda, Memoranda of Conversations, External, June–July 1976.

President Carter's change in US foreign policy towards South Africa: see the website of the State Department's Office of the Historian, https://history.state.gov/departmenthistory/short-history/carter.

Carter's ban on sharing military intelligence with South Africa: 'US Is Said to Give Pretoria Intelligence on Rebel Organization', *New York Times*, 23 July 1986.

President Carter's vote for UN arms sanctions and discussion of economic sanctions: Alex Thomson, *U.S. Foreign Policy Towards Apartheid South Africa, 1948–1994*.

Andrew Young's stance on South Africa and Steve Biko's refusal to meet him. Andrew DeRoche, *Andrew Young: Civil Rights Ambassador* (Rowman & Littlefield, 2003).

The hiring of Sydney Baron: Department of Justice, Foreign Agents Registration Office's Report of the Attorney General to the Congress of the United States for the Administration of the Foreign Agents Registration Act, 1976; and individual lobbying disclosure documents.

Sydney Baron's comment about South Africa not being 'Disneyland': Julian Burgess, *The Great White Hoax*.

Rhoodie's comments on why he hired the firm and Andrew Hatcher: Eschel Rhoodie, *The Real Information Scandal*.

Hatcher's appointment to the Kennedy administration: Nicholas Bryant, *The Bystander: John F. Kennedy and the Struggle for Black Equality* (Basic Books, 2006)

Business conferences organised by Andrew Hatcher and paid for by the South African government: 'Some US Blacks Visit South Africa on Business', *New York Times*, 2 July 1976 and Y.G.M. Lulat, *United States Relations with South Africa* (Peter Lang, 2008). Lulat discusses former President Gerald Ford speaking at a conference in Houston, Texas, organised by Hatcher.

Hatcher's appearance before the 100 Black Men organisation: 'Some US Blacks Visit South Africa on Business', *New York Times*, 2 July 1976. Hatcher's appearance on NBC in defence of the South African government is detailed in the same article and a transcript of the NBC's *Today* show, 23 June 1976.

Hatcher's attempt to stop Les Payne of *New York Newsday* from visiting South Africa: author's interview with Payne (12 March 2014) and Payne's self-published report 'White Power, Black Revolt' (2011).

Hatcher's appearance at Transkei independence: *Spokesman-Review*, 25 October 1976, and US State Department diplomatic cable, 14 April 1977, taken from Wikileaks. Andrew Hatcher's other media appearances: *Jet Magazine*, 15 June 1976, and Shelly Pitterman, 'A Fine Face for Apartheid' (The Africa Fund, 1978).

Bernard Katzen and Jay Parker: Department of Justice, Foreign Agents Registration Office's Report of the Attorney General to the Congress of the United States for the Administration of the Foreign Agents Registration Act, 1978.

Parker's television appearance with Hatcher and De Villiers: WCBS 'Channel 2/ The People', 8 October 1976. Additional information on Parker: David T. Tyson, *Courage to Put My Country above Color: The Jay Parker Story* (2009).

United Nations vote on Transkei: http://daccess-dds-ny.un.org/doc/ RESOLUTION/GEN/NR0/301/89/IMG/NR030189.pdf?OpenElement.

5

Muldergate

Death of Steve Biko: Donald Woods, *Biko* (Henry Holt, 1978); Helen Zille, 'No Sign of Hunger Strike: Biko Doctors', *Rand Daily Mail*, 7 October 1977.

Jimmy Kruger's comments on death of Biko: 'Inquest in Pretoria Ready for Testimony on How Black Leader Died', *New York Times*, 14 November 1977.

Gerald Sparrow: 'I, Said the Sparrow', *The Spectator*, 28 July 1979.

On Muldergate: Mervyn Rees and Chris Day, *Muldergate*; Eschel Rhoodie, *The Real Information Scandal*; Les de Villiers, *Secret Information*; 'South Africa's Scandal Spreads to the West and Beyond', *Washington Post*, 25 March 1979.

John McGoff and his role in Muldergate: 'The McGoff Grab', *Columbia Journalism Review*, November/December 1979.

Andrew Hatcher's and Sydney Baron's role in Muldergate and South Africa's attempt to influence US elections: *Der Spiegel*, 15 October 1979; Eschel Rhoodie, *The Real Information Scandal*; 'South African Role in Iowa Voting Charged', *New York Times*, 22 March 1979.

Senator Dick Clark's meeting with Biko: Xolela Mangcu, *Biko: A Biography* (I.B. Tauris, 2013).

Stephen Bisenius was interviewed by the author on 21 July 2014.

South African financing of Roger Jepsen's election: 'AWACS Vote-Getting Crusade Turns Out to Have Embarrassing Results', *Lawrence-Daily World*, 24

December 1981. See the Federal Election Commission General Counsel's file at www.fec.gov/disclosure_data/mur/971.pdf on why the agency declined to investigate the allegations of South African involvement in the Iowa elections.

P.W. Botha and Muldergate: Mervyn Rees and Chris Day, *Muldergate* and Carmel Rickard, *Thank You, Judge Mostert* (Penguin, 2012).

6

Constructive Engagement

The election of Ronald Reagan and his new policy of 'constructive engagement': J.E. Davies, *Constructive Engagement?: Chester Crocker and American Policy in South Africa, Namibia and Angola 1981–8* (Boydell & Brewer, 2007); also see Dickson A. Mungazi, *The Struggle for Social Change in Southern Africa: Visions of Liberty* (Taylor & Francis, 1989)

Reagan's comment on detesting apartheid: Douglas Brinkley (ed.), *The Reagan Diaries* (HarperCollins, 2007).

Margaret Thatcher's position on sanctions and South Africa: Nicholas Wapshott, *Ronald Reagan and Margaret Thatcher: A Political Marriage* (Penguin, 2007).

Denis Thatcher's business ties with South Africa: 'How Margaret Thatcher Helped End Apartheid. Despite Herself', *The Guardian*, 10 April 2013.

Thatcher's comments on sanctions hardening attitudes: speech on 17 October 1987 at a press conference at the Vancouver Commonwealth Summit, www.margaretthatcher.org/document/106948.

P.W. Botha's visit to London: 'National Archive: Margaret Thatcher Barely Mentions Mandela in Talks', *Daily Telegraph*, 3 January 2014.

Thatcher's long ties with Botha and their meeting in 1974: 'Margaret Thatcher's Shameful Support of Apartheid', *Mail & Guardian*, 19 April 2013.

Thatcher's calling the ANC a terrorist organisation: speech on 17 October 1987 at a press conference at the Vancouver Commonwealth Summit.

The ANC listed as a terrorist organisation: 'U.S. Report Stirs Furore in South Africa', *New York Times*, 14 January 1989.

Reagan and the normalising of trade with South Africa: *Public Papers of the Presidents of the United States: Ronald Reagan, 1987*, US National Archives.

Restoration of aid to Unita: 'White House Statement on the President's Meeting with Jonas Savimbi of Angola', *The American Presidency Project*, 30 June 1988, University of California, Santa Barbara.

Reagan administration's intelligence sharing with South Africa: 'U.S. Is Said to Have Given Pretoria Intelligence on Rebel Organization', *New York Times*, 23 July 1986.

South Africa's lobbying in the US: Department of Justice, Foreign Agents Registration Office's Reports of the Attorney General to the Congress of the United States for the Administration of the Foreign Agents Registration Act, 1981–1988; and Richard Leonard, 'Apartheid Whitewash: South African Propaganda in the United States'.

The Sears lobbying controversy: 'Law Firm's Split Airs Lobbying by South Africa', *Washington Post*, 12 March 1984.

American conservative think-tanks' support of apartheid South Africa: Thomas Frank, *The Wrecking Crew: How Conservatives Rule* (Henry Holt, 2008); 'An Investment Strategy to Undermine Apartheid in South Africa', *Heritage Foundation Backgrounder*, 427 (30 April 1985); Anthony J. Hall, *American Empire and the Fourth World: The Bowl with One Spoon, Part One* (McGill-Queen's Press, 2003); and Y.G.M. Lulat, *United States Relations with South Africa*.

South Africa's lobbying campaign against Howard Wolpe: 'Apartheid under Siege: Challenges from the Churches, Sanctions and the White Right', *Africa Today*, 36, 1 (1st quarter 1989).

South Africa Foundation: Department of Justice, Foreign Agents Registration Office's Reports of the Attorney General to the Congress of the United States for the Administration of the Foreign Agents Registration Act, 1981–1988; 'South Africa's Lobbyists', *New York Times*, 13 October 1985.

John Chettle's claims about the ANC leadership and South African Communist Party: testimony of 3 June 1986 before the Advisory Committee on South Africa, appointed by the US Secretary of State, http://digitalcollections.library.cmu.edu/awweb/awarchive?type=file&item=541831.

Trips sponsored by the South Africa Foundation: 'US Promoters Aid in Pretoria's Race for Respect', *Chicago Tribune*, 10 August 1986. Additional information about the foundation from author interview with John Chettle, 3 March 2014.

South African propaganda efforts in the US education system: Richard Leonard, 'Apartheid Whitewash: South African Propaganda in the United States'.

Lobbying by Strategy Network International: 'Attack of the Sleaze: How Apartheid Regime Set Out to Woo Tories', *The Independent*, 26 October 1994; House of Commons Committee on Standards and Privileges, Seventh Report, 31 July 1997.

Michael Colvin's remarks about his dealings with SNI: 'Tory No. 3 in Cash Row', *Daily Mail*, 25 October 1994.

Marion Roe's visit to Unita: 'Diary', *The Guardian*, 7 July 1989.

South African lobbying in UK: Members' Register of Interests for the years 1975 to 1990, House of Commons Parliamentary Library.

David Cameron's trip to South Africa: Francis Elliott and James Hanning, *Cameron: The Rise of the New Conservative* (HarperCollins, 2009).

The author made an attempt to interview Patrick Watson on 28 June 2014; follow-up emails were sent on the same day.

Author interview with Steven Govier on 16 August 2014. Govier provided additional information on the network of public relations firms hired by Sean Cleary's Transcontinental Consultancy, in emails sent on 18 August 2014 and 28 August 2014. Further information on Volker Stoltz: 'In the Bush', *Der Spiegel*, 29 December 1986.

Marion H. Smoak and Carl L. Shipley: author communication with Bruce Brager, former staffer at the Namibia News Bureau, on 28 August 2014, and an interview on 2 September 2014.

Lobbying information for the Namibia News Bureau: Department of Justice, Foreign Agents Registration Office's Reports of the Attorney General to the Congress of the United States for the Administration of the Foreign Agents Registration Act, Volume 2, Part 3: 1988–1991.

Lobbying by the Bophuthatswana International Affairs Office: testimony by Ian Findlay before House of Commons Select Committee on Members' Interests, 25 April 1989, House of Commons Parliamentary Library, also 'Attack of the Sleaze. How Apartheid Regime Set Out to Woo Tories', *The Independent*, 26 October 1994.

The Human Rights Watch report on Bophuthatswana: 'Out of Sight: The Misery in Bophuthatswana', 16 September 1991.

Lobbying by Ted Cobb for Bophuthatswana: 'Black Americans Play into S. Africa's Hands', *Washington Post*, 15 December 1980.

William Timmons's lobbying efforts for Bophuthatswana: Department of Justice, Foreign Agents Registration Office's Reports of the Attorney General to the Congress of the United States for the Administration of the Foreign Agents Registration Act, 1983 through 1986.

The dissolution of Bophuthatswana International Affairs Office: documents filed with Companies House, the United Kingdom's Register for Companies.

7

Free South Africa

The beginnings of the Free South Africa Movement, TransAfrica and Randall Robinson: Randall Robinson, *Defending the Spirit* (Penguin, 1998) and Francis Njubi Nesbitt, *Race for Sanctions*.

Robinson's quote: 'On Mandela Day, Founders of DC Free South Africa

Movement Look Back', *Washington Post*, 17 July 2013.

Robinson's early interest in Africa: 'Lobby Views Success as Being out of Favor', *New York Times*, 29 November 1983.

Robinson and TransAfrica's first national attention: 'Documents Link Namibia Solution to Better US Ties to South Africa', *New York Times*, 30 May 1981.

Rosa Parks's arrest at the South African embassy: 'Anti-Apartheid Rally Joined by Rosa Parks', UPI, 11 December 1984. On others arrested: 'Let's Recall the Americans Who Supported Mandela', *Progressive* magazine, 12 December 2013.

The arrest of Lowell Weicker: 'Under Arrest! A Senator Joins the Protest against S. Africa', *People* magazine, 4 February 1985.

Desmond Tutu's role in the protest: 'Tutu Cheers Anti-Apartheid Protest at S. African Embassy', *Los Angeles Times*, 9 January 1986.

Herman Nickel's comments on Tutu: 1986 memo to the assistant secretary of state on the South Africa Public Diplomacy Initiative, National Security Archives, George Washington University, Washington DC.

Tutu speech's about Reagan and the policy of 'constructive engagement': John Allen, *Desmond Tutu: Rabble Rouser for Peace: The Authorized Biography* (Chicago Review Press, 2008).

Barack Obama's role in the anti-apartheid movement: 'On Mandela Day, Founders of DC Free South Africa Movement Look Back', *Washington Post*, 17 July 2013.

Reagan's criticism of Pretoria on human rights: speech given on International Human Rights Day, 10 December 1984, *The Public Papers of the Presidents of the United States: Ronald Reagan, 1984*.

P.W. Botha's offer of dual citizenship: 'Citizenship Plan Offered by Botha', *New York Times*, 12 September 1985.

Letter to Brand Fourie from 35 conservative law-makers: 'South Africa Image in US Shatters', *Christian Science Monitor*, 10 December 1984.

8

Stopping the Anti-Apartheid Movement

William Keyes: 'South Africa's Newest Lobbyist Is a Black American', *Washington Post*, 21 November 1985.

Louis Nel was interviewed by the author on 3 June 2013.

Keyes's lobbying: US Department of Justice, Foreign Agents Registration Office, Registration Statement Exhibit A, 30 August 1985. A copy of Keyes's contract with the South African embassy is attached to the registration statement. The contract, which was signed on 28 August 1985, lays out the work the lobbyist was supposed to perform on behalf of the South African government. See also US Department of Justice, Foreign Agents Registration Office, Supplementary Statements, 10 October 1986 and 10 April 1987.

Keyes's comments to CNN: 'South Africa's Newest Lobbyist Is a Black American', *Washington Post*, 21 November 1985.

William Keyes's BlackPac: Federal Election Commission files on the organisation, 24 December 1991.

South African state of emergency: 'State of Emergency Imposed Throughout South Africa; More than 1,000 Rounded Up', *New York Times*, 13 June 1986.

The 'Rubicon speech': www.nelsonmandela.org/omalley/index.php/site/q/03lv 01538/04lv01600/05lv01638/06lv01639.htm.

Ronald V. Dellums and the first sanctions bill: http://history.house.gov/People/ Detail?id=12109.

Reagan's executive order to pre-empt sanctions against South Africa: *The Public Papers of the Presidents of the United States, 1985, Ronald Reagan*. The order is signed 9 September 1985. Democrats calling the executive order 'watered down': 'Senate Upholds Reagan's Sanctions Position', *Santa Cruz Sentinel*, 11 September 1985.

Reagan's plans to appoint a black businessman as first black ambassador to South Africa: 'US Says Pretoria Was Told of a Black Nominee', *New York Times*, 16 June 1986.

William B. Robertson's address at the International Conference Against Apartheid: *US State Department Current Policy* No. 787, February 1986.

Other White House officials sent on public outreach missions: notes of the International Political Committee (IPC) meeting at the US State Department, 8 November 1985, National Security Archives, George Washington University, Washington DC.

Anti-Apartheid Movement and Thatcher: author's communication with Peter Hain, 17 September 2014, and Peter Hain, *Outsiders In*.

The student boycott against Barclays Bank: www.aamarchives.org/file view/ category/27-barclays-and-shell.html.

Disagreement between Queen Elizabeth and Thatcher: 'Queen Dismayed by Uncaring Thatcher', *Sunday Times*, 20 July 1986.

The Commonwealth's attempts to impose sanctions: 'Commonwealth Leaders Agree on Limited Sanctions Against South Africa', *New York Times*, 21 October 1985.

The South African government meeting with lobbyists and their subsequent lobbying in Washington: 'US Promoters Aid in Pretoria's Race for Respect',

Chicago Tribune, 10 August 1986.

United States Corporate Council on South Africa: 'Business Protest on Apartheid Grows', *New York Times*, 2 December 1985.

The Reagan administration's role in the United States Corporate Council on South Africa: memo of 24 October 1985 from Chester Crocker to George Shultz, 'United States Corporate Council on South Africa', National Security Archives, George Washington University, Washington DC. The council is also mentioned in a memo of 11 October 1985 from Nicholas Platt, executive secretary at the State Department, to Robert C. McFarlane, a national security adviser at the Reagan White House.

Leon Sullivan, the 'Sullivan principles' and the United States Corporate Council on South Africa: 'Sullivan Asks End of Business Links with South Africa', *New York Times*, 4 June 1987.

United States Corporate Council on South Africa's secret lobbying campaign: memo of 11 October 1985 from Nicholas Platt to Robert C. McFarlane.

Carl 'Spitz' Channell's role in the South African lobbying campaign: letter of 23 October 1986 from Channell to Marl Maseng, deputy assistant to the president and director of public liaison at the White House, National Security Archives, George Washington University, Washington DC. The campaign is also mentioned in a second letter dated 17 October 1986 to Mitch Daniels, assistant to the president for political and intergovernmental affairs at the White House.

Memo of 28 September 1985 that suggested bringing in representatives from the CIA, the FBI and the Department of Defense: National Security Decisions Directives 187, *US Policy Towards South Africa*, Federation of American Scientists, Washington DC.

The passing of the Comprehensive Anti-Apartheid Act of 1986: 'Sanctions Win, Reagan Loses', *Chicago Tribune*, 3 October 1986.

European Community sanctions: 'Senate, 78 to 21, Overrides Reagan's Veto and Imposes Sanctions on South Africa', *New York Times*, 3 October 1986.

Six members of the Commonwealth adopting more stringent sanctions against South Africa: 'London Talks Fail to Agree on Sanctions', *Los Angeles Times*, 5 August 1986.

Brian Mulroney's role in sanctions on South Africa: 'How Brian Mulroney Spearheaded Canadian Push to End Apartheid in South Africa and Free Mandela', *National Post*, 5 December 2013, and 'Brian Mulroney Recalls Fight Against Apartheid and Friendship with Nelson Mandela', *Global and Mail*, 11 December 2013. See also Brian Mulroney, *Brian Mulroney: Memories 1939–1993* (Douglas Gibson, 2007).

Reagan's veto of the Comprehensive Anti-Apartheid Act of 1986 and the US Congress override: 'Sanctions Win, Reagan Loses', *Chicago Tribune*, 3 October 1986.

Pik Botha's calls to US senators before the vote on the Comprehensive Anti-Apartheid Act: 'S. African Ties US Sanctions to Grain Deals: Foreign Minster Calls Senators, Threatens to End Purchases', *Los Angeles Times*, 2 October 1986.

James Baker's and Reagan's regret for his veto: CBS, 'Face the Nation', 8 December 2013.

Reagan on sanctions as misguided: statement of 2 October 1985, www.reagan. utexas.edu/archives/speeches/1986/100286d.htm.

Japanese sanctions against South Africa: 'Japan OKs Limited South Africa Sanctions', *Chicago Tribune*, 20 September 1986. The Japanese sanctions came after the US Congress voted to impose sanctions on 12 September 1986.

Black Americans emerging as a force in US foreign policy: Francis Njubi Nesbitt, *Race for Sanctions*.

Sylvia Hill's interview with author was conducted on 23 February 2013.

9

Sanctions Only Hurt Blacks

The Reagan administration's failure to support international economic sanctions at the UN: 'A Crime in the US: Vetoing South African Sanctions', *Chicago Tribune*, 9 March 1987.

The Government Accountability Office report on the Reagan administration's not fully enforcing US sanctions: 'South Africa: Status Report on the Implementation of the Comprehensive Anti Apartheid Act', 21 October 1987.

The Coalition on Southern Africa: 'South Africa: US Blacks Form New Coalition Favoring Black Ties', IPS-Inter Press Service, 10 September 1987.

The coalition's letter to the Reagan administration: Richard Leonard, 'Apartheid's Whitewash: South African Propaganda in the United States'.

Gilbert Caldwell's arrest: 'Apartheid Protest Met Arrest', Associated Press, 26 January 1985. The article ran in the *Victoria Advocate* newspaper.

Gilbert Caldwell hearing King speak at the 1957 'prayer pilgrimage': from a press announcement for an appearance by Caldwell at Shenandoah University, 15 January 2015, www.su.edu/blog/2015/01/15/civil-rights-movement-veteran-friend-dr-martin-luther-king-jr-speak-universitys-mlk-day-observance/.

Gilbert Caldwell inviting King to speak at Boston College: www.umc.org/news-and-media/the-rev.-gil-caldwell-sharing-mlks-dream.

Clyde Williams's statement on South Africa: 'US Blacks Form New Coalition

Favoring Black Ties', IPS-Inter Press Service, 10 September 1987.

The coalition's visit to South Africa and Oprah Winfrey's donation: 'Morning Report: TV&Video', *Los Angeles Times*, 22 July 1988.

Richard Fisher's statement: 'US Blacks Form New Coalition Favoring Black Ties', IPS-Inter Press Service, 10 September 1987.

William Raspberry article: 'Apartheid: Some Help for the Victims', *Washington Post*, 18 September 1987.

Interfaith Center on Corporate Responsibility and the Neptune Strategy: 'South Africa: US Clergy Group Linked to Shell Oil', IPS-Inter Press Service, 7 October 1987, and 'Shell Mounts Campaign Against Critics', United Press International, 1 October 1987. Additional information about Shell Oil and the Neptune Strategy: Richard Leonard, 'Apartheid's Whitewash: South African Propaganda in the United States'.

The Neptune Strategy and two university-based projects: *Boycott Shell Bulletin* (published by the Interfaith Center on Corporate Responsibility), 9 (9 February 1988).

Shell's operations in South Africa: testimony by Richard Knight of the American Committee on Africa at the United Nations hearings on the oil embargo against South Africa, 12–13 April 1989.

Shell's role in breaking the oil embargo: 'Shell Earns Secret Millions in Sanction-busting Deals', *The Observer*, 5 August 1984, and 'Shell Linked to New South African Oil Deal', *The Observer*, 12 August 1984.

Donna Katzin was interviewed by the author on 9 May 2013.

Additional revelations about the Coalition on Southern Africa and its ties to Shell and other American companies with operations in South Africa: 'Black Group Opposes Sanctions', *Ellensburg Daily Record*, 7 May 1989.

Timothy Smith was interviewed by the author on 7 May 2013.

Centrality of business to the apartheid economy: Truth and Reconciliation Commission Report, Volume Four, 29 October 2013.

Members of the Coalition on Southern Africa quitting: 'Black Group Opposes Sanctions', *Ellensburg Daily Record*, 7 May 1989. Additional information from *Boycott Shell Bulletin*, 9 (9 February 1988).

Gilbert Caldwell was interviewed by the author on 26 April 2013.

Gilbert H. Caldwell Justice Ministry Award inaugural ceremony: http://umc-gbcs.org/faith-in-action/caldwell-honored-by-church-within-a-church-movement.

10

The Fixer

Robert Brown: interview with the author on 14 May 2013; and Brown's company website, www.bandcinternational.com/who-we-are/our-founder/.

Robert Brown's support: 'South African Schools Boycotted, US Weighs Naming Black Envoy: A Signal to Pretoria', *New York Times*, 15 July 1986.

The 'working group' where Robert Brown came to the attention of the Reagan administration: National Security Decisions Directives 187, *US Policy Towards South Africa*, Federation of American Scientists, Washington DC.

Jesse Jackson urging Robert Brown not to take the 'suicide mission' as ambassador to South Africa: 'US Press Plan for Black Envoy', *New York Times*, 17 July 1986.

George Shultz's opposition to Robert Brown as ambassador: 'Buying Time on Sanctions: US Choice of Envoy Part of Reagan Tactic', *New York Times*, 16 July 1986.

Brown's close ties to Umaru Dikko: 'Envoy Role Details in Nigeria', *New York Times*, 19 July 1986.

Accusations against Robert Brown: 'US Said to Drop Black for Pretoria Post', *New York Times*, 20 July 1986.

Robert Brown's International Concern Foundation: see Brown's letter of 28 February 1989 to *New York Times.*

Tax information on the foundation: Guidestar.org, which provides tax information about nongovernmental organisations operating in the US.

Brown and Winnie Madikizela Mandela: author's interview with Brown on 14 May 2013.

Brown's prison meeting with Mandela: 'Who Speaks for Nelson Mandela?', *New York Times*, 30 July 1988.

Brown's soliciting of money for Winnie Mandela's home: 'US Ties Could Hurt Mandela', *The Hour*, 13 March 1989.

Brown paying for Mandela children to attend college: 'Mandela Family Friend from Triad to Attend Funeral', *Greensboro News and Record*, 8 December 2013.

Coalition on Southern Africa event in Alexandra: 'Government Publicizes Event Involving Black Activist', Associated Press, 22 July 1988.

Robert Brown on his work with the Coalition on Southern Africa: interview of 14 May 2013 with the author.

Jack Anderson crediting Brown with being a founder of the coalition: 'Black Group in US Oppose Sanctions', *Toledo Blade*, 7 March 1989.

Donna Katzin was interviewed by the author on 9 May 2013.

The South African BookSmart Foundation, now called the International BookSmart Foundation: www.internationalbooksmart.org/.

Robert Brown on Nelson Mandela: 'Republican Robert Brown Known as Maverick in Politics and Business', *Baltimore Afro-American*, 25 September 2013.

11

Operation Heartbreak

Kenneth Frazier and Operation Heartbreak: 'Motives of South African Children Lobby Questioned', Associated Press, 8 June 1988; press release from the Wake Up America Coalition dated the same day; and the Africa Fund's 1989 report 'Apartheid's Whitewash: South African Propaganda in the United States' by Richard Leonard, http://africanactivist.msu.edu/document_metadata.php?objectid=32-130-F6B. Mwiza Munthali, an information specialist with TransAfrica, also provided information about Frazier, in an interview with the author on 25 June 2013. Kenneth Frazier's background information is taken from a 8 June 1988 press release issued by the Wake Up America Coalition, which ran Operation Heartbreak.

Frazier's California lecture on the ANC: 'Speakers Attack Apartheid, but Agreements Ends There', *Los Angeles Times*, 28 November 1985.

Frazier's launching of Operation Heartbreak: 'Motives of South African Children Lobby Questioned', Associated Press, 8 June 1988. See also the press release of 7 June 1988 from the Wake Up America Coalition, taken from PR Newswire.

Washington DC schools saying they were duped by Frazier: Richard Leonard, 'Apartheid's Whitewash: South African Propaganda in the United States'.

Frazier's meeting with William Keyes: Supplementary Statement of the International Public Affairs Consultants, Inc. (Keyes's lobbying firm), filed with the US Department of Justice on 6 April 1988.

Frazier as a member of the Church Universal and Triumphant: email from Chris Kelley, Communications Office of the president of the church, to the church board, 30 July 1999.

Founding of the Church Universal and Triumphant by Elizabeth Clare Prophet: 'Elizabeth Prophet, 70, Church Founder, Is Dead', *New York Times*, 16 October 2009.

The Church Universal and Triumphant and its anti-communism: Peter B. Clarke and Peter Beyer, *The World's Religions: Continuities and Transformations* (Routledge, 2009).

Elizabeth Prophet's views on South Africa: Elizabeth Prophet, *Pearls of Wisdom, 1978: Spoken by Elohim*, ed. by Mark L. Prophet and Elizabeth Prophet (Summit University Press, 1980).

Panel at the Church Universal and Triumphant to discuss South Africa: Elizabeth Clare Prophet, *Year of Prophecy* (Summit University Press, 1987). The session was held on 3 July 1987.

Uys Viljoen, James W. Kendricks and Gene Vosseler: from biographies of the participants in the Summit University's forums at Freedom 1987 programme.

James W. Kendricks and his ties to William Keyes and Jay Parker: Supplementary Statements of the International Public Affairs Consultants, Inc., filed with the US Department of Justice, including those dated 10 October 1986 and 23 March 1988. The documents show Kendricks served as a consultant to Keyes, lobbying for South Africa.

Gene Vosseler and his relationship with David W. Balsiger: Sara Diamond, *Spiritual Warfare: The Politics of the Christian Right* (Black Rose Books, 1990).

David W. Balsiger: Richard Leonard, 'Apartheid's Whitewash: South African Propaganda in the United States'.

Aida Parker Newsletter: Gordon Winter, *Inside B.O.S.S.: Inside South Africa's Secret Police* (Penguin Books, 1981).

The TRC on Project Villa Marie: Truth and Reconciliation Commission Report, Volume Two, Chapter 6, 29 October 1998.

Louis Nel was interviewed by the author on 3 June 2013.

12

The Anti-Sanctions Videos

J. Morgan Hodges and his videos: *Missionary Seer* magazine, Volumes 87–90, 1988, published by the Department of Overseas Missions of the AME Zion Church; and Richard Leonard, 'Apartheid's Whitewash: South African Propaganda in the United States'.

J. Morgan Hodges as lobbyist registered with Congress: lobbying disclosure forms filed with the US Senate Office of Public Records, 26 June 1986, National Archives, Washington DC.

Hodges's meeting with Congress. *Missionary Seer* magazine, Volumes 87 90, 1988.

South Africa: A Closer Look (video): Walter E. Fauntroy Collection, Special Collections Research Center, Gelman Library, George Washington University, Washington DC.

Hodges as minister of the Universal Holiness Church and board member of the NRB: 'Building a Dream on Prison Walls', *Washington Post*, 6 December 1979; Records of National Religious Broadcasters Collection 309, Billy Graham Center and Museum, Wheaton College, Illinois.

NRB visits to South Africa: Sara Diamond, *Spiritual Warfare*.

South African Tourism Corporation at the NRB convention, March 1988: 'How U.S. Evangelicals Bless Apartheid', *Penthouse*, March 1988.

NRB award to Pik Botha: 'Foreign Minister Honored by US Religious Broadcasters', Associated Press, 21 May 1987.

NRB hosting Bishop Isaac Mokoena: 'How U.S. Evangelicals Bless Apartheid', *Penthouse*, March 1988.

Paul F. Crouch and the South African government: 'TV Empire: Satellites Spread Scripture', *Los Angeles Times*, 26 January 1989.

Jerry Falwell's support for the South African government: Michael Sean Winters, *God's Right Hand: How Jerry Falwell Made God a Republican and Baptized the American Right* (HarperOne, 2012).

Jimmy Swaggart's and Pat Robertson's involvement in South Africa: 'How U.S. Evangelicals Bless Apartheid', *Penthouse*, March 1988; Richard Leonard, 'Apartheid's Whitewash: South African Propaganda in the United States'; and Sara Diamond, *Spiritual Warfare*.

The effects of the tax increase on companies doing business in South Africa, due to an amendment to the Budget Reconciliation Act of 1987: see the testimony of Richard Knight of the American Committee on Africa at the United Nations hearings on the oil embargo against South Africa, 12–13 April 1989.

Mobil Oil's withdrawal from South Africa: S. Prakash Sethi and Oliver F. Williams, *Economic Imperatives and Ethical Values in Global Business: The South African Experience and International Codes Today* (Springer Science & Business Media, 2012).

Business Day's estimate that the company lost $5 million a year: 'Mobil Reported to Plan South African Pullout', *New York Times*, 27 April 1989.

J. Morgan Hodges's obituary: *Washington Post*, 10 August 2012.

13

Apartheid's Man in Angola

Jonas Savimbi's appearance at the National Press Club and his meeting with President Reagan: 'Savimbi Says Reagan Backs Plan', Associated Press, 30 June 1988.

Savimbi being transported in the car of George Shultz: US State Department memo, 6 February 1986, National Security Archives, George Washington University, Washington DC.

Savimbi's visit to France: 'Cuba Annual Report: 1986', Voice of America-Radio Marti Program, Office of Research and Policy, United States Information Agency.

Britain keeping Savimbi at arm's length and Lonrho's lobbying: Foreign and Commonwealth memo, 'Angola: Visit of Savimbi to London', 24 June 1980, United Kingdom Parliamentary Archives.

Savimbi and Unita: William Minter, *King Solomon's Mines Revisited*; 'The Three Men Who Control Angola's Warring Faction', *New York Times*, 23 December 1975.

TRC on the apartheid government's support of Savimbi: Truth and Reconciliation Report, Volume Two, Chapter 6, 29 October 1998.

Lobbying on behalf of Unita by Black, Manafort, Stone & Kelly: 'Red Carpet for a Rebel, or How a Star Is Born', *New York Times*, 7 February 1986; 'The Selling of Jonas Savimbi: Success and a $600,000 Tab', *Washington Post*, 8 February 1986; and 'How Lobbyist Briefed a Rebel Leader', *Washington Post*, 8 October 1990.

Unita's effort to win the support of black Americans: 'The Politics of Survival: Unita in Angola, Africa', *Africa Notes*, 18 February 1993, published by the African Studies Program of the Georgetown University Center for Strategic and International Studies.

The Congressional Black Caucus and other black American groups refusing to meet with Savimbi: 'US Black Groups Rap Savimbi Visit', Associated Press, 9 December 1981.

TransAfrica's comments on Unita: author's interview with Mwiza Munthali, an information specialist with TransAfrica, 25 June 2013.

OAU denunciation of Unita: 'Jonas Savimbi: Washington's Freedom Fighter, Africa's Terrorist', *Foreign Policy in Focus*, 1 February 2002, published by the Institute for Policy Studies, Washington DC.

Sylvia Hill on Unita: interview with the author on 23 February 2013.

The courting of black Americans by Unita from the 1970s: 'Jonas Savimbi: US-Sponsored Terrorist?', *Final Call*, 11 February 2002.

Support of Unita by Edward Vaughn and Nana Akpan: 'The Photographic and Political Legacy of Nano Kwadwo O. Akpan', *Michigan Citizen*, 19 August 2008.

Unita's hiring of Florence Tate: 'The Politics of Survival: Unita in Angola, Africa', *Africa Notes*, 18 February 1993, and Department of Justice, Foreign Agents Registration Office's Reports of the Attorney General to the Congress of the United States for the Administration of the Foreign Agents Registration Act, 1980 through 1983.

Savimbi and Ralph Abernathy: 'Savimbi Says Reagan Backs Plan', Associated Press, 30 June 1988. Abernathy's relationship with Martin Luther King Jr: Adam Fairclough, *To Redeem the Soul of America: The SCLC and Martin Luther King, Jr* (University of Georgia Press, 1987).

Lobbying by Clarence McKee and Maurice Dawkins: Richard Leonard,

'Apartheid's Whitewash: South African Propaganda in the United States'; and Department of Justice, Foreign Agents Registration Office's Reports of the Attorney General to the Congress of the United States for the Administration of the Foreign Agents Registration Act, 1987 through 1988.

McKee's article on his visit to South Africa: 'A Black American Visits South Africa', *Lincoln Review*, 3, 2 (Fall 1982).

Savimbi's visit to Mississippi: 'Angolan Guerrilla Leader Gets Medgar Evers Award', *Jackson Clarion-Ledger*, 26 June 1988; 'Savimbi's Visit Generates Controversy', *Washington Post*, 26 June 1988; and author's interview with Charles Evers, 14 October 2014.

Jonas Savimbi's visit to Alabama: 'Savimbi Seeks Black Support in Alabama', *Washington Post*, 27 June 1988.

Unita's criticism of the MPLA: 'The Politics of Survival: Unita in Angola, Africa', *Africa Notes*, 18 February 1993.

Savimbi's ties to South Africa being downplayed before black audiences: 'Jonas Savimbi: US-Sponsored Terrorist?', *Final Call*, 11 February 2002.

Savimbi referring to P.W. Botha as a friend: Piero Gleijeses, *Visions of Freedom: Havana, Washington, Pretoria, and the Struggle for Southern Africa, 1976–1991* (UNC Press Books, 2013).

Savimbi and the South African government agree to criticise each other publicly: UK Foreign and Commonwealth Office memo, 2 July 1980, United Kingdom Parliamentary Archives.

Author interview with Clarence McKee, 11 June 2013.

South Africa cutting off aid to Unita: Truth and Reconciliation Commission Report, Volume Two, Chapter 6, 29 October 1998.

Savimbi offered the vice-presidency of Angola: 'Rebel Leader Savimbi Gets One Offer: Vice Presidency', *Orlando Sentinel*, 30 August 1995.

Savimbi and Unita continuing to fight after peace accords: 'Angolan Rebel Leader Still Has the Oratory, but Not the Territory', *Washington Post*, 9 February 1995.

UN condemnation of Unita: United Nations Security Council Resolution 864, 15 September 1993.

Savimbi's death: 'Luanda Celebrates Savimbi's Death', BBC News, 23 February 2002.

14

Apartheid's Last Gasp

International Freedom Foundation: 'Front for Apartheid', *Newsday*, 16 July 1995;

and 'How Apartheid Conned the West', *The Observer*, 16 July 1995. Most of the quotes and activities described in this chapter come from these two articles.

Mandela's visit to New York City: 'The Mandela Visit: Mandela Takes His Message to Rally at Yankee Stadium', *New York Times*, 22 June 1990.

Xavier Suarez's statement on Nelson Mandela was released on 26 June 1990 and signed by the mayors of several other South Florida cities near Miami. The statement was entered into the US House of Representatives Congressional Record on the same day by congressman Ira William 'Bill' McCollum, a Republican from Florida.

Black Americans in Florida protest over the treatment of Mandela: 'Miami Journey: Boycott over Visit of Mandela Lives On', *New York Times*, 21 July 1991.

International Freedom Foundation flyers about Mandela at Wembley Stadium: 'Anatomy of a Cause Concert', *Spin* magazine, September 1988.

South African government's financial support of the International Freedom Foundation: Truth and Reconciliation Commission Report, Volume Two, Chapter 6, 29 October 1998.

Herman Cohen on the International Freedom Foundation: 'The Tale of "Red Scorpion"', *Salon* magazine, 17 August 2005.

Craig Williamson and his work in Geneva. Tor Sellström, *Sweden and National Liberation in Southern Africa: Solidarity and Assistance, 1970–1994* (Nordic Africa Institute, 2002).

Anders Hasselbohm's interview about Williamson: 'S. African Killer Repeats Palme Claim', *Los Angeles Times*, 28 September 1996.

GMR company: Stephen Ellis, 'Africa and International Corruption: The Strange Case of South Africa and Seychelles', *African Affairs*, 95 (1996).

GMR's role in the distribution of videos targeting the ANC: US Department of Justice, Amendment to Registration Statement filed by About My Father's Business, 26 February 1990.

Author's interview with Richard Schmidt was conducted on 8 October 2014.

Craig Williamson's testimony before the TRC: www.justice.gov.za/trc/special%5Cmedia/media03.htm.

David Hoile's 'Hang Mandela' controversy: 'T-Shirt Test', *The Guardian*, 5 October 2001. Hoile's book *Understanding Sanctions* was published by the International Freedom Foundation in 1988.

Marc Gordon's criticism of Oxfam: interview with BBC Radio 4, 31 January 1989.

Oxfam's role in South Africa: see 'Oxfam's Responses to the Death of Nelson Mandela', www.oxfam.org/en/pressroom/reactions/oxfams-response-death-nelson-mandela; and Maggie Black, *A Cause for Our Times: Oxfam – The First Fifty Years* (Oxfam Press, 1992).

Author's interview with Jack Abramoff was conducted on 17 September 2014.

Author's interview with Ken Silverstein was conducted on 21 September 2014.

South African government's propaganda projects: De Wet Potgieter, *Total Onslaught: Apartheid's Dirty Tricks Exposed* (Struik Publishers, 2008).

Léon Delbecque and his role in Algeria: 'Plotter for Dissidents: Léon Delbecque', *New York Times*, 14 June 1958. His lobbying for the apartheid government in France: Daniel C. Bach, *La France et l'Afrique du Sud: histoire, mythes et enjeux contemporains* (Karthala Editions, 1990). (Dr Mark Lee Hunter, Adjunct Professor and Senior Research Fellow, INSEAD Social Innovation Centre, Paris, located this book for me.) Translation from French by the author.

Acoda, its members and ties to the South African government: 'Acoda: In Whose Interest', *Eltsa Southern Africa Briefing*, No. 2, published by the UK research organisation End Loans to Southern Africa. The organisation was established in 1974 and campaigned for sanctions against South Africa. The journal was obtained from the Eltsa archives, Library of Commonwealth and African Studies, Rhodes House, University of Oxford. See also 'Pretoria Link to EC Think Tank', *The Guardian*, 3 February 1992.

Guy Guermeur: www.assemblee-nationale.fr/histoire/trombinoscope/Vrepublique/Legis06/guermeur-guy-11011930.asp; www.europarl.europa.eu/meps/en/1656/GUY+JEAN_GUERMEUR_history.html; 'Beaucoup d'amis', *Droit et Liberté*, 379 (April 1979).

Acoda representatives visit South Africa: 'Sanksies moet weg om streek te help', *Beeld*, 30 October 1990; also in Acoda's newsletter *Info*, 1, 1 (December 1990).

Acoda German delegation's visit to South Africa: 'Duitsers wil help by Onderstepoort: Parlementslede by navorsingsentrum', *Beeld*, 31 May 1991.

The author interviewed Professor Jack Spence on 21 October 2014.

The TRC on Acoda: Truth and Reconciliation Commission Report, Volume Two, Chapter 6, 29 October 1998.

Sean Leary's role in Acoda: 'Pretoria Link to EC Think Tank', *The Guardian*, 3 February 1992.

Nico Basson's disclosures: 'Pretoria Ran Trial of Plot Against ANC', *The Guardian*, 11 June 1991.

President De Klerk shutting down the National Security Management System: 'De Klerk Moves to Curb Security Forces', *Los Angeles Times*, 29 November 1989.

The phasing out of secret projects and lobbying: Truth and Reconciliation Commission Report, Volume Two, Chapter 6, 29 October 1998; and Department of Justice, Foreign Agents Registration Office's Reports of the Attorney General to the Congress of the United States for the Administration of the Foreign Agents Registration Act, 1990 through 1993.

15
The End of Apartheid

De Klerk lifting the ban on the ANC: 'South Africa Lifts Ban on ANC: De Klerk Promises Mandela Freedom', *Philadelphia Inquirer*, 3 February 1990.

The first democratic elections: 'Mandela Named President, Closing the Era of Apartheid', *New York Times*, 10 May 1994.

Mandela's praise of the sanctions movement: Foreword to William Minter, Gail Hovey and Charles Cobb Jr, *No Easy Victories*.

The systematic destruction of records related to the apartheid government's propaganda activities: Mpho Ngoepe, 'To Hell or Heaven? Sanitisation of Records in Apartheid and Democratic South Africa: Implications for Social Memory', Department of Information Science, University of South Africa, 12–14 February 2014.

Destruction of records dating back to Muldergate era: Truth and Reconciliation Commission Report, Volume One, Chapter 8, 2 June 1993; and Richard J. Cox and David Wallace, *Archives and the Public Good: Accountability and Records in Modern Society* (Greenwood Publishing Group, 2002).

The rejection letter to the author's request under the Promotion of Access to Information Act for documents used by the Truth and Reconciliation Commission is dated 19 September 2014.

The author's interview with Stephen Bisenius was conducted on 21 July 2014.

Karen Rothmyer, 'The South Africa Lobby', *The Nation*, 19 April 1980.

The author's interview with Sylvia Hill was conducted on 23 February 2013.

Assessment of South Africa's propaganda: Garth Jowett and Victoria O'Donnell, *Propaganda and Persuasion* (Sage Publications, 2006).

Acknowledgements

Writing a book is a lonely endeavour. There are days of staring at blank pages wondering what will come next, or if anything will come at all. There is the waiting for interviews and documents, some of which will never come. And finally wondering, what am I going to do with all of these papers, books, reports after I finish the book?

Still, despite the feeling of loneliness in producing this book, it could not have been done without the contribution of several individuals and organisations.

I am indebted to the staff of the US Library of Congress, the US National Archives, the US National Security Archives at George Washington University, the US State Department Office of the Historian, the US Justice Department's Office of Foreign Agents Registration, the Moorland-Spingarn Center at Howard University, the New York City Library's Schomburg Center for Research in Black Culture, the Black Studies Center in the Martin Luther King Jr. Memorial Library in Washington DC, the Paul H. Nitze School of Advanced International Studies Library at Johns Hopkins University in Washington DC, the Bodleian Library at Oxford University, the South African National Archives, and the Historical Papers Department at Wits University Library in Johannesburg. I would also like to thank the Gelman Library at George Washington University, the British Parliamentary Library, the International Institute of Social History, and the European Commission.

Special thanks go to Anton Harber, director of the Wits University Journalism School, for first encouraging me to write the story of the apartheid government's global lobbying efforts as an ebook. I am grateful to Anton for sharing his knowledge of the apartheid era when he worked as a reporter at the *Rand Daily Mail* and as editor of the *Weekly Mail*: the history lesson was invaluable. And thank you for giving me a home at Wits Journalism. I am grateful to my colleagues at Wits: Lesley Cowling, Dinesh Balliah, J0-Anne Richards, Brigitte Read, Pierre Miller, Franz Kruger, Kenichi Serino, Ruth Hopkins, Nooshin Erfani-Ghadimi and Carolyn Raphaely. And special thanks to Margaret Renn, the Taco Kuiper Visiting Fellow in Investigative Journalism at Wits, for giving me the opportunity to make repeated trips to South Africa.

Thanks to Julian Rademeyer of Africa Check for helping me with his unbelievable number of sources in places where most people fear to tread. Thank you also for your advice and friendship. Julian is truly one of the greatest investigative reporters that I have had the pleasure of knowing. Gwen Lister of *The Namibian* provided valuable information on the apartheid government's propaganda efforts in Namibia and the links to the US and Europe.

A special thank-you is due to Kitty Bennett, my friend and *New York Times* researcher. If Kitty can't find it, it doesn't exist. Alain Delaquérière, also a researcher at the *New York Times*, contributed by finding several hard-to-get research papers, contact information and corporate records. Thank you, Alain; I couldn't have done it without your help.

Thanks to Richard Prince for promoting the book before it was even published and for giving me an opportunity to talk about it over dinner during the monthly journalism roundtables he organises in Washington DC.

Thanks to Elena Egawhary, my little sister in the United Kingdom, for your Saturday research trips on my behalf to the British Parliamentary Archives. Love you, little sis! Zeenat Abdool, my former student at Wits and good friend, did legwork for me at the National Archives in Pretoria. Thank you, Zee!

Thanks also go to my deskmates at the *New York Times*: Eric Lichtblau and Jim Risen, two of the best investigative reporters I know. They both served as sounding boards for the book and offered useful suggestions for finding people and documents. Scott Shane, who covers intelligence issues at the *Times*, also provided invaluable advice. To Orville Buddo and Brian Kennedy of the *New York Times* bestsellers: thank you for acting as sounding boards and for being my brothers. Thanks to Dean Baquet, editor of the *New York Times*, for hiring me in the Washington office of the *Times* and giving me a chance to write about foreign and domestic policy issues. Thanks also to Carolyn Ryan, Washington bureau chief of the *New York Times*; Elisabeth Bumiller, deputy bureau chief and my former editor; and Mike Tackett, my present editor.

I am grateful to professors Yanick Rice Lamb, Ingrid Sturgis and Clint Wilson of Howard University for their support. To Portia Kobue, thank you for the laughter and words of encouragement, and for showing me the cool spots in Jo'burg. I owe Damilola Oyedele very special thanks for reading early drafts of the book and making valuable editorial suggestions.

Very special thanks to Russell Martin, publisher at Jacana Media, for seeing that I had a book in me and for guiding me through several drafts until the final product.

I am forever indebted to the late Danny Schechter, filmmaker and activists, whose series 'Rights and Wrongs: Human Rights Television' featured some of my earliest work on global lobbying. RIP, Danny. To Damu Smith, long-time anti-apartheid, peace and environmental activist, who passed away in 2006: most of what I know about these movements comes from you. RIP, Damu.

Thanks to my family: Lillie Sanders, Marketta and Luis Valentin,

Ronnie Nixon Jr, Ronald Nixon and Courtney Williams Jr, Laura and Miles Parish. To my brother Timothy Nixon and to Makani Themba: thank you for years of support and love and saying that I had a book, or two, in me.

Finally, to my wife LaRaye Brown, for your love, caring and support through the years and especially during the process of writing this book. I couldn't have done this without you.

Ron Nixon

Index